M000280179

Integral Calculus

INTEGRAL CALCULUS

BY

H. B. PHILLIPS, Ph. D.

Assistant Professor of Mathematics in the Massachusetts Institute of Technology

FIRST EDITION

NEW YORK

JOHN WILEY & SONS, Inc.

London: CHAPMAN & HALL, Limited

1917

COPYRIGHT, 1917,

BY

H. B. PHILLIPS

Stanhope Press
F. H. GILSON COMPANY
BOSTON, U.S.A.

PREFACE

THIS text on Integral Calculus completes the course in mathematics begun in the Analytic Geometry and continued in the Differential Calculus. Throughout this course I have endeavored to encourage individual work and to this end have presented the detailed methods and formulas rather as suggestions than as rules necessarily to be followed.

The book contains more exercises than are ordinarily needed. As material for review, however, a supplementary list of exercises is placed at the end of the text.

The appendix contains a short table of integrals which includes most of the forms occurring in the exercises. Through the courtesy of Prof. R. G. Hudson I have taken a two-page table of natural logarithms from his Engineers' Manual.

I am indebted to Professors H. W. Tyler, C. L. E. Moore, and Joseph Lipka for suggestions and assistance in preparing the manuscript.

H. B. PHILLIPS.

CAMBRIDGE, MASS.
June, 1917.

CONTENTS

INTEGRAL CALCULUS

CHAPTER I

INTEGRATION

1. Integral. — A function $F(x)$ whose differential is equal to $f(x)\,dx$ is called an *integral* of $f(x)\,dx$. Such a function is represented by the notation $\int f(x)\,dx$. Thus

$$F(x) = \int f(x)\,dx, \qquad dF(x) = f(x)\,dx,$$

are by definition equivalent equations. The process of finding an integral of a given differential is called *integration*.

For example, since $d(x^2) = 2x\,dx$,

$$\int 2x\,dx = x^2.$$

Similarly,

$$\int \cos x\,dx = \sin x, \qquad \int e^x\,dx = e^x.$$

The test of integration is to differentiate the integral. If it is correct, its differential must be the expression integrated.

2. Constant of Integration. — If C is any constant,

$$d\,[F(x) + C] = d\,F(x).$$

If then $F(x)$ is one integral of a given differential, $F(x) + C$ is another. For example,

$$\int 2x\,dx = x^2 + C, \qquad \int \cos x\,dx = \sin x + C,$$

where C is any constant.

1

We shall now prove that, *if two continuous functions of one variable have the same differential, their difference is constant.*

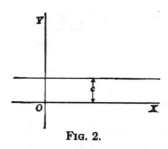

FIG. 2.

Suppose $F_1(x)$ and $F_2(x)$ are functions having the same differential. Then

$$dF_1(x) = dF_2(x).$$

Let $y = F_2(x) - F_1(x)$ and plot the locus representing y as a function of x. The slope of this locus is

$$\frac{dy}{dx} = \frac{dF_2(x) - dF_1(x)}{dx} = 0.$$

Since the slope is everywhere zero, the locus is a horizontal line. The equation of such a line is $y = C$. Therefore,

$$F_2(x) - F_1(x) = C,$$

which was to be proved.

If then $F(x)$ is one continuous integral of $f(x)\,dx$, any other continuous integral has the form

$$\int f(x)\,dx = F(x) + C. \tag{2}$$

Any value can be assigned to C. It is called an *arbitrary constant*.

3. Formulas. — Let a and n be constants, u, v, w, variables.

    I. $\displaystyle\int du \pm dv \pm dw = \int du \pm \int dv \pm \int dw.$

    II. $\displaystyle\int a\,du = a\int du.$

    III. $\displaystyle\int u^n\,du = \frac{u^{n+1}}{n+1} + C,$ if n is not -1.

    IV. $\displaystyle\int u^{-1}\,du = \int \frac{du}{u} = \ln u + C.$

These formulas are proved by showing that the differential of the right member is equal to the expression under the integral sign. Thus to prove III we differentiate the right side and so obtain

$$d\left(\frac{u^{n+1}}{n+1}+C\right) = \frac{(n+1)\,u^n\,du}{n+1} = u^n\,du.$$

Formula I expresses that the integral of an algebraic sum of differentials is obtained by integrating them separately and adding the results.

Formula II expresses that a constant factor can be transferred from one side of the symbol $\int$ to the other without changing the result. A variable cannot be transferred in this way. Thus it is not correct to write

$$\int x\,dx = x\int dx = x^2.$$

Example 1. $\int x^5\,dx.$

Apply Formula III, letting $u = x$ and $n = 5$. Then $dx = du$ and

$$\int x^5\,dx = \frac{x^{5+1}}{5+1}+C = \frac{x^6}{6}+C.$$

Ex. 2. $\int 3\sqrt{x}\,dx.$

By Formula II we have

$$\int 3\sqrt{x}\,dx = 3\int x^{\frac{1}{2}}\,dx = \frac{3\,x^{\frac{3}{2}}}{\frac{3}{2}}+C = 2\,x^{\frac{3}{2}}+C.$$

Ex. 3. $\int (x-1)\,(x+2)\,dx.$

We expand and integrate term by term.

$$\int (x-1)\,(x+2)\,dx = \int (x^2+x-2)\,dx$$
$$= \tfrac{1}{3}x^3 + \tfrac{1}{2}x^2 - 2\,x + C.$$

Ex. 4. $\displaystyle\int \frac{x^2 - 2x + 1}{x^3}\, dx.$

Dividing by x^3 and using negative exponents, we get

$$\int \frac{x^2 - 2x + 1}{x^3}\, dx = \int (x^{-1} - 2x^{-2} + x^{-3})\, dx$$

$$= \ln x + 2x^{-1} - \tfrac{1}{2} x^{-2} + C$$

$$= \ln x + \frac{2}{x} - \frac{1}{2x^2} + C.$$

Ex. 5. $\displaystyle\int \sqrt{2x + 1}\, dx.$

If $u = 2x + 1$, $du = 2\, dx$. We therefore place a factor 2 before dx and $\tfrac{1}{2}$ outside the integral sign to compensate for it.

$$\int \sqrt{2x + 1}\, dx = \tfrac{1}{2} \int (2x + 1)^{\frac{1}{2}} 2\, dx = \tfrac{1}{2} \int u^{\frac{1}{2}}\, du$$

$$= \frac{1}{2} \frac{u^{\frac{3}{2}}}{\frac{3}{2}} + C = \frac{1}{3} (2x + 1)^{\frac{3}{2}} + C.$$

Ex. 6. $\displaystyle\int \frac{x\, dx}{x^2 + 1}.$

Apply IV with $u = x^2 + 1$. Then $du = 2x\, dx$ and

$$\int \frac{x\, dx}{x^2 + 1} = \frac{1}{2} \int \frac{2x\, dx}{x^2 + 1} = \frac{1}{2} \int \frac{du}{u} = \frac{1}{2} \ln u + C = \ln \sqrt{x^2 + 1} + C.$$

Ex. 7. $\displaystyle\int \frac{4x + 2}{2x - 1}\, dx.$

By division, we find

$$\frac{4x + 2}{2x - 1} = 2 + \frac{4}{2x - 1}.$$

Therefore

$$\int \frac{4x + 2}{2x - 1}\, dx = \int \left(2 + \frac{4}{2x - 1}\right) dx = 2x + 2 \ln (2x - 1) + C.$$

EXERCISES

Find the values of the following integrals:

1. $\int (x^4 - 3x^3 + 5x^2)\, dx.$

2. $\int \left(x^2 - \dfrac{1}{x^2}\right) dx.$

3. $\int \left(\sqrt{x} + \dfrac{1}{\sqrt{x}}\right) dx.$

4. $\int \left(\sqrt{2x} - \dfrac{1}{\sqrt{2x}}\right) dx.$

5. $\int \big(\sqrt{x}\,(x^2) + 2x + 1\big)\, dx.$

6. $\int (\sqrt{a} - \sqrt{x})^3\, dx.$

7. $\int x\,(x + a)\,(x + b)\, dx.$

8. $\int \dfrac{2x + 3}{x}\, dx.$

9. $\int \dfrac{(y + 2)^2}{y}\, dy.$

10. $\int \dfrac{(x^2 + 1)\,(x^3 - 2)}{x^{\frac{2}{3}}}\, dx.$

11. $\int \dfrac{dx}{x + 1}.$

12. $\int \dfrac{dx}{(x + 1)^2}.$

13. $\int \dfrac{dx}{\sqrt{2x + 1}}.$

14. $\int \dfrac{x\, dx}{x^2 + 2}.$

15. $\int \dfrac{x\, dx}{\sqrt{x^2 - 1}}.$

16. $\int \dfrac{x\, dx}{(a + bx^2)^3}$

17. $\int x.\sqrt{a^2 - x^2}\, dx.$

18. $\int \dfrac{x^2\, dx}{a^3 + x^3}.$

19. $\int x^2\,\sqrt{x^3 - 1}\, dx.$

20. $\int \dfrac{2x + a}{x^2 + ax + b}\, dx.$

21. $\int \dfrac{(2x + a)\, dx}{\sqrt{x^2 + ax + b}}.$

22. $\int \dfrac{t^4\, dt}{1 - at^6}.$

23. $\int t\,(a^2 - t^2)^{\frac{3}{2}}\, dt.$

24. $\int \dfrac{x + 1}{x - 2}\, dx.$

25. $\int \left(2 + \dfrac{1}{2x^2 + 1}\right) \dfrac{x\, dx}{2x^2 + 1}.$

26. $\int \left(1 - \dfrac{1}{x}\right)^3 \dfrac{dx}{x^2}.$

27. $\int \dfrac{x^{n-1}\, dx}{(x^n + a)^n}.$

28. $\int (\sqrt{2x} - \sqrt{2a})^{10}\, \dfrac{dx}{\sqrt{x}}.$

29. $\int \dfrac{x^3 - 2}{x^3 + 2}\, x^2\, dx.$

30. $\int (x^3 - 1)^2\, x\, dx.$

4. Motion of a Particle. — Let the acceleration of a particle moving along a straight line be a, the velocity v, and the distance passed over s. Then, $k = const \checkmark$

$$a = \frac{dv}{dt}, \qquad v = \frac{ds}{dt}.$$

Consequently,

$$dv = a\, dt, \qquad ds = v\, dt.$$

If then a is a known function of the time or a constant,

$$v = \int a\,dt + C_1, \qquad s = \int v\,dt + C_2. \qquad (4)$$

If the particle moves along a curve and the components of velocity or acceleration are known, each coördinate can be found in a similar way.

Example 1.   A body falls from rest under the constant acceleration of gravity g.   Find its velocity and the distance traversed as functions of the time t.

In this case

$$a = \frac{dv}{dt} = g.$$

Hence

$$v = \int g\,dt = gt + C.$$

Since the body starts from rest, $v = 0$ when $t = 0$.   These values of v and t must satisfy the equation $v = gt + C$. Hence

$$0 = g{\cdot}0 + C,$$

whence $C = 0$ and $v = gt$.   Since $v = \frac{ds}{dt}$, $ds = gt\,dt$ and

$$s = \int gt\,dt + C = \tfrac{1}{2}gt^2 + C.$$

When $t = 0$, $s = 0$.   Consequently, $C = 0$ and $s = \tfrac{1}{2}gt^2$.

Ex. 2.   A projectile is fired with a velocity v_0 in a direction making an angle α with the horizontal plane.   Neglecting the resistance of the air, find its motion.

Pass a vertical plane through the line along which the particle starts.   In this plane take the starting point as origin, the horizontal line as x-axis, and the vertical line as y-axis.   The only acceleration is that of gravity acting downward and equal to g.   Hence

$$\frac{d^2x}{dt^2} = 0, \qquad \frac{d^2y}{dt^2} = -g.$$

Integration gives,

$$\frac{dx}{dt} = C_1, \qquad \frac{dy}{dt} = -gt + C_2.$$

When $t = 0$, $\frac{dx}{dt}$ and $\frac{dy}{dt}$ are the components of v_0. Hence $C_1 = v_0 \cos \alpha, C_2 = v_0 \sin \alpha$, and

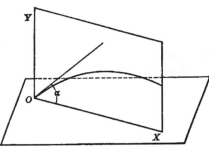

$$\frac{dx}{dt} = v_0 \cos \alpha,$$

$$\frac{dy}{dt} = v_0 \sin \alpha - gt.$$

Integrating again, we get

$$x = v_0 t \cos \alpha,$$
$$y = v_0 t \sin \alpha - \tfrac{1}{2} g t^2,$$

FIG. 4.

the constants being zero because x and y are zero when $t = 0$.

5. Curves with a Given Slope. — If the slope of a curve is a given function of x,

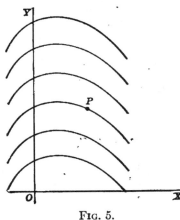

$$\frac{dy}{dx} = f(x),$$

then

$$dy = f(x)\, dx$$

and

$$y = \int f(x)\, dx + C$$

is the equation of the curve.

Since the constant can have any value, there are an infinite number of curves having the given slope. If the curve is required to pass through a given point P, the

FIG. 5.

value of C can be found by substituting the coördinates of P in the equation after integration.

Example 1. Find the curve passing through (1, 2) with slope equal to 2 x.

In this case

$$\frac{dy}{dx} = 2\,x.$$

Hence

$$y = \int 2\,x\,dx = x^2 + C.$$

Since the curve passes through (1, 2), the values $x = 1$, $y = 2$ must satisfy the equation, that is

$$2 = 1 + C.$$

Consequently, $C = 1$ and $y = x^2 + 1$ is the equation of the curve.

Ex. 2. On a certain curve

$$\frac{d^2y}{dx^2} = x.$$

If the curve passes through $(-2, 1)$ and has at that point the slope -2, find its equation.

By integration we get

$$\frac{dy}{dx} = \int \frac{d^2y}{dx^2}\,dx = \int x\,dx = \frac{1}{2}x^2 + C.$$

At $(-2, 1)$, $x = -2$ and $\frac{dy}{dx} = -2$. Hence

$$-2 = 2 + C,$$

or $C = -4$. Consequently,

$$y = \int (\tfrac{1}{2}x^2 - 4)\,dx = \tfrac{1}{6}x^3 - 4\,x + C.$$

Since the curve passes through $(-2, 1)$,

$$1 = -\tfrac{4}{3} + 8 + C.$$

Consequently, $C = -5\tfrac{2}{3}$, and

$$y = \tfrac{1}{6}x^3 - 4\,x - 5\tfrac{2}{3}$$

is the equation of the curve.

6. Separation of the Variables. — The integration formulas contain only one variable. If a differential contains two or more variables, it must be reduced to a form in which each term contains a single variable. If this cannot be done, we cannot integrate the differential by our present methods.

Example 1. Find the curves such that the part of the tangent included between the coördinate axes is bisected at the point of tangency.

Let $P(x, y)$ be the point at which AB is tangent to the curve. Since P is the middle point of AB,

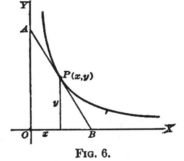

$$OA = 2y, \qquad OB = 2x.$$

The slope of the curve at P is

$$\frac{dy}{dx} = -\frac{OA}{OB} = -\frac{y}{x}.$$

This can be written

$$\frac{dy}{y} + \frac{dx}{x} = 0.$$

FIG. 6.

Since each term contains a single variable, we can integrate and so get

$$\ln y + \ln x = C.$$

This is equivalent to

$$\ln xy = C.$$

Hence

$$xy = e^C = k.$$

C, and consequently k, can have any value. The curves are rectangular hyperbolas with the coördinate axes as asymptotes.

Ex. 2. According to Newton's law of cooling,

$$\frac{d\theta}{dt} = -k(\theta - a).$$

when k is constant, a the temperature of the air, and θ the temperature at the time t of a body cooling in the air. Find θ as a function of t.

Multiplying by dt and dividing by $\theta - a$, Newton's equation becomes

$$\frac{d\theta}{\theta - a} = -k\,dt.$$

Integrating both sides, we get

$$\ln(\theta - a) = -kt + C.$$

Hence

$$\theta - a = e^{-kt+C} = e^C e^{-kt}.$$

When $t = 0$, let $\theta = \theta_0$. Then

$$\theta_0 - a = e^C e^0 = e^C,$$

and so

$$\theta - a = (\theta_0 - a)\,e^{-kt}$$

is the equation required.

Ex. 3. The retarding effect of fluid friction on a rotating disk is proportional to the angular speed ω. Find ω as a function of the time t.

The statement means that the rate of change of ω is proportional to ω, that is,

$$\frac{d\omega}{dt} = k\omega,$$

where k is constant. Separating the variables, we get

$$\frac{d\omega}{\omega} = k\,dt,$$

whence

$$\ln \omega = kt + C,$$

and

$$\omega = e^{kt+C} = e^C e^{kt}.$$

Let ω_0 be the value of ω when $t = 0$. Then

$$\omega_0 = e^{k \cdot 0} e^C = e^C.$$

Replacing e^C by ω_0, the previous equation becomes

$$\omega = \omega_0 e^{kt},$$

which is the result required.

Ex. 4. A cylindrical tank full of water has a leak at the bottom. Assuming that the water escapes at a rate proportional to the depth and that $\frac{1}{10}$ of it escapes the first day, how long will it take to half empty?

Let the radius of the tank be a, its height h and the depth of the water after t days x. The volume of the water at any time is $\pi a^2 x$ and its rate of change

$$- \pi a^2 \frac{dx}{dt}.$$

This is assumed to be proportional to x, that is,

$$\pi a^2 \frac{dx}{dt} = kx,$$

where k is constant. Separating the variables,

$$\frac{\pi a^2 \, dx}{x} = k \, dt.$$

Integration gives

$$\pi a^2 \ln x = kt + C.$$

When $t = 0$ the tank is full and $x = h$. Hence

$$\pi a^2 \ln h = C.$$

Subtracting this from the preceding equation, we get

$$\pi a^2 \ln \frac{x}{h} = kt.$$

When $t = 1$, $x = \frac{9}{10} h$. Consequently,

$$\pi a^2 \ln \tfrac{9}{10} = k.$$

When $x = \frac{1}{2} h$,

$$t = \frac{\pi a^2 \ln \dfrac{x}{h}}{k} = \frac{\ln \frac{1}{2}}{\ln \frac{9}{10}} = 6.57 \text{ days.}$$

EXERCISES

1. If the velocity of a body moving along a line is $v = 2t + 3t^2$, find the distance traversed between $t = 2$ and $t = 5$.

2. Find the distance a body started vertically downward with a velocity of 30 ft./sec. will fall in the time t.

3. From a point 60 ft. above the street a ball is thrown vertically upward with a speed of 100 ft./sec. Find its height as a function of the time. Also find the highest point reached.

4. A rifle ball is fired through a 3-inch plank the resistance of which causes a negative constant acceleration. If its velocity on entering the plank is 1000 ft./sec. and on leaving it 500 ft./sec., how long does it take the ball to pass through?

5. A particle starts at (1, 2). After t seconds the component of its velocity parallel to the x-axis is $2t - 1$ and that parallel to the y-axis is $1 - t$. Find its coördinates as functions of the time. Also find the equation of its path.

6 A bullet is fired at a velocity of 3000 ft./sec. at an angle of 45° from a point 100 ft. above the ground. Neglecting the resistance of the air, find where the bullet will strike the ground.

7. Find the motion of a particle started from the origin with velocity v_0 in the vertical direction, if its acceleration is a constant K in a direction making 30° with the horizontal plane.

8. Find the equation of the curve with slope $2 - x$ passing through (1, 0).

9. Find the equation of the curve with slope equal to y passing through (0, 1).

10. On a certain curve

$$\frac{dy}{dx} = 2x + 3.$$

If the curve passes through (1, 2), find its lowest point.

11. On a certain curve

$$\frac{d^2y}{dx^2} = x - 1.$$

If the curve passes through (− 1, 1) and has at that point the slope 2, find its equation.

12. On a certain curve

$$\frac{d^2y}{dx^2} = 2 - 3x.$$

If the slope is − 1 at $x = 0$, find the difference of the ordinates at $x = 3$ and $x = 4$.

13. The pressure of the air p and altitude above sea level h are connected by the equation

$$\frac{dp}{dh} = - kp,$$

where k is constant. Show that $p = p_0 e^{-kh}$, when p_0 is the pressure at sea level.

14. Radium decomposes at a rate proportional to the amount present. If half the original quantity disappears in 1800 years, what percentage disappears in 100 years?

15. When bacteria grow in the presence of unlimited food, they increase at a rate proportional to the number present. Express that number as a function of the time.

16. Cane sugar is decomposed into other substances through the presence of acids. The rate at which the process takes place is proportional to the mass x of sugar still unchanged. Show that $x = ce^{-kt}$. What does c represent?

17. The rate at which water flows from a small opening at the bottom of a tank is proportional to the square root of the depth of the water. If half the water flows from a cylindrical tank in 5 minutes, find the time required to empty the tank.

18. Solve Ex. 17, when the cylindrical tank is replaced by a conical funnel.

19. A sum of money is placed at compound interest at 6 per cent per annum, the interest being added to the principal at each instant. How many years will be required for the sum to double?

20. The amount of light absorbed in penetrating a thin sheet of water is proportional to the amount falling on the surface and approximately proportional to the thickness of the sheet, the approximation increasing as the thickness approaches zero. Show that the rate of change of illumination is proportional to the depth and so find the illumination as a function of the depth.

CHAPTER II

FORMULAS AND METHODS OF INTEGRATION

7. Formulas. — The following is a short list of integration formulas. In these u is any variable or function of a single variable and du is its differential. The constant is omitted but it should be added to each function determined by integration. A more extended list of formulas is given in the Appendix.

I. $\displaystyle\int u^n \, du = \frac{u^{n+1}}{n+1}$, if n is not -1. $\;\displaystyle\int \frac{dv}{v} = \ln v + c$

II. $\displaystyle\int \frac{du}{u} = \ln u.$

III. $\displaystyle\int \cos u \, du = \sin u.$

IV. $\displaystyle\int \sin u \, du = -\cos u.$

V. $\displaystyle\int \sec^2 u \, du = \tan u.$

VI. $\displaystyle\int \csc^2 u \, du = -\cot u.$

VII. $\displaystyle\int \sec u \tan u \, du = \sec u.$

VIII. $\displaystyle\int \csc u \cot u \, du = -\csc u.$

IX. $\displaystyle\int \tan u \, du = -\ln \cos u.$

X. $\displaystyle\int \cot u \, du = \ln \sin u.$

XI. $\displaystyle\int \sec u \, du = \ln (\sec u + \tan u).$

14

XII. $\displaystyle\int \csc u \, du = \ln\left(\csc u - \cot u\right).$

XIII. $\displaystyle\int \frac{du}{\sqrt{a^2 - u^2}} = \sin^{-1}\frac{u}{a}.$ *

XIV. $\displaystyle\int \frac{du}{u^2 + a^2} = \frac{1}{a}\tan^{-1}\frac{u}{a}.$

XV. $\displaystyle\int \frac{du}{u\sqrt{u^2 - a^2}} = \frac{1}{a}\sec^{-1}\frac{u}{a}.$ *

XVI. $\displaystyle\int \frac{du}{\sqrt{u^2 \pm a^2}} = \ln\left(u + \sqrt{u^2 \pm a^2}\right).$

XVII. $\displaystyle\int \frac{du}{u^2 - a^2} = \frac{1}{2a}\ln\frac{u - a}{u + a}.$

XVIII. $\displaystyle\int e^u \, du = e^u.$

Any one of these formulas can be proved by showing that the differential of the right member is equal to the expression under the integral sign. Thus to show that

$$\int \sec u \, du = \ln\left(\sec u + \tan u\right),$$

we note that

$$d\ln\left(\sec u + \tan u\right) = \frac{\left(\sec u \tan u + \sec^2 u\right) du}{\sec u + \tan u} = \sec u \, du.$$

8. Integration by Substitution. — When some function of the variable is taken as u, a given differential may assume the form of the differential in one of the integration formulas or differ from such form only by a constant factor. Integration accomplished in this way is called integration by substitution.

Each differential is the product of a function of u by du. More errors result from failing to pay attention to the du

* In Formulas XIII and XV it is assumed that $\sin^{-1}\frac{u}{a}$ is an angle in the 1st or 4th quadrant, and $\sec^{-1}\frac{u}{a}$ an angle in the 1st òr 2nd quadrant. In other cases the algebraic sign of the result must be changed.

than from any other one cause. Thus the student may carelessly conclude from Formula III that the integral of a cosine is a sine and so write

$$\int \cos 2x \, dx = \sin 2x.$$

If, however, we let $2x = u$, dx is not du but $\frac{1}{2} du$ and so

$$\int \cos 2x \, dx = \frac{1}{2} \int \cos u \, du = \frac{1}{2} \sin u = \frac{1}{2} \sin 2x.$$

Example 1. $\int \sin^3 x \cos x \, dx.$

If we let $u = \sin x$, $du = \cos x \, dx$ and

$$\int \sin^3 x \cos x \, dx = \int u^3 \, du = \frac{1}{4} u^4 + C = \frac{1}{4} \sin^4 x + C.$$

Ex. 2. $\int \dfrac{\sin \frac{1}{3} x \, dx}{1 + \cos \frac{1}{3} x}.$

We observe that $\sin \frac{1}{3} x \, dx$ differs only by a constant factor from the differential of $1 + \cos \frac{1}{3} x$. Hence we let

$$u = 1 + \cos \tfrac{1}{3} x.$$

Then $du = -\frac{1}{3} \sin \frac{1}{3} x \, dx,$ $\sin \frac{1}{3} x \, dx = -3 \, du,$

and $\displaystyle \int \frac{\sin \frac{1}{3} x \, dx}{1 + \cos \frac{1}{3} x} = -3 \int \frac{du}{u} = -3 \ln u + C$

$$= -3 \ln \left(1 + \cos \tfrac{1}{3} x\right) + C.$$

Ex. 3. $\int (\tan x + \sec x) \sec x \, dx.$

Expanding we get

$$\int (\tan x + \sec x) \sec x \, dx = \int \tan x \sec x \, dx + \int \sec^2 x \, dx$$

$$= \sec x + \tan x + C.$$

Ex. 4. $\int \dfrac{3 \, dx}{\sqrt{2 - 3x^2}}.$

This resembles the integral in formula XIII. Let $u = x\sqrt{3}$, $a = \sqrt{2}$. Then $du = \sqrt{3}\,dx$ and

$$\int \frac{3\,dx}{\sqrt{2-3\,x^2}} = \int \frac{3\,\dfrac{du}{\sqrt{3}}}{\sqrt{a^2-u^2}} = \sqrt{3}\int \frac{du}{\sqrt{a^2-u^2}}$$

$$= \sqrt{3}\,\sin^{-1}\frac{u}{a} + C = \sqrt{3}\,\sin^{-1}\frac{x\sqrt{3}}{\sqrt{2}} + C.$$

Ex. 5. $\displaystyle\int \frac{dt}{t\sqrt{4\,t^2-9}}.$

This suggests the integral in formula XV. Let $u = 2\,t$, $a = 3$. Then

$$\int \frac{dt}{t\sqrt{4\,t^2-9}} = \int \frac{2\,dt}{2\,t\sqrt{4\,t^2-9}} = \int \frac{du}{u\sqrt{u^2-a^2}}$$

$$= \frac{1}{a}\sec^{-1}\frac{u}{a} + C = \frac{1}{3}\sec^{-1}\frac{2\,t}{3} + C.$$

Ex. 6. $\displaystyle\int \frac{x\,dx}{\sqrt{2\,x^2+1}}.$

This may suggest formula XVI. If, however, we let $u = x\sqrt{2}$, $du = \sqrt{2}\,dx$, which is not a constant times $x\,dx$. We should let

$$u = 2\,x^2 + 1.$$

Then $x\,dx = \frac{1}{4}\,du$ and

$$\int \frac{x\,dx}{\sqrt{2\,x^2+1}} = \frac{1}{4}\int \frac{du}{\sqrt{u}} = \frac{1}{4}\int u^{-\frac{1}{2}}\,du$$

$$= \frac{1}{2}\sqrt{u} + C = \frac{1}{2}\sqrt{2\,x^2+1} + C.$$

Ex. 7. $\displaystyle\int e^{\tan x}\sec^2 x\,dx.$

If $u = \tan x$, by formula XVIII

$$\int e^{\tan x}\sec^2 x\,dx = \int e^u\,du = e^u + C = e^{\tan x} + C.$$

EXERCISES

Determine the values of the following integrals:

1. $\int (\sin 2x - \cos 3x)\, dx.$

2. $\int \cos \left(\dfrac{2x-3}{5} \right) dx.$

3. $\int \sin (nt + \alpha)\, dt.$

4. $\int \sec^2 \tfrac{1}{3} \theta\, d\theta.$

5. $\int \csc \dfrac{\theta}{4} \cot \dfrac{\theta}{4}\, d\theta.$

6. $\int \cos \theta \sin \theta\, d\theta.$

7. $\int \dfrac{dx}{\cos^3 x}.$

8. $\int \dfrac{dx}{\sin^2 2x}.$

9. $\int \dfrac{\cos x\, dx}{\sin^2 x}.$

10. $\int \dfrac{\sin x\, dx}{\cos^5 x}.$

11. $\int \left(\csc \dfrac{\theta}{2} - \cot \dfrac{\theta}{2} \right) \csc \dfrac{\theta}{2}\, d\theta.$

12. $\int \cos (x^2 - 1)\, x\, dx.$

13. $\int \dfrac{1 + \sin 3x}{\cos^2 3x}\, dx.$

14. $\int (\sec x - 1)^2\, dx.$

15. $\int \dfrac{1 - \sin x}{\cos x}\, dx.$

16. $\int (\cos \theta - \sin \theta)^2\, d\theta.$

17. $\int \dfrac{(\cos x + \sin x)^2}{\sin x}\, dx.$

18. $\int \sin^2 x \cos x\, dx.$

19. $\int \tan^3 x \sec^2 x\, dx.$

20. $\int \sec^2 x \tan x\, dx.$

21. $\int \cos^5 x \sin x\, dx.$

22. $\int \dfrac{\sec^2 x\, dx}{1 + 2 \tan x}.$

23. $\int \dfrac{\cos 2x\, dx}{1 - \sin 2x}.$

24. $\int \dfrac{\sec^2 (ax)\, dx}{1 + \tan (ax)}.$

25. $\int \dfrac{dx}{\sqrt{3 - 2x^3}}.$

26. $\int \dfrac{2\, dx}{3x^2 + 4}.$

27. $\int \dfrac{dx}{x \sqrt{3x^2 - 4}}.$

28. $\int \dfrac{dy}{12 y^2 + 3}.$

29. $\int \dfrac{dx}{\sqrt{7x^2 + 1}}.$

30. $\int \dfrac{dx}{x \sqrt{a^2 x^2 - 9}}.$

31. $\int \dfrac{dx}{3 - 4x^2}.$

32. $\int \dfrac{dx}{\sqrt{4x^2 - 3}}.$

33. $\int \dfrac{(3x - 2)\, dx}{\sqrt{4 - x^2}}.$

34. $\int \dfrac{2x + 3}{\sqrt{x^2 + 4}}\, dx.$

35. $\int \dfrac{x + 4}{4x^2 - 5}\, dx.$

36. $\int \dfrac{5x - 2}{\sqrt{3x^2 - 9}}\, dx.$

37. $\int \dfrac{\cos x\, dx}{\sqrt{2 - \sin^2 x}}.$

38. $\int \dfrac{\sin x \cos x\, dx}{\sqrt{2 - \sin^2 x}}.$

39. $\int \dfrac{\cos x\, dx}{1 + \sin^2 x}.$

40. $\int \dfrac{\sec^2 x\, dx}{\tan x \sqrt{\tan^2 x - 1}}.$

41. $\int \dfrac{\sec x \tan x\, dx}{\sqrt{\sec^2 x + 1}}.$

42. $\int \dfrac{\sin \theta\, d\theta}{\sqrt{1 - \cos \theta}}.$

43. $\int \dfrac{dx}{x\,[4 - (\ln x)^2]}.$

44. $\int \dfrac{\sin x \cos x\, dx}{\sqrt{\cos^2 x - \sin^2 x}}.$

45. $\int \dfrac{x\, dx}{\sqrt{a^4 - x^4}}.$

46. $\int e^{-k^2 x}\, dx.$

47. $\int (e^{ax} + e^{-ax})^2\, dx.$

48. $\int \dfrac{e^{3x}\, dx}{1 + e^{3x}}.$

49. $\int \dfrac{e^x - e^{-x}}{e^x + e^{-x}}\, dx.$

50. $\int e^{-\frac{1}{x}} \dfrac{dx}{x^2}.$

51. $\int \dfrac{e^x\, dx}{1 + e^{2x}}.$

52. $\int \dfrac{e^{-x}\, dx}{1 - e^{-2x}}.$

53. $\int \dfrac{e^{ax}\, dx}{\sqrt{1 - e^{2ax}}}.$

54. $\int \dfrac{dx}{e^x + e^{-x}}.$

9. Integrals Containing $ax^2 + bx + c.$ Integrals containing a quadratic expression $ax^2 + bx + C$ can often be reduced to manageable form by completing the square of $ax^2 + bx.$

Example 1. $\displaystyle\int \dfrac{dx}{3x^2 + 6x + 5}.$

Completing the square, we get

$$3x^2 + 6x + 5 = 3(x^2 + 2x + 1) + 2 = 3(x + 1)^2 + 2.$$

If then $u = (x + 1)\sqrt{3},$

$$\int \dfrac{dx}{3x^2 + 6x + 5} = \int \dfrac{d(x + 1)}{3(x + 1)^2 + 2} = \dfrac{1}{\sqrt{3}} \int \dfrac{du}{u^2 + 2}$$

$$= \dfrac{1}{\sqrt{6}} \tan^{-1} \dfrac{(x + 1)\sqrt{3}}{\sqrt{2}} + C.$$

Ex. 2. $\displaystyle\int \dfrac{2\, dx}{\sqrt{2 - 3x - x^2}}.$

The coefficient of x^2 being negative, we place the terms x^2 and $3x$ in a parenthesis preceded by a minus sign. Thus

$$2 - 3x - x^2 = 2 - (x^2 + 3x) = \tfrac{17}{4} - (x + \tfrac{3}{2})^2.$$

If then, $u = x + \frac{3}{2}$, we have

$$\int \frac{2\,dx}{\sqrt{2-3x-x^2}} = 2\int \frac{du}{\sqrt{\frac{17}{4}-u^2}} = 2\sin^{-1}\frac{x+\frac{3}{2}}{\frac{1}{2}\sqrt{17}} + C.$$

Ex. 3. $\int \dfrac{(2x-1)\,dx.}{\sqrt{4x^2+4x+2}}$.

Since the numerator contains the first power of x, we resolve the integral into two parts,

$$\int \frac{(2x-1)\,dx}{\sqrt{4x^2+4x+2}} = \frac{1}{4}\int \frac{(8x+4)\,dx}{\sqrt{4x^2+4x+2}} - 2\int \frac{dx}{\sqrt{4x^2+4x+2}}.$$

In the first integral on the right the numerator is taken equal to the differential of $4x^2+4x+2$. In the second the numerator is dx. The outside factors $\frac{1}{4}$ and -2 are chosen so that the two sides of the equation are equal. The first integral has the form

$$\frac{1}{4}\int \frac{du}{\sqrt{u}} = \frac{1}{2}\sqrt{u} = \frac{1}{2}\sqrt{4x^2+4x+2}.$$

The second integral is evaluated by completing the square. The final result is

$$\int \frac{(2x-1)\,dx}{\sqrt{4x^2+4x+2}} = \frac{1}{2}\sqrt{4x^2+4x+2}$$
$$- \ln\left(2x+1+\sqrt{4x^2+4x+2}\right) + C.$$

EXERCISES

1. $\int \dfrac{dx}{x^2+6x+13}$.

2. $\int \dfrac{dx}{\sqrt{2+4x-4x^2}}$.

3. $\int \dfrac{dx}{\sqrt{3x^2+4x+2}}$.

4. $\int \dfrac{dx}{\sqrt{1+5x-5x^2}}$.

5. $\int \dfrac{dx}{(x-3)\sqrt{2x^2-12x+15}}$.

6. $\int \dfrac{dx}{(x+a)(x+b)}$.

7. $\int \dfrac{(2x+5)\,dx}{4x^2-4x-2}$.

8. $\int \dfrac{(2x-1)\,dx}{\sqrt{3x^2-6x+1}}$.

9. $\int \dfrac{x\,dx}{3x^2+2x+2}$.

10. $\int \dfrac{(2x+3)\,dx.}{(2x+1)\sqrt{4x^2+4x-1}}$.

11. $\int \dfrac{(3x-3)\,dx}{(x^2-2x+3)^{\frac{1}{2}}}$.

12. $\int \sqrt{\dfrac{x+1}{x-2}}\,dx$.

13. $\int \dfrac{e^x\,dx}{2e^{2x}+3e^x-1}$.

10. Integrals of Trigonometric Functions. — A power of a trigonometric function multiplied by its differential can be integrated by Formula I. Thus, if $u = \tan x$,

$$\int \tan^4 x \cdot \sec^2 x \, dx = \int u^4 \, du = \tfrac{1}{5} \tan^5 x + C.$$

Differentials can often be reduced to the above form by trigonometric transformations. This is illustrated by the following examples.

Example 1. $\int \sin^4 x \cos^3 x \, dx.$

If we take $\cos x \, dx$ as du and use the relation $\cos^2 x = 1 - \sin^2 x$, the other factors can be expressed in terms of $\sin x$ *without introducing radicals.* Thus

$$\int \sin^4 x \cos^3 x \, dx = \int \sin^4 x \cos^2 x \cdot \cos x \, dx$$

$$= \int \sin^4 x \, (1 - \sin^2 x) \, d \sin x = \tfrac{1}{5} \sin^5 x - \tfrac{1}{7} \sin^7 x + C.$$

Ex. 2. $\int \tan^3 x \sec^4 x \, dx.$

If we take $\sec^2 x \, dx$ as du and use the relation $\sec^2 x = 1 + \tan^2 x$, the other factors can be expressed in terms of $u = \tan x$ without introducing radicals. Thus

$$\int \tan^3 x \sec^4 x \, dx = \int \tan^3 x \cdot \sec^2 x \cdot \sec^2 x \, dx$$

$$= \int \tan^3 x \, (1 + \tan^2 x) \, d \tan x$$

$$= \tfrac{1}{4} \tan^4 x + \tfrac{1}{6} \tan^6 x + C.$$

Ex. 3. $\int \tan^3 x \sec^3 x \, dx.$

If we take $\tan x \sec x \, dx = d \sec x$ as du, and use the relation $\tan^2 x = \sec^2 x - 1$, the integral takes the form

$$\int \tan^3 x \sec^3 x \, dx = \int \tan^2 x \cdot \sec^2 x \cdot \tan x \sec x \, dx$$

$$= \int (\sec^2 x - 1) \sec^2 x \cdot d \sec x$$

$$= \tfrac{1}{5} \sec^5 x - \tfrac{1}{3} \sec^3 x + C.$$

Ex. 4. $\displaystyle\int \sin 2 x \cos 3 x \, dx.$

This is the product of the sine of one angle and the cosine of another. This product can be resolved into a sum or difference by the formula

$$\sin A \cos B = \tfrac{1}{2} [\sin (A + B) + \sin (A - B)].$$

Thus

$$\sin 2 x \cos 3 x = \tfrac{1}{2} [\sin 5 x + \sin (- x)]$$
$$= \tfrac{1}{2} [\sin 5 x - \sin x]$$

Consequently,

$$\int \sin 2 x \cos 3 x \, dx = \tfrac{1}{2} \int (\sin 5 x - \sin x) \, dx$$

$$= - \tfrac{1}{10} \cos 5 x + \tfrac{1}{2} \cos x + C.$$

Ex. 5. $\displaystyle\int \tan^5 x \, dx.$

If we replace $\tan^2 x$ by $\sec^2 x - 1$, the integral becomes

$$\int \tan^5 x \, dx = \int \tan^3 x \, (\sec^2 x - 1) \, dx = \tfrac{1}{4} \tan^4 x - \int \tan^3 x \, dx.$$

The integral is thus made to depend on a simpler one $\displaystyle\int \tan^3 x \, dx.$ Similarly,

$$\int \tan^3 x \, dx = \int \tan x \, (\sec^2 x - 1) \, dx = \tfrac{1}{2} \tan^2 x + \ln \cos x.$$

Hence finally

$$\int \tan^5 x \, dx = \tfrac{1}{4} \tan^4 x - \tfrac{1}{2} \tan^2 x - \ln \cos x + C.$$

11. Even Powers of Sines and Cosines. — Integrals of the form

$$\int \sin^m x \cos^n x \, dx,$$

where m or n is odd can be evaluated by the methods of Art. 10. If both m and n are even, however, those methods fail. In that case we can evaluate the integral by the use of the formulas

$$\left. \begin{array}{l} \sin^2 u = \dfrac{1 - \cos 2u}{2}, \\[2mm] \cos^2 u = \dfrac{1 + \cos 2u}{2}, \\[2mm] \sin u \cos u = \dfrac{\sin 2u}{2}. \end{array} \right\} \tag{11}$$

Example 1. $\displaystyle \int \cos^4 x \, dx.$

By the above formulas

$$\int \cos^4 x \, dx = \int (\cos^2 x)^2 \, dx = \int \left(\frac{1 + \cos 2x}{2} \right)^2 dx$$

$$= \int (\tfrac{1}{4} + \tfrac{1}{2} \cos 2x + \tfrac{1}{4} \cos^2 2x)$$

$$= \int [\tfrac{1}{4} + \tfrac{1}{2} \cos 2x + \tfrac{1}{8}(1 + \cos 4x)] \, dx$$

$$= \tfrac{3}{8} x + \tfrac{1}{4} \sin 2x + \tfrac{1}{32} \sin 4x + C.$$

Ex. 2. $\displaystyle \int \cos^2 x \sin^2 x \, dx.$

$$\int \cos^2 x \sin^2 x \, dx = \int \tfrac{1}{4} \sin^2 2x \, dx = \int \tfrac{1}{8}(1 - \cos 4x) \, dx$$

$$= \tfrac{1}{8} x - \tfrac{1}{32} \sin 4x + C.$$

12. Trigonometric Substitutions. — Differentials containing $\sqrt{a^2 - x^2}$, $\sqrt{a^2 + x^2}$, or $\sqrt{x^2 - a^2}$, which are not reduced to manageable form by taking the radical as a new variable, can often be integrated by one of the following substitutions:

For $\sqrt{a^2 - x^2}$, let $x = a \sin \theta$.

For $\sqrt{a^2 + x^2}$, let $x = a \tan \theta$.

For $\sqrt{x^2 - a^2}$, let $x = a \sec \theta$.

Example 1. $\int \sqrt{a^2 - x^2}\, dx$.

Let $x = a \sin \theta$.   Then

$$\sqrt{a^2 - x^2} = a \cos \theta, \quad dx = a \cos \theta\, d\theta.$$

Consequently,

$$\int \sqrt{a^2 - x^2}\, dx = a^2 \int \cos^2 \theta\, d\theta = \frac{a^2}{2}\left(\theta + \frac{1}{2}\sin 2\theta\right) + C.$$

Since $x = a \sin \theta$,

$$\theta = \sin^{-1}\frac{x}{a}, \qquad \frac{1}{2}\sin 2\theta = \sin \theta \cos \theta = \frac{x\sqrt{a^2 - x^2}}{a^2}.$$

Hence finally

$$\int \sqrt{a^2 - x^2}\, dx = \frac{a^2}{2}\sin^{-1}\frac{x}{a} + \frac{x}{2}\sqrt{a^2 - x^2} + C.$$

Ex. 2. $\int \dfrac{dx}{(x^2 + a^2)^2}$.

If we let $x = a \tan \theta$, $x^2 + a^2 = a^2 \sec^2 \theta$, $dx = a \sec^2 \theta\, d\theta$, and

$$\int \frac{dx}{(x^2 + a^2)^2} = \frac{1}{a^3}\int \frac{d\theta}{\sec^2 \theta} = \frac{1}{a^3}\int \cos^2 \theta\, d\theta$$

$$= \frac{1}{2\, a^3}(\theta + \sin \theta \cos \theta) + C.$$

Since

$$x = a \tan \theta, \quad \theta = \tan^{-1}\frac{x}{a}, \quad \sin \theta \cos \theta = \frac{ax}{a^2 + x^2}.$$

Hence

$$\int \frac{dx}{(x^2 + a^2)^2} = \frac{1}{2\, a^3}\left[\tan^{-1}\frac{x}{a} + \frac{ax}{a^2 + x^2}\right] + C.$$

EXERCISES

1. $\int \sin^3 x \, dx.$

2. $\int \cos^5 x \, dx.$

3. $\int (\cos x + \sin x)^3 \, dx.$

4. $\int \cos^2 x \sin^3 x \, dx.$

5. $\int \sin^4 \tfrac{1}{2} x \cos^5 \tfrac{1}{2} x \, dx.$

6. $\int \sin^5 3\theta \cos^3 3\theta \, d\theta.$

7. $\int (\cos^2 \theta - \sin^2 \theta) \sin \theta \, d\theta.$

8. $\int \dfrac{\cos^3 x \, dx}{1 - \sin x}.$

9. $\int \dfrac{\cos^2 x \, dx}{\sin x}.$

10. $\int \dfrac{\sin^5 \theta \, d\theta}{\cos \theta}.$

11. $\int \sec^4 x \, dx.$

12. $\int \csc^{10} y \, dy.$

13. $\int \tan^2 x \, dx.$

14. $\int \dfrac{\sec^3 \theta + \tan^3 \theta}{\sec \theta + \tan \theta} \, d\theta.$

15. $\int \tan \tfrac{1}{2} x \sec^3 \tfrac{1}{2} x \, dx.$

16. $\int \tan^5 2x \sec^3 2x \, dx.$

17. $\int \cot^3 x \, dx.$

18. $\int \tan^7 x \, dx.$

19. $\int \dfrac{\cos^3 x \, dx}{\sin^6 x}.$

20. $\int \sec^3 x \csc x \, dx.$

21. $\int \sin^2 ax \, dx.$

22. $\int \cos^2 ax \, dx.$

23. $\int \cos^6 x \sin^4 x \, dx.$

24. $\int \cos^4 \tfrac{1}{2} x \sin^2 \tfrac{1}{2} x \, dx.$

25. $\int \sin^6 x \, dx.$

26. $\int \dfrac{dx}{1 - \sin x}.$

27. $\int \dfrac{dx}{1 + \cos x}.$

28. $\int \sqrt{1 + \sin \theta} \, d\theta.$

29. $\int \sqrt{x^2 - a^2} \, dx.$

30. $\int \sqrt{x^2 + a^2} \, dx.$

31. $\int \dfrac{x^3 \, dx}{\sqrt{x^2 + a^2}}.$

32. $\int \dfrac{dx}{(x^2 - a^2)^{\frac{3}{2}}}.$

33. $\int \dfrac{dx}{x \sqrt{a^2 - x^2}}.$

34. $\int \dfrac{dx}{x \sqrt{2ax - x^2}}.$

35. $\int \dfrac{x \, dx}{(a^2 - x^2)^{\frac{3}{2}}}.$

36. $\int x^3 \sqrt{x^2 + a^2} \, dx.$

37. $\int \dfrac{dx}{x^2 \sqrt{x^2 + a^2}}.$

38. $\int \sqrt{x^2 - 4x + 5} \, dx.$

39. $\int \dfrac{(x^2 - x) \, dx}{\sqrt{2 - 2x - 4x^2}}.$

13. Integration of Rational Fractions. — A fraction, such as

$$\frac{x^3 + 3x}{x^2 - 2x - 3},$$

whose numerator and denominator are polynomials is called a *rational fraction*.

If the degree of the numerator is equal to or greater than that of the denominator, the fraction should be reduced by division. Thus

$$\frac{x^3 + 9x + 12}{x^2 - 2x - 3} = x + 2 + \frac{10x + 6}{x^2 - 2x + 3}.$$

A fraction with numerator of lower degree than its denominator can be resolved into a sum of *partial* fractions with denominators that are factors of the original denominator. Thus

$$\frac{10x + 6}{x^2 - 2x - 3} = \frac{10x + 6}{(x - 3)(x + 1)} = \frac{9}{x - 3} + \frac{1}{x + 1}.$$

These fractions can often be found by trial. If not, proceed as in the following examples.

CASE 1.   Factors of the denominator all of the first degree and none repeated.

Ex. 1. $\int \frac{x^4 + 2x + 6}{x^3 + x^2 - 2x}\, dx.$

Dividing numerator by denominator, we get

$$\frac{x^4 + 2x + 6}{x^3 + x^2 - 2x} = x - 1 + \frac{3x^2 + 6}{x^3 + x^2 - 2x}$$

$$= x - 1 + \frac{3x^2 + 6}{x(x - 1)(x + 2)}.$$

Assume

$$\frac{3x^2 + 6}{x(x - 1)(x + 2)} = \frac{A}{x} + \frac{B}{x - 1} + \frac{C}{x + 2}.$$

The two sides of this equation are merely different ways of

writing the same function.   If then we clear of fractions, the
two sides of the resulting equation

$$3\,x^2 + 6 = A\,(x-1)\,(x+2) + Bx\,(x+2) + Cx\,(x-1)$$
$$= (A+B+C)\,x^2 + (A+2B-C)\,x - 2\,A$$

are identical.   That is

$$A+B+C = 3, \quad A+2B-C = 0, \quad -2\,A = 6.$$

Solving these equations, we get

$$A = -3, \quad B = 3, \quad C = 3.$$

Conversely, if A, B, C, have these values, the above equations are identically satisfied.   Therefore

$$\int \frac{x^4 + 2\,x + 6}{x^3 + x^2 - 2\,x}\,dx = \int \left(x - 1 - \frac{3}{x} + \frac{3}{x-1} + \frac{3}{x+2} \right) dx$$
$$= \tfrac{1}{2}\,x^2 - x - 3\ln x + 3\ln(x-1) + 3\ln(x+2) + C$$
$$= \frac{1}{2}x^2 - x + 3\ln \frac{(x-1)\,(x+2)}{x} + C.$$

The constants can often be determined more easily by
substituting particular values for x on the two sides of the
equation.   Thus, the equation above,

$$3\,x^2 + 6 = A\,(x-1)\,(x+2) + Bx\,(x+2) + Cx\,(x-1)$$

is an identity, that is, it is satisfied by all values of x.   In
particular, if $x = 0$, it becomes

$$6 = -2\,A,$$

whence $A = -3$.   Similarly, by substituting $x = 1$ and
$x = -2$, we get

$$9 = 3\,B, \quad 18 = 6\,C,$$

whence $\qquad\qquad B = 3, \qquad C = 3.$

CASE 2.   Factors of the denominator all of first degree
but some repeated.

Ex. 2. $\displaystyle \int \frac{(8\,x^3 + 7)\,dx}{(x+1)\,(2\,x+1)^3}.$

Assume

$$\frac{8\,x^3+7}{(x+1)\,(2\,x+1)^3} = \frac{A}{x+1} + \frac{B}{(2\,x+1)^3} + \frac{C}{(2\,x+1)^2} + \frac{D}{2\,x+1}.$$

Corresponding to the repeated factor $(2\,x+1)^3$, we thus introduce fractions with $(2\,x+1)^3$ and all lower powers as denominators. Clearing and solving as before, we find

$$A = 1, \quad B = 12, \quad C = -6, \quad D = 0.$$

Hence

$$\int \frac{8\,x^3+7}{(x+1)\,(2\,x+1)^3}\,dx = \int \left[\frac{1}{x+1} + \frac{12}{(2\,x+1)^3} - \frac{6}{(2\,x+1)^2} \right] dx$$

$$= \ln\,(x+1) - \frac{3}{(2\,x+1)^2} + \frac{3}{2\,x+1} + C.$$

CASE 3. Denominator containing factors of the second degree but none repeated.

Ex. 3. $\int \dfrac{4\,x^2+x+1}{x^3-1}\,dx.$

The factors of the denominator are $x-1$ and x^2+x+1. Assume

$$\frac{4\,x^2+x+1}{x^3-1} = \frac{A}{x-1} + \frac{Bx+C}{x^2+x+1}.$$

With the quadratic denominator x^2+x+1, we thus use a numerator that is not a single constant but a linear function $Bx+C$. Clearing fractions and solving for A, B, C, we find

$$A = 2, \quad B = 2, \quad C = 1.$$

Therefore

$$\int \frac{4\,x^2+x+1}{x^3-1}\,dx = \int \left(\frac{2}{x-1} + \frac{2\,x+1}{x^2+x+1} \right) dx$$

$$= 2\ln\,(x-1) + \ln\,(x^2+x+1) + C.$$

CASE 4. Denominator containing factors of the second degree, some being repeated.

Ex. 4. $\int \dfrac{x^3+1}{x\,(x^2+1)^2}\,dx.$

Assume

$$\frac{x^3+1}{x\,(x^2+1)^2} = \frac{A}{x} + \frac{Bx+C}{(x^2+1)^2} + \frac{Dx+E}{x^2+1}.$$

Corresponding to the repeated second degree factor $(x^2+1)^2$, we introduce partial fractions having as denominators $(x^2+1)^2$ and all lower powers of x^2+1, the numerators being all of first degree. Clearing fractions and solving for A, B, C, D, E, we find

$$A = 1, \quad B = -1, \quad C = -1, \quad D = -1, \quad E = 1.$$

Hence

$$\int \frac{x^3+1}{x\,(x^2+1)^2}\,dx = \int \left[\frac{1}{x} - \frac{x+1}{(x^2+1)^2} - \frac{x-1}{x^2+1}\right]dx$$

$$= \ln\frac{x}{\sqrt{x^2+1}} + \frac{1}{2}\tan^{-1}x - \frac{x-1}{2\,(x^2+1)} + C.$$

14. Integrals Containing $(ax+b)^{\frac{p}{q}}$. — Integrals containing $(ax+b)^{\frac{p}{q}}$ can be rationalized by the substitution

$$ax + b = z^q.$$

If several fractional powers of the same linear function $ax+b$ occur, the substitution

$$ax + b = z^n$$

may be used, n being so chosen that all the roots can be extracted.

Example 1. $\displaystyle\int \frac{dx}{1+\sqrt{x}}.$

Let $x = z^2$. Then $dx = 2\,z\,dz$ and

$$\int\frac{dx}{1+\sqrt{x}} = \int\frac{2\,z\,dz}{1+z} = \int\left(2 - \frac{2}{1+z}\right)dz$$

$$= 2z - 2\ln(1+z) + C$$

$$= 2\sqrt{x} - 2\ln(1+\sqrt{x}) + C.$$

Ex. 2. $\displaystyle\int \frac{(2x-3)^{\frac{1}{2}}\,dx}{(2x-3)^{\frac{1}{3}}+1}.$

To rationalize both $(2x-3)^{\frac{1}{2}}$ and $(2x-3)^{\frac{1}{3}}$, let $2x-3=z^6$. Then

$$\int \frac{(2x-3)^{\frac{1}{2}}\,dx}{(2x-3)^{\frac{1}{3}}+1} = \int \frac{3z^8\,dz}{z^2+1} = 3\int\left(z^6-z^4+z^2-1+\frac{1}{z^2+1}\right)dz$$

$$= 3\left(\frac{z^7}{7}-\frac{z^5}{5}+\frac{z^3}{3}-z+\tan^{-1}z\right)+C$$

$$= \tfrac{3}{7}(2x-3)^{\frac{7}{6}}-\tfrac{3}{5}(2x-3)^{\frac{5}{6}}+(2x-3)^{\frac{1}{2}}$$

$$-3(2x-3)^{\frac{1}{6}}+\tan^{-1}(2x-3)^{\frac{1}{6}}+C.$$

EXERCISES

1. $\int \dfrac{x^3+x^2}{x^2-3x+2}\,dx.$

2. $\int \dfrac{2x+3}{x^2+x}\,dx.$

3. $\int \dfrac{x^2+1}{x(x^2-1)}\,dx.$

4. $\int \dfrac{x^3-1}{4x^3-x}\,dx.$

5. $\int \dfrac{x\,dx}{(x+1)(x+3)(x+5)}.$

6. $\int \dfrac{16x\,dx}{(2x-1)(2x-3)(2x-5)}.$

7. $\int \dfrac{x^3+1}{x^3-x^2}\,dx.$

8. $\int \dfrac{x^2\,dx}{(x+1)(x-1)^2}.$

9. $\int \dfrac{dx}{(x^2-1)^2}.$

10. $\int \left(\dfrac{x-1}{x+1}\right)^4 dx$

11. $\int \dfrac{dx}{x^5-x^4}.$

12. $\int \dfrac{x^2\,dx}{(x^2-4)^2}.$

13. $\int \dfrac{x\,dx}{(x^2-4)^2}.$

14. $\int \dfrac{x^4\,dx}{x^4-1}.$

15. $\int \dfrac{dx}{x^3+1}.$

16. $\int \dfrac{x^2\,dx}{x^3+1}.$

17. $\int \dfrac{dx}{x^5-x^3+x^2-1}.$

18. $\int \dfrac{2x^2+x-2}{(x^2-1)^2}\,dx.$

19. $\int \dfrac{x^4+24x^2-8x}{(x^3-8)^2}\,dx.$

20. $\int \dfrac{(x+1)^{\frac{1}{2}}\,dx}{x}.$

21. $\int \dfrac{x^{\frac{1}{2}}-x^{\frac{1}{3}}+1}{x^{\frac{1}{3}}-x^{\frac{1}{6}}}\,dx.$

22. $\int x\sqrt{ax+b}\,dx.$

23. $\int \dfrac{\sqrt{x+2}-1}{x+3}\,dx.$

24. $\int \dfrac{dx}{(x^{\frac{1}{2}}-1)(x^{\frac{1}{3}}+1)}.$

25. $\int \dfrac{dx}{\sqrt{x+1}-\sqrt{x-1}}.$

15. Integration by Parts. — From the formula

$$d(uv) = u\,dv + u\,dv$$

we get

$$u\,dv = d(uv) - v\,du,$$

whence

$$\int u\,dv = uv - \int v\,du. \tag{15}$$

If $\int v\,du$ is known this gives $\int v\,du$. Integration by the use of this formula is called *integration by parts*.

Example 1. $\int \ln x\,dx$.

Let $u = \ln x$, $dv = dx$. Then $du = \dfrac{dx}{x}$, $v = x$, and

$$\int \ln x\,dx = \ln x \cdot x - \int x \cdot \frac{dx}{x}$$

$$= x(\ln x - 1) + C.$$

Ex. 2. $\int x^2 \sin x\,dx$.

Let $u = x^2$ and $dv = \sin x\,dx$. Then $du = 2\,x\,dx$, $v = -\cos x$, and

$$\int x^2 \sin x\,dx = -x^2 \cos x + \int 2\,x \cos x\,dx.$$

A second integration by parts with $u = 2\,x$, $dv = \cos x\,dx$ gives

$$\int 2\,x \cos x\,dx = 2\,x \sin x - \int 2 \sin x\,dx$$

$$= 2\,x \sin x + 2 \cos x + C.$$

Hence finally

$$\int x^2 \sin x\,dx = -x^2 \cos x + 2\,x \sin x + 2 \cos x + C.$$

The method of integration by parts applies particularly to functions that are simplified by differentiation, like ln x, or to products of functions of different classes, like $x \sin x$. In applying the method the given differential must be resolved into a product $u \cdot dv$. The part called dv must have a known integral and the part called u should usually be simplified by differentiation.

Sometimes after integration by parts a multiple of the original differential appears on the right side of the equation. It can be transposed to the other side and the integral can be solved for algebraically. This is shown in the following examples.

Ex. 3. $\displaystyle\int \sqrt{a^2 - x^2}\, dx.$

Integrating by parts with $u = \sqrt{a^2 - x^2}$, $dv = dx$, we get

$$\int \sqrt{a^2 - x^2}\, dx = x \sqrt{a^2 - x^2} - \int \frac{-x^2\, dx}{\sqrt{a^2 - x^2}}.$$

Adding a^2 to the numerator of the integral and subtracting an equivalent integral, this becomes

$$\int \sqrt{a^2 - x^2}\, dx = x \sqrt{a^2 - x^2} - \int \frac{a^2 - x^2}{\sqrt{a^2 - x^2}}\, dx + a^2 \int \frac{dx}{\sqrt{a^2 - x^2}}$$

$$= x \sqrt{a^2 - x^2} - \int \sqrt{a^2 - x^2}\, dx + a^2 \int \frac{dx}{\sqrt{a^2 - x^2}}.$$

Transposing $\displaystyle\int \sqrt{a^2 - x^2}\, dx$ and dividing by 2, we get

$$\int \sqrt{a^2 - x^2}\, dx = \frac{x}{2} \sqrt{a^2 - x^2} + \frac{a^2}{2} \sin^{-1} \frac{x}{a} + C.$$

Ex. 4. $\displaystyle\int e^{ax} \cos bx\, dx.$

Integrating by parts with $u = e^{ax}$, $dv = \cos bx\, dx$, we get

$$\int e^{ax} \cos bx\, dx = \frac{e^{ax} \sin bx}{b} - \frac{a}{b} \int e^{ax} \sin bx\, dx.$$

Integrating by parts again with $u = e^{ax}$, $dv = \sin bx\, dx$, this becomes

$$\int e^{ax} \cos bx\, dx = \frac{e^{ax} \sin bx}{b} - \frac{a}{b}\left[-\frac{e^{ax} \cos bx}{b} + \frac{a}{b} \int e^{ax} \sin bx\, dx \right]$$

$$= e^{ax}\left(\frac{b \sin bx + a \cos bx}{b^2}\right) - \frac{a^2}{b^2}\int e^{ax} \sin bx\, dx.$$

Transposing the last integral and dividing by $1 + \dfrac{b^2}{a^2}$, this gives

$$\int e^{ax} \cos bx\, dx = e^{ax}\left(\frac{b \sin bx + a \cos bx}{a^2 + b^2}\right).$$

16. Reduction Formulas. — Integration by parts is often used to make an integral depend on a simpler one and so to obtain a formula by repeated application of which the given integral can be determined.

To illustrate this take the integral

$$\int \sin^n x\, dx,$$

where n is a positive integer. Integrating by parts with $u = \sin^{n-1} x$, $dv = \sin x\, dx$, we get

$$\int \sin^n x\, dx = -\sin^{n-1} x \cos x + \int (n-1) \sin^{n-2} x \cos^2 x\, dx$$

$$= -\sin^{n-1} x \cos x + (n-1) \int \sin^{n-2} x\, (1 - \sin^2 x)\, dx$$

$$= -\sin^{n-1} x \cos x + (n-1) \int \sin^{n-2} x\, dx$$

$$- (n-1) \int \sin^n x\, dx.$$

Transposing the last integral and dividing by n, we get

$$\int \sin^n x\, dx = -\frac{\sin^{n-1} x \cos x}{n} + \frac{n-1}{n} \int \sin^{n-2} x\, dx.$$

By successive application of this formula we can make $\int \sin^n x\, dx$ depend on $\int dx$ or $\int \sin x\, dx$ according as n is even or odd.

Example. $\displaystyle\int \sin^6 x \, dx.$

By the formula just proved

$$\int \sin^6 x \, dx = -\frac{\sin^5 x \cos x}{6} + \frac{5}{6} \int \sin^4 x \, dx$$

$$= -\frac{\sin^5 x \cos x}{6} + \frac{5}{6}\left[-\frac{\sin^3 x \cos x}{4} + \frac{3}{4}\int \sin^2 x \, dx\right]$$

$$= -\frac{\sin^5 x \cos x}{6} - \frac{5}{24}\sin^3 x \cos x - \frac{5}{16}\sin x \cos x + \frac{5}{16}x + C.$$

EXERCISES

1. $\displaystyle\int x \cos 2x \, dx.$

2. $\displaystyle\int \ln x \cdot x \, dx.$

3. $\displaystyle\int \sin^{-1} x \, dx.$

4. $\displaystyle\int x \tan^{-1} x \, dx.$

5. $\displaystyle\int \ln \left(x + \sqrt{a^2 + x^2}\right) dx.$

6. $\displaystyle\int \frac{\ln x \, dx}{\sqrt{x-1}}.$

7. $\displaystyle\int \ln (\ln x) \frac{dx}{x}.$

8. $\displaystyle\int x^2 \sec^{-1} x \, dx.$

9. $\displaystyle\int e^{-x} \ln (e^x + 1) \, dx.$

10. $\displaystyle\int x^2 e^x \, dx.$

11. $\displaystyle\int x^3 e^{-x} \, dx.$

12. $\displaystyle\int (x-1)^2 \sin (2x) \, dx.$

13. $\displaystyle\int \sqrt{x^2 - a^2} \, dx.$

14. $\displaystyle\int \sqrt{a^2 + x^2} \, dx.$

15. $\displaystyle\int e^{2x} \sin 3x \, dx.$

16. $\displaystyle\int e^x \cos x \, dx.$

17. $\displaystyle\int e^{-x} \sin 2x \, dx.$

18. $\displaystyle\int \sec^3 \theta \, d\theta.$

19. $\displaystyle\int \sin 2x \cos 3x \, dx.$

20. Prove the formula

$$\int \sec^n (x) \, dx = \frac{\sec^{n-2} x \tan x}{n-1} + \frac{n-2}{n-1} \int \sec^{n-2} (x) \, dx.$$

and use it to integrate $\displaystyle\int \sec^5 x \, dx.$

21. Prove the formula

$$\int (a^2 - x^2)^n \, dx = \frac{x(a^2 - x^2)^n}{2n+1} + \frac{2na^2}{2n+1} \int (a^2 - x^2)^{n-1} \, dx$$

and use it to integrate $\displaystyle\int (a^2 - x^2)^{\frac{3}{2}} \, dx.$

CHAPTER III

DEFINITE INTEGRALS

17. Summation. — Between $x = a$ and $x = b$ let $f(x)$ be a continuous function of x. Divide the interval between a and b into any number of equal parts Δx and let $x_1, x_2, \ldots x_n$, be the points of division. Form the sum

$$f(a)\,\Delta x + f(x_1)\,\Delta x + f(x_2)\,\Delta x + \cdots + f(x_n)\,\Delta x.$$

This sum is represented by the notation

$$\sum_a^b f(x)\,\Delta x.$$

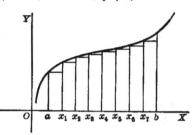

FIG. 17a.

Since $f(a)$, $f(x_1)$, $f(x_2)$, etc., are the ordinates of the curve $y = f(x)$ at $x = x_1, x_2$, etc., the terms $f(a)\,\Delta x, f(x_1)\,\Delta x, f(x_2)\,\Delta x$, etc., represent the areas of the rectangles in Fig. 17a, and $\sum_a^b f(x)\,\Delta x$ is the sum of those rectangles.

Example 1. Find the value of $\sum_1^2 x^2\,\Delta x$ when $\Delta x = \frac{1}{4}$.

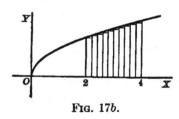

FIG. 17b.

The interval between 1 and 2 is divided into parts of length $\Delta x = \frac{1}{4}$. The points of division are $1\frac{1}{4}$, $1\frac{1}{2}$, $1\frac{3}{4}$. Therefore

$$\sum_1^2 x^2\,\Delta x = 1^2 \cdot \Delta x + (\tfrac{5}{4})^2\,\Delta x +$$
$$(\tfrac{3}{2})^2\,\Delta x + (\tfrac{7}{4})^2\,\Delta x$$
$$= \tfrac{63}{8}\,\Delta x = \tfrac{63}{8} \cdot \tfrac{1}{4} = 1.97.$$

Ex. 2. Find approximately the area bounded by the x-axis, the curve $y = \sqrt{x}$, and the ordinates $x = 2, x = 4$.

From Fig. 17b it appears that a fairly good approxima-

35

tion will be obtained by dividing the interval between 2 and 4 into 10 parts each of length 0.2. The value of the area thus obtained is

$$\sum_{2}^{4}\sqrt{x}\,\Delta x = (\sqrt{2}+\sqrt{2.2}+\sqrt{2.4}+ \cdots +\sqrt{3.8})(0.2)=3.39.$$

The area correct to two decimals (given by the method of Art. 20) is 3.45.

18. Definite and Indefinite Integrals. — If we increase indefinitely the number of parts into which $b - a$ is divided, the intervals Δx approach zero and $\sum_{a}^{b} f(x)\,\Delta x$ usually approaches a limit. This limit is called the *definite* integral of $f(x)\,dx$ between $x = a$ and $x = b$. It is represented by the notation $\int_{a}^{b} f(x)\,dx$. That is

$$\int_{a}^{b} f(x)\,dx = \lim_{\Delta x \doteq 0} \sum_{a}^{b} f(x)\,\Delta x. \tag{18}$$

The number a is called the *lower limit*, b the *upper limit* of the integral.

In contradistinction to the definite integral (which has a definite value), the integral that we have previously used (which contains an undetermined constant) is called an *indefinite* integral. The connection between the two integrals will be shown in Art. 21.

19. Geometrical Representation.—If the curve $y = f(x)$ lies above the x-axis and $a < b$, as in Fig. 17a, $\int_{a}^{b} f(x)\,dx$ represents

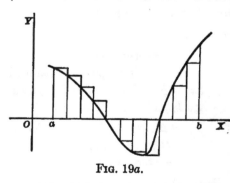

Fig. 19a.

the limit approached by the sum of the inscribed rectangles and that limit is the area between $x = a$ and $x = b$ bounded by the curve and the x-axis.

At a point below the x-axis the ordinate $f(x)$ is negative and so the product $f(x)\,\Delta x$ is the negative of the area of the corresponding rectangle. Therefore (Fig. 19a)

$$\sum_a^b f(x)\,\Delta x = \text{(sum of rectangles above } OX)$$
$$- \text{(sum of rectangles below } OX),$$

and in the limit

$$\int_a^b f(x)\,dx = \text{(area above } OX) - \text{(area below } OX) \quad (19a)$$

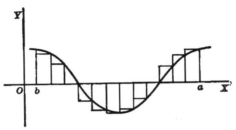

FIG. 19b.

If, however, $a > b$, as in Fig. 19b, x decreases as we pass from a to b, Δx is negative and instead of the above equation we have

$$\int_a^b f(x)\,dx = \text{(area below } OX) - \text{(area above } OX). \quad (19b)$$

Example 1.   Show graphically that $\displaystyle\int_0^{2\pi} \sin^3 x\,dx = 0$.

The curve $y = \sin^3 x$ is shown in Fig. 19c. Between $x = 0$ and $x = 2\pi$ the areas above and below the x-axis are equal. Hence

FIG. 19c.

$$\int_0^{2\pi} \sin^3 x\,dx = A_1 - A_2 = 0.$$

Ex. 2.   Show that

$$\int_{-1}^1 e^{-x^2}\,dx = 2\int_0^1 e^{-x^2}\,dx.$$

The curve $y = e^{-x^2}$ is shown in Fig. 19a. It is symmetrical with respect to the y-axis. The area between $x = -1$ and $x = 0$ is therefore equal to that between $x = 0$ and $x = 1$. Consequently

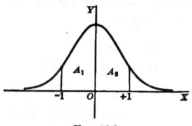

FIG. 19d.

$$\int_{-1}^{1} e^{-x^2} \, dx = A_1 + A_2 = 2 A_2$$

$$= 2 \int_{0}^{1} e^{-x^2} dx.$$

EXERCISES

Find the values of the following sums:

1. $\sum_{0}^{2} x \, \Delta x, \qquad \Delta x = \frac{1}{4}.$

2. $\sum_{1}^{10} \frac{\Delta x}{x}, \qquad \Delta x = 1.$

3. $\sum_{-2}^{2} \sqrt[3]{x} \, \Delta x, \qquad \Delta x = \frac{1}{4}.$

4. Show that

$$\sum_{0}^{\frac{\pi}{6}} \sin x \, \Delta x = 1 - \cos \frac{\pi}{6}$$

approximately. Use a table of natural sines and take $\Delta x = \frac{\pi}{60}$.

5. Calculate π approximately by the formula

$$\pi = 4 \sum_{0}^{1} \frac{\Delta x}{1 + x^2}, \qquad \Delta x = 0.1.$$

6. Find correct to one decimal the area bounded by the parabola $y = x^2$, the x-axis, and the ordinates $x = 0$, $x = 2$. The exact area is $\frac{8}{3}$.

7. Find correct to one decimal the area of the circle $x^2 + y^2 = 4$.

By representing the integrals as areas prove graphically the following equations:

8. $\int_{0}^{\pi} \sin (2 x) \, dx = 0.$

9. $\int_{0}^{2\pi} \cos^7 x \, dx = 0.$

10. $\int_{0}^{\pi} \sin^5 x \, dx = 2 \int_{0}^{\frac{\pi}{2}} \sin^5 x \, dx.$

11. $\int_{-a}^{+a} \frac{x\,dx}{1+x^4} = 0.$

12. $\int_{-1}^{1} \frac{dx}{1+x^4} = 2\int_{0}^{1} \frac{dx}{1+x^4}.$

13. $\int_{0}^{a} f(x)\,dx = \int_{0}^{a} f(a-x)\,dx.$

20. Derivative of Area. — The area A bounded by a curve

$$y = f(x),$$

a fixed ordinate $x = a$, and a movable ordinate MP, is a function of the abscissa x of the movable ordinate.

Let x change to $x + \Delta x$. The increment of area is

$$\Delta A = MPQN.$$

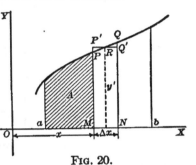

Construct the rectangle $MP'Q'N$ equal in area to $MPQN$. If some of the points of the arc PQ are above $P'Q'$, others must be below to make $MPQN$ and $MP'Q'N$ equal. Hence $P'Q'$ intersects PQ at some point R. Let y' be the ordinate of R. Then y' is the altitude of $MP'Q'N$ and so

$$\Delta A = MPQN = MP'Q'N = y'\,\Delta x.$$

FIG. 20.

Consequently

$$\frac{\Delta A}{\Delta x} = y'.$$

When Δx approaches zero, if the curve is continuous, y' approaches y. Therefore in the limit

$$\frac{dA}{dx} = y = f(x). \tag{20a}$$

Let the indefinite integral of $f(x)\,dx$ be

$$\int f(x)\,dx = F(x) + C.$$

From equation (20a) we then have

$$A = \int f(x)\,dx = F(x) + C.$$

The area is zero when $x = a$. Consequently

$$0 = F(a) + C,$$

whence $C = -F(a)$ and

$$A = F(x) - F(a).$$

This is the area from $x = a$ to the ordinate MP with abscissa x. The area between $x = a$ and $x = b$ is then

$$A = F(b) - F(a). \tag{20b}$$

The difference $F(b) - F(a)$ is often represented by the notation $F(x)\Big|_a^b$, that is,

$$F(x)\Big|_a^b = F(b) - F(a). \tag{20c}$$

21. Relation of the Definite and Indefinite Integrals. — The definite integral $\int_a^b f(x)\,dx$ is equal to the area bounded by the curve $y = f(x)$, the x-axis, and the ordinates $x = a$, $x = b$. If

$$\int f(x)\,dx = F(x) + C,$$

by equation (20b) this area is $F(b) - F(a)$. We therefore conclude that

$$\int_a^b f(x)\,dx = F(x)\Big|_a^b = F(b) - F(a), \tag{21}$$

that is, *to find the value of the definite integral* $\int_a^b f(x)\,dx$, *substitute $x = a$, and $x = b$ in the indefinite integral* $\int f(x)\,dx$ *and subtract the former from the latter result.*

Example. Find the value of the integral

$$\int_0^1 \frac{dx}{1+x^2}.$$

The value required is

$$\int_0^1 \frac{dx}{1+x^2} = \tan^{-1} x \Big|_0^1 = \tan^{-1} 1 - \tan^{-1} 0 = \frac{\pi}{4}.$$

22. Properties of Definite Integrals. — A definite integral has the following simple properties:

I. $\displaystyle\int_a^b f(x)\,dx = -\int_b^a f(x)\,dx.$

II. $\displaystyle\int_a^c f(x)\,dx = \int_a^b f(x)\,dx + \int_b^c f(x)\,dx.$

III. $\displaystyle\int_a^b f(x)\,dx = (b - a)f(x_1), \qquad a \lesseqgtr x_1 \lesseqgtr b.$

The first of these is due to the fact that if Δx is positive when x varies from a to b, it is negative when x varies from b to a. The two integrals thus represent the same area with different algebraic signs.

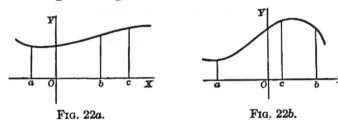

FIG. 22a.   FIG. 22b.

The second property expresses that the area from a to c is equal to the sum of the areas from a to b and b to c. This is the case not only when b is between a and c, as in Fig. 22a, but also when b is beyond c, as in Fig. 22b. In the latter case $\int_b^c f(x)\,dx$ is negative and the sum

$$\int_a^b f(x)\,dx + \int_b^c f(x)\,dx$$

is equal to the difference of the two areas.

Equation III expresses that the area $PQMN$ is equal to

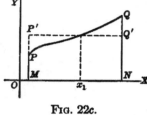

FIG. 22c.

that of a rectangle $P'Q'MN$ with altitude between MP and NQ.

23. Infinite Limits. — It has been assumed that the limits a and b were finite. If the integral

$$\int_a^b f(x)\, dx$$

approaches a limit when b increases indefinitely, that limit is defined as the value of $\int_a^\infty f(x)\, dx$. That is,

$$\int_a^\infty f(x)\, dx = \lim_{b=\infty} \int_a^b f(x)\, dx. \qquad (23)$$

If the indefinite integral

$$\int f(x)\, dx = F(x)$$

approaches a limit when x increases indefinitely,

$$\int_a^\infty f(x)\, dx = \lim_{b=\infty} [F(b) - F(a)] = F(\infty) - F(a).$$

The value is thus obtained by equation (21) just as if the limits were finite.

Example 1.　$\displaystyle \int_0^\infty \frac{dx}{1 + x^2}.$

The indefinite integral is

$$\int \frac{dx}{1 + x^2} = \tan^{-1} x.$$

When x approaches infinity, this approaches $\dfrac{\pi}{2}$. Hence

$$\int_0^\infty \frac{dx}{1 + x^2} = \tan^{-1} x \Big|_0^\infty = \frac{\pi}{2}.$$

Ex. 2. $\int_0^\infty \cos x\, dx.$

The indefinite integral $\sin x$ does not approach a limit when x increases indefinitely.   Hence

$$\int_0^\infty \cos x\, dx$$

has no definite value.

24. Infinite Values of the Function. — If the function $f(x)$ becomes infinite when $x = b$, $\int_a^b f(x)\, dx$ is defined as the limit

$$\int_a^b f(x)\, dx = \lim_{z=b} \int_a^z f(x)\, dx,$$

z being between a and b.

Similarly, if $f(a)$ is infinite,

$$\int_a^b f(x)\, dx = \lim_{z=a} \int_z^b f(x)\, dx,$$

z being between a and b.

If the function becomes infinite at a point c between a and b, $\int_a^b f(x)\, dx$ is defined by the equation

$$\int_a^b f(x)\, dx = \int_a^c f(x)\, dx + \int_c^b f(x)\, dx. \qquad (24)$$

Example 1. $\int_{-1}^1 \dfrac{dx}{\sqrt[3]{x}}.$

When $x = 0$, $\dfrac{1}{\sqrt[3]{x}}$ is infinite.   We therefore divide the integral into two parts:

$$\int_{-1}^1 \frac{dx}{\sqrt[3]{x}} = \int_{-1}^0 \frac{dx}{\sqrt[3]{x}} + \int_0^1 \frac{dx}{\sqrt[3]{x}} = -\frac{3}{2} + \frac{3}{2} = 0.$$

Ex. 2. $\displaystyle\int_{-1}^{1}\frac{dx}{x^2}$.

If we use equation (21), we get

$$\int_{-1}^{1}\frac{dx}{x^2} = -\frac{1}{x}\bigg|_{-1}^{1} = -2.$$

Since the integral is obviously positive, the result -2 is absurd. This is due to the fact that $\dfrac{1}{x^2}$ becomes infinite when $x = 0$. Resolving the integral into two parts, we get

$$\int_{-1}^{1}\frac{dx}{x^2} = \int_{-1}^{0}\frac{dx}{x^2} + \int_{0}^{1}\frac{dx}{x^2} = \infty + \infty = \infty.$$

25. Change of Variable. — If a change of variable is made in evaluating an integral, the limits can be replaced by the corresponding values of the new variable. To see this, suppose that when x is expressed in terms of t,

$$\int f(x)\, dx = F(x)$$

is changed into

$$\int \phi(t)\, dt = \Phi(t).$$

If t_0, t_1, are the values of t, corresponding to x_0, x_1,

$$F(x_0) = \Phi(t_0), \qquad F(x_1) = \Phi(t_1),$$

and so

$$F(x_1) - F(x_0) = \Phi(t_1) - \Phi(t_0),$$

that is

$$\int_{x_0}^{x_1} f(x)\, dx = \int_{t_0}^{t_1} \phi(t)\, dt.$$

If more than one value of t corresponds to the same value of x, care should be taken to see that when t varies from t_0 to t_1, x varies from x_0 to x_1, and that for all intermediate values, $f(x)\, dx = \phi(t)\, dt$.

Example. $\displaystyle\int_{-a}^{a}\sqrt{a^2 - x^2}\, dx$.

Substituting $x = a \sin \theta$, we find

$$\int \sqrt{a^2 - x^2}\, dx = a^2 \int \cos^2 \theta\, d\theta = \frac{a^2}{2}\left[\theta + \frac{\sin 2\theta}{2}\right].$$

When $x = a$, $\sin \theta = 1$, and $\theta = \frac{\pi}{2}$. When $x = -a$, $\sin \theta = -1$ and $\theta = -\frac{\pi}{2}$. Therefore

$$\int_{-a}^{a} \sqrt{a^2 - x^2}\, dx = a^2 \int_{-\frac{\pi}{2}}^{\frac{\pi}{2}} \cos^2 \theta\, d\theta = \frac{a^2}{2}\left[\theta + \frac{1}{2}\sin 2\theta\right]_{-\frac{\pi}{2}}^{\frac{\pi}{2}} = \frac{\pi a^2}{2}.$$

Since $\sin \frac{3}{2}\pi = -1$, it might seem that we could use $\frac{3}{2}\pi$ as the lower limit. We should then get

$$a^2 \int_{\frac{3\pi}{2}}^{\frac{\pi}{2}} \cos^2 \theta\, d\theta = -\frac{\pi a^2}{2}.$$

This is not correct because in passing from $\frac{3}{2}\pi$ to $\frac{1}{2}\pi$, θ crosses the third and second quadrants. There $\cos \theta$ is negative and

$$\sqrt{a^2 - x^2}\, dx = (-a \cos \theta) \cos \theta\, d\theta,$$

and not $a^2 \cos^2 \theta\, d\theta$ as assumed above.

EXERCISES

Find the values of the following definite integrals:

1. $\int_{\frac{\pi}{6}}^{\frac{\pi}{4}} \sec^2 x\, dx.$

2. $\int_{\frac{a}{2}}^{a} \frac{dx}{\sqrt{a^2 - x^2}}.$

3. $\int_{-2}^{2} (x-1)^3\, dx.$

4. $\int_{-5}^{0} \frac{x\, dx}{\sqrt{x^2 + 144}}.$

5. $\int_{-\pi}^{\frac{3}{2}\pi} \sin^3 \theta\, d\theta.$

6. $\int_{2}^{3} x \ln x\, dx.$

7. $\int_{3}^{4} \frac{dx}{x^2 - 3x + 2}.$

8. $\int_{-\frac{\pi}{4}}^{\frac{\pi}{4}} \tan x\, dx.$

9. $\int_{0}^{a \ln 2} \left(e^{\frac{x}{a}} + e^{-\frac{x}{a}}\right) dx.$

10. $\int_{0}^{1} \frac{dx}{\sqrt{x}}.$

11. $\int_{-\frac{\pi}{2}}^{\frac{\pi}{2}} \csc^2 x \, dx$.

12. $\int_1^\infty \frac{dx}{x \sqrt{x^2 - 1}}$.

13. $\int_0^\infty e^{-k^2 x^2} x \, dx$.

14. $\int_2^\infty \frac{dx}{x^2 - 1}$.

Evaluate the following definite integrals by making the change of variable indicated:

15. $\int_{-1}^1 \frac{dx}{(1 + x^2)^2}$, $x = \tan \theta$.

16. $\int_1^5 \frac{\sqrt{x - 1}}{x} \, dx$, $x - 1 = z^2$.

17. $\int_{\frac{1}{2}}^{\frac{2}{3}} \frac{dz}{z \sqrt{z^2 + 1}}$, $z = \frac{1}{x}$.

18. $\int_0^{\frac{\pi}{2}} \frac{\cos \theta \, d\theta}{6 - 5 \sin \theta + \sin^2 \theta}$, $\sin \theta = z$.

19. $\int_0^a \frac{x^3 \, dx}{a^2 + x^2}$, $a^2 + x^2 = z^2$.

CHAPTER IV

SIMPLE AREAS AND VOLUMES

26. Area Bounded by a Plane Curve. Rectangular Coördinates. — The area bounded by the curve $y = f(x)$, the x-axis and two ordinates $x = a$, $x = b$, is the limit approached by the sum of rectangles $y \, \Delta x$. That is,

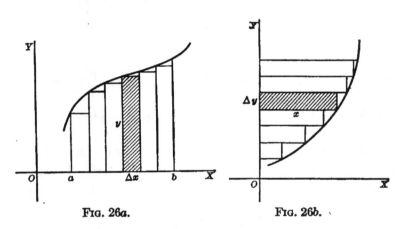

Fig. 26a.   Fig. 26b.

$$A = \lim_{\Delta x \doteq 0} \sum_{a}^{b} y \, \Delta x = \int_{a}^{b} y \, dx = \int_{a}^{b} f(x) \, dx. \quad (26a)$$

Similarly, the area bounded by a curve, the abscissas $y = a, y = b$, and the y-axis is

$$A = \lim_{\Delta y \doteq 0} \sum x \, \Delta y = \int_{a}^{b} x \, dy. \quad (26b)$$

Example 1.   Find the area bounded by the curve $x = 2 + y - y^2$ and the y-axis.

47

The curve (Fig. 26c) crosses the y-axis at $y = -1$ and $y = 2$. The area required is, therefore,

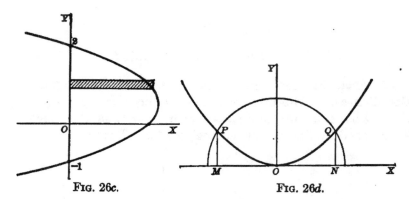

FIG. 26c.   FIG. 26d.

$$A = \int_{-1}^{2} x\, dy = \int_{-1}^{2} (2 + y - y^2)\, dy = 2y + \frac{y^2}{2} - \frac{y^3}{3} \Big|_{-1}^{2} = 4\tfrac{1}{2}.$$

Ex. 2. Find the area within the circle $x^2 + y^2 = 16$ and parabola $x^2 = 6y$.

Solving the equations simultaneously, we find that the parabola and circle intersect at $P(-2\sqrt{3}, 2)$ and $Q(2\sqrt{3}, 2)$. The area $MPQN$ (Fig. 26d) under the circle is

$$\int_{-2\sqrt{3}}^{2\sqrt{3}} y\, dx = \int_{-2\sqrt{3}}^{2\sqrt{3}} \sqrt{16 - x^2}\, dx = \frac{16}{3}\pi + 4\sqrt{3}.$$

The area $MPO + OQN$ under the parabola is

$$\int_{-2\sqrt{3}}^{2\sqrt{3}} \frac{x^2}{6}\, dx = \frac{8}{3}\sqrt{3}.$$

The area between the curves is the difference

$$MPQN - MPO - OQN = \tfrac{16}{3}\pi + \tfrac{4}{3}\sqrt{3}.$$

Ex. 3. Find the area within the hypocycloid $x = a\sin^3\phi$, $y = a\cos^3\phi$.

The area OAB in the first quadrant is

$$\int_0^a y\, dx = \int_0^{\frac{\pi}{2}} a \cos^3 \phi \cdot 3\, a \sin^2 \phi \cos \phi\, d\phi$$

$$= 3\, a^2 \int_0^{\frac{\pi}{2}} \cos^4 \phi \sin^2 \phi\, d\phi = \tfrac{3}{32} \pi\, a^2.$$

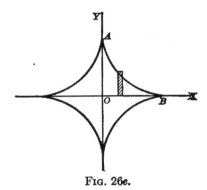

FIG. 26e.

The entire area is then

$$4 \cdot OAB = \tfrac{3}{8} \pi\, a^2.$$

EXERCISES

1. Find the area bounded by the line $2\,y - 3\,x - 5 = 0$, the x-axis, and the ordinates $x = 1$, $x = 3$.

2. Find the area bounded by the parabola $y = 3\,x^2$, the y-axis, and the abscissas $y = 2$, $y = 4$.

3. Find the area bounded by $y^3 = x$, the line $y = -2$, and the ordinates $x = 0$, $x = 3$.

4. Find the area bounded by the parabola $y = 2\,x - x^2$ and the x-axis.

5. Find the area bounded by $y = \ln x$, the x-axis, and the ordinates $x = 2$, $x = 8$.

6. Find the area enclosed by the ellipse

$$\frac{x^2}{a^2} + \frac{y^2}{b^2} = 1.$$

7. Find the area bounded by the coördinate axes and the curve $x^{\frac{1}{2}} + y^{\frac{1}{2}} = a^{\frac{1}{2}}$.

8. Find the area within a loop of the curve $x^2 = y^2 (4 - y^2)$. ✓

9. Find the area within the loop of the curve $y^2 = (x - 1)(x - 2)^2$.

10. Show that the area bounded by an arc of the hyperbola $xy = k^2$, the x-axis and the ordinates at its ends, is equal to the area bounded by the same arc, the y-axis and the abscissas at its ends.

11. Find the area bounded by the curves $y^2 = 4\,ax$, $x^2 = 4\,ay$.]

12. Find the area bounded by the parabola $y = 2\,x - x^2$ and the line $y = -x$.

13. Find the areas of the two parts into which the circle $x^2 + y^2 = 8$ is divided by the parabola $y^2 = 2\,x$.

14. Find the area within the parabola $x^2 = 4\,y + 4$ and the circle $x^2 + y^2 = 16$.

15. Find the area bounded by $y^2 = 4\,x$, $x^2 = 4\,y$, and $x^2 + y^2 = 5$.

16. Find the area of a circle by using the parametric equations $x = a \cos \theta$, $y = a \sin \theta$.

17. Find the area bounded by the x-axis and one arch of the cycloid.

$$x = a\,(\phi - \sin \phi), \ y = a\,(1 - \cos \phi).$$

18. Find the area within the cardioid

$$x = a \cos \theta\,(1 - \cos \theta), \ y = a \sin \theta\,(1 - \cos \theta).$$

19. Find the area bounded by an arch of the trochoid,

$$x = a\phi - b \sin \phi, \qquad y = a - b \cos \phi,$$

and the tangent at the lowest points of the curve.

20. Find the area of the ellipse $x^2 - xy + y^2 = 3$.

21. Find the area bounded by the curve $y^2 = \dfrac{x^3}{2\,a - x}$ and its asymptote $x = 2\,a$.

22. Find the area within the curve

$$\frac{x^2}{a^2} + \left(\frac{y}{b}\right)^{\!3} = 1.$$

27. Area Bounded by a Plane Curve. Polar Coördinates. — To find the area of the sector POQ bounded by two radii OP, OQ and the arc PQ of a given curve.

Divide the angle POQ into any number of equal parts $\Delta\theta$ and construct the circular sectors shown in Fig. 27a. One of these sectors ORS has the area

$$\tfrac{1}{2}\,OR^2\,\Delta\theta = \tfrac{1}{2}\,r^2\,\Delta\theta.$$

If α and β are the limiting values of θ, the sum of all the sectors is then

$$\sum_{\alpha}^{\beta} \tfrac{1}{2}\, r^2\, \Delta\theta.$$

As $\Delta\theta$ approaches zero, this sum approaches the area A of the sector POQ.   Therefore

$$A = \lim_{\Delta\theta \to 0} \sum_{\alpha}^{\beta} \tfrac{1}{2}\, r^2\, \Delta\theta = \int_{\alpha}^{\beta} \tfrac{1}{2}\, r^2\, d\theta. \tag{27}$$

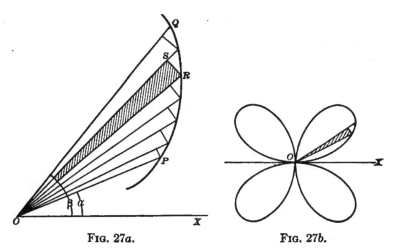

FIG. 27a.   FIG. 27b.

In this equation r must be replaced by its value in terms of θ from the equation of the curve.

Example. Find the area of one loop of the curve $r = a \sin 2\,\theta$ (Fig. 27b).

· A loop of the curve extends from $\theta = 0$ to $\theta = \dfrac{\pi}{2}$.   Its area is

$$A = \int_0^{\frac{\pi}{2}} \frac{1}{2}\, r^2\, d\theta = \int_0^{\frac{\pi}{2}} \frac{a^2}{2} \sin^2 (2\,\theta)\, d\theta$$

$$= \frac{a^2}{4} \int_0^{\frac{\pi}{2}} (1 - \cos 4\,\theta)\, d\theta = \frac{\pi a^2}{8}.$$

EXERCISES

1. Find the area of the circle $r = a$.

2. Find the area of the circle $r = a \cos \theta$.

3. Find the area bounded by the coördinate axes and the line $r = a \sec \left(\theta - \frac{\pi}{3} \right)$.

4. Find the area bounded by the initial line and the first turn of the spiral $r = ae^{\theta}$.

5. Find the area of one loop of the curve $r^2 = a^2 \cos 2\theta$.

6. Find the area enclosed by the curve $r = \cos \theta + 2$.

7. Find the area within the cardioid $r = a (1 + \cos \theta)$.

8. Find the area bounded by the parabola $r = a \sec^2 \frac{\theta}{2}$ and the y-axis.

9. Find the area bounded by the parabola

$$r = \frac{2\,a}{1 - \cos \theta}$$

and the radii $\theta = \frac{\pi}{4}$, $\theta = \frac{\pi}{2}$.

10. Find the area bounded by the initial line and the second and third turns of the spiral $r = a\theta$.

11. Find the area of the curve $r = 2\,a \cos 3\,\theta$ outside the circle $r = a$.

12. Show that the area of the sector bounded by any two radii of the spiral $r\theta = a$ is proportional to the difference of those radii.

13. Find the area common to the two circles $r = a \cos \theta$, $r = a \cos \theta + a \sin \theta$.

14. Find the entire area enclosed by the curve $r = a \cos^3 \frac{\theta}{3}$.

15. Find the area within the curve $(r - a)^2 = a^2 (1 - \theta^2)$.

16. Through a point within a closed curve a chord is drawn. Show that, if either of the areas determined by the chord and curve is a maximum or minimum, the chord is bisected by the fixed point.

28. Volume of a Solid of Revolution. — To find the volume generated by revolving the area $ABCD$ about the x-axis.

Inscribe in the area a series of rectangles as shown in Fig. 28a. One of these rectangles $PQSR$ generates a circular cylinder with radius y and altitude Δx.   The volume of this cylinder is

$$\pi y^2 \, \Delta x.$$

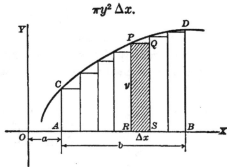

FIG. 28a.

If a and b are the limiting values of x, the sum of the cylinders is

$$\sum_{a}^{b} \pi y^2 \, \Delta x.$$

The volume generated by the area is the limit of this sum

$$v = \lim_{\Delta x \doteq 0} \sum_{a}^{b} \pi y^2 \, \Delta x = \int_{a}^{b} \pi y^2 \, dx. \qquad (28)$$

If the area does not reach the axis, as in Fig. 28b, let y_1 and y_2 be the distances from the axis to the bottom and top

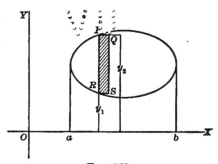

FIG. 28b.

of the rectangle $PQRS$.   When revolved about the axis, it generates a hollow cylinder, or washer, of volume

$$\pi \left(y_2{}^2 - y_1{}^2 \right) \Delta x.$$

The volume generated by the area is then

$$v = \lim_{\Delta x \doteq 0} \sum_a^b \pi \left(y_2{}^2 - y_1{}^2\right) \Delta x = \int_a^b \pi \left(y_2{}^2 - y_1{}^2\right) dx.$$

If the area is revolved about some other axis, y in these formulas must be replaced by the perpendicular from a point of the curve to the axis and x by the distance along the axis to that perpendicular.

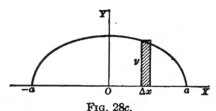

FIG. 28c.

Example 1. Find the volume generated by revolving the ellipse

$$\frac{x^2}{a^2} + \frac{y^2}{b^2} = 1$$

about the x-axis.

From the equation of the curve we get

$$y^2 = \frac{b^2}{a^2} \left(a^2 - x^2\right).$$

The volume required is, therefore,

$$v = \int_{-a}^a \pi y^2 \, dx = \frac{\pi b^2}{a^2} \int_{-a}^a \left(a^2 - x^2\right) dx = \frac{4}{3} \pi a b^2.$$

Ex. 2. A circle of radius a is revolved about an axis in its plane at the distance b (greater than a) from its center. Find the volume generated.

Revolve the circle, Fig. 28d, about the line CD. The rectangle MN generates a washer with radii

$$R_1 = b - x = b - \sqrt{a^2 - y^2},$$
$$R_2 = b + x = b + \sqrt{a^2 - y^2}.$$

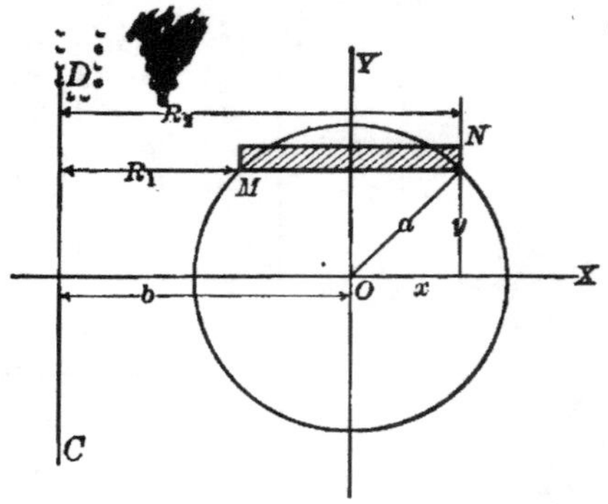

FIG. 28d.

The volume of the washer is

$$\pi \left(R_2{}^2 - R_1{}^2\right) = 4 \pi b \sqrt{a^2 - y^2} \, \Delta y.$$

The volume required is then

$$v = \int_{-a}^{a} 4\,\pi b \,\sqrt{a^2 - y^2}\, dy = 2\,\pi^2 a^2 b.$$

Ex. 3. Find the volume generated by revolving the circle $r = a \sin \theta$ about the x-axis.

In this case

$$y = r \sin \theta = a \sin^2 \theta,$$
$$x = r \cos \theta = a \cos \theta \sin \theta.$$

The volume required is

$$v = \int \pi y^2 \, dx = \int_{\pi}^{0} \pi a^3 \sin^4 \theta \,(\cos^2 \theta - \sin^2 \theta)\, d\theta = \frac{\pi^2 a^3}{4}.$$

The reason for using π as the lower limit and 0 as the upper is to make dx positive along the upper part ABC of the curve.

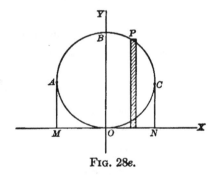

FIG. 28e.

As θ varies from π to 0, the point P describes the path $OABCO$. Along OA and CO dx is negative. The integral thus gives the volume generated by $MABCN$ minus that generated by OAM and OCN.

EXERCISES

1. Find the volume of a sphere by integration.
2. Find the volume of a right cone by integration.
3. Find the volume generated by revolving about the x-axis the area bounded by the x-axis and the parabola $y = 2\,x - x^2$.

4. Find the volume generated by revolving about OY the area bounded by the coördinate axes and the parabola $x^{\frac{1}{2}} + y^{\frac{1}{2}} = a^{\frac{1}{2}}$.

5. Find the volume generated by revolving about the x-axis the area bounded by the catenary $y = \dfrac{a}{2}\left(e^{\frac{x}{a}} + e^{\frac{-x}{a}}\right)$, the x-axis and the lines $x = \pm a$.

6. Find the volume generated by revolving one arch of the sine curve $y = \sin x$ about OX.

7. A cone has its vertex on the surface of a sphere and its axis coincides with a diameter of the sphere. Find the common volume.

8. Find the volume generated by revolving about the y-axis, the part of the parabola $y^2 = 4\,ax$ cut off by the line $x = a$.

9. Find the volume generated by revolving about $x = a$ the part of the parabola $y^2 = 4\,ax$ cut off by the line $x = a$.

10. Find the volume generated by revolving about $y = -2\,a$ the part of the parabola $y^2 = 4\,ax$ cut off by the line $x = a$.

11. Find the volume generated by revolving one arch of the cycloid

$$x = a\,(\phi - \sin\phi), \qquad y = a\,(1 - \cos\phi)$$

about the x-axis.

12. Find the volume generated by revolving the curve

$$x = a\cos^3\phi, \qquad y = a\sin^3\phi$$

about the y-axis.

13. Find the volume generated by revolving the cardioid $r = a\,(1 + \cos\theta)$ about the initial line.

14. Find the volume generated by revolving the cardioid $r = a\,(1 + \cos\theta)$ about the line $x = -\dfrac{a}{4}$.

15. Find the volume generated by revolving the ellipse

$$x^2 + xy + y^2 = 3$$

about the x-axis.

16. Find the volume generated by revolving about the line $y = x$ the part of the parabola $x^{\frac{1}{2}} + y^{\frac{1}{2}} = a^{\frac{1}{2}}$ cut off by the line $x + y = a$.

29. Volume of a Solid with Given Area of Section. — Divide the solid into slices by parallel planes. Let X be the area of section at distance x from a fixed point. The plate $PQRS$ with lateral surface perpendicular to PQR has the volume

$$PQR \cdot \Delta x = X\,\Delta x.$$

If a and b are the limiting values of x, the sum of such plates is

$$\sum_{a}^{b} X \, \Delta x.$$

The volume required is the limit of this sum

$$v = \lim_{\Delta x \doteq 0} \sum_{a}^{b} X \, \Delta x = \int_{a}^{b} X \, dx. \qquad (29)$$

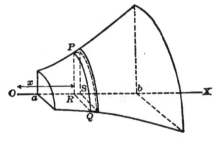

FIG. 29a.

Example 1.   Find the volume of the ellipsoid

$$\frac{x^2}{a^2} + \frac{y^2}{b^2} + \frac{z^2}{c^2} = 1.$$

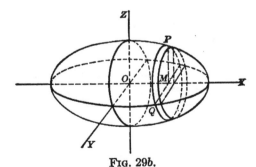

FIG. 29b.

The section perpendicular to the x-axis at the distance x from the center is an ellipse

$$\frac{y^2}{b^2} + \frac{z^2}{c^2} = 1 - \frac{x^2}{a^2}.$$

The semi-axes of this ellipse are

$$MP = c\sqrt{1 - \frac{x^2}{a^2}}, \qquad MQ = b\sqrt{1 - \frac{x^2}{a^2}}.$$

By exercise 6, page 49, the area of this ellipse is

$$\pi \cdot MP \cdot MQ = \pi bc\left(1 - \frac{x^2}{a^2}\right).$$

The volume of the ellipsoid is, therefore,

$$\int_{-a}^{a} \pi bc\left(1 - \frac{x^2}{a^2}\right) dx = \frac{4}{3}\pi abc.$$

Ex. 2.   The axes of two equal right circular cylinders intersect at right angles.   Find the common volume.

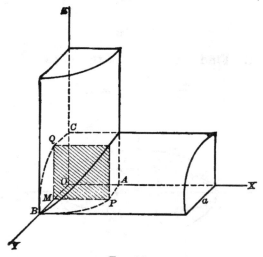

FIG. 29c.

In Fig. 29c, the axes of the cylinders are OX and OZ and $OABC$ is $\frac{1}{8}$ of the common volume.   The section of $OABC$ by a plane perpendicular to OY is a square of side

$$MP = MQ = \sqrt{a^2 - y^2}.$$

The area of the section is therefore

$$MP \cdot MQ = a^2 - y^2,$$

and the required volume is

$$v = 8 \int_0^a (a^2 - y^2)\, dy = \frac{16\, a^3}{3}.$$

EXERCISES

1. Find the volume of a pyramid by integration.

2. A wedge is cut from the base of a right circular cylinder by a plane passing through a diameter of the base and inclined at an angle α to the base. Find the volume of the wedge.

3. Two circles have a diameter in common and lie in perpendicular planes. A square moves in such a way that its plane is perpendicular to the common diameter and its diagonals are chords of the circles. Find the volume generated.

4. The plane of a moving circle is perpendicular to that of an ellipse and the radius of the circle is an ordinate of the ellipse. Find the volume generated when the circle moves from one vertex of the ellipse to the other.

5. The plane of a moving triangle is perpendicular to a fixed diameter of a circle, its base is a chord of the circle, and its vertex lies on a line parallel to the fixed diameter at distance h from the plane of the circle. Find the volume generated by the triangle in moving from one end of the diameter to the other.

6. A triangle of constant area A rotates about a line perpendicular to its plane while advancing along the line. Find the volume swept out in advancing a distance h.

7. Show that if two solids are so related that every plane parallel to a fixed plane cuts from them sections of equal area, the volumes of the solids are equal.

8. A cylindrical surface passes through two great circles of a sphere which are at right angles. Find the volume within the cylindrical surface and sphere.

9. Two cylinders of equal altitude h have a common upper base and their lower bases are tangent. Find the volume common to the two cylinders.

10. A circle moves with its center on the z-axis and its plane parallel to a fixed plane inclined at 45° to the z-axis. If the radius of the circle is always $r = \sqrt{a^2 - z^2}$, where z is the coördinate of its center, find the volume described.

CHAPTER V

OTHER GEOMETRICAL APPLICATIONS

30. Infinitesimals of Higher Order. — In the applications of the definite integral that we have previously made, the quantity desired has in each case been a limit of the form

$$\lim_{\Delta x \doteq 0} \sum_{a}^{b} f(x) \, \Delta x.$$

We shall now consider cases involving limits of the form

$$\lim_{\Delta x \doteq 0} \sum_{a}^{b} F(x, \Delta x)$$

when $F(x, \Delta x)$ is only approximately expressible in the form $f(x) \, \Delta x$. Such cases are usually handled by neglecting infinitesimals of higher order than Δx. That such neglect does not change the limit is indicated by the following theorem:

If for values of x between a and b, $F(x, \Delta x)$ differs from $f(x) \, \Delta x$ by an infinitesimal of higher order than Δx,

$$\lim_{\Delta x \doteq 0} \sum_{a}^{b} F(x, \Delta x) = \lim_{\Delta x \doteq 0} \sum_{a}^{b} f(x) \, \Delta x.$$

To show this let ϵ be a number so chosen that

$$F(x, \Delta x) = f(x) \, \Delta x + \epsilon \, \Delta x.$$

If $F(x, \Delta x)$ and $f(x) \, \Delta x$ differ by an infinitesimal of higher order than Δx, $\epsilon \, \Delta x$ is of higher order than Δx and so ϵ approaches zero as Δx approaches zero (Differential Calculus, Art. 9). The difference

$$\sum_{a}^{b} F(x, \Delta x) - \sum_{a}^{b} f(x) \, \Delta x = \sum_{a}^{b} \epsilon \, \Delta x$$

is graphically represented by a sum of rectangles (Fig. 30), whose altitudes are the various values of ϵ. Since all these values approach zero * with Δx, the total area approaches zero and so

$$\lim_{\Delta x \doteq 0} \sum_{a}^{b} F(x, \Delta x) = \lim_{\Delta x \doteq 0} \sum_{a}^{b} f(x) \Delta x,$$

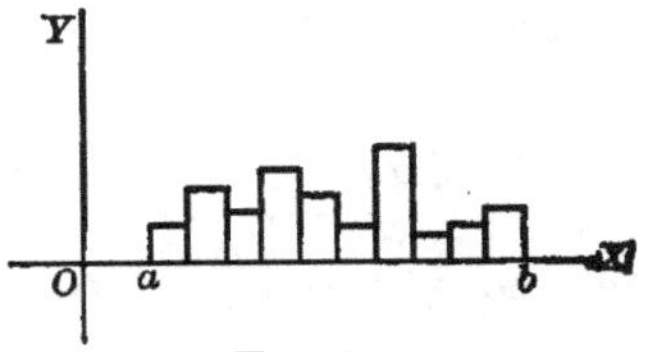

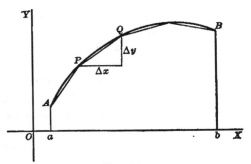

FIG. 30.

which was to be proved.

31. Length of a Curve. Rectangular Coördinates. — In the arc AB of a curve inscribe a series of chords. The length of one of these chords PQ is

$$\sqrt{\Delta x^2 + \Delta y^2} = \sqrt{1 + \left(\frac{\Delta y}{\Delta x}\right)^2}\, \Delta x,$$

FIG. 31a.

and the sum of their lengths is

$$\sum_{a}^{b} \sqrt{1 + \left(\frac{\Delta y}{\Delta x}\right)^2}\, \Delta x.$$

The length of the arc AB is defined as the limit approached by this sum when the number of chords is increased indefinitely, their lengths approaching zero.

* For the discussion to be strictly accurate it must be shown that there is a number larger than any of the ϵ's which approaches zero. In the language of higher mathematics, the approach to the limit must be uniform. In ordinary cases that certainly would be true. A similar remark applies to all the applications of the above theorem.

The quantity $\sqrt{1+\left(\frac{\Delta y}{\Delta x}\right)^2}$ is not a function of x alone. When Δx approaches zero, however, the difference of $\sqrt{1+\left(\frac{\Delta y}{\Delta x}\right)^2}$ and $\sqrt{1+\left(\frac{dy}{dx}\right)^2}$ approaches zero. If then we replace $\sqrt{1+\left(\frac{\Delta y}{\Delta x}\right)^2}\,\Delta x$ by $\sqrt{1+\left(\frac{dy}{dx}\right)^2}\,\Delta x$, the error is an infinitesimal of higher order than Δx. Therefore the length of arc is

$$s = \lim_{\Delta x \to 0} \sum \sqrt{1+\left(\frac{dy}{dx}\right)^2}\,\Delta x = \int_a^b \sqrt{1+\left(\frac{dy}{dx}\right)^2}\,dx.$$

In applying this formula $\frac{dy}{dx}$ must be determined from the equation of the curve. The result can also be written

$$s = \int_A^B \sqrt{dx^2 + dy^2}. \tag{31}$$

In this formula, y may be expressed in terms of x, or x in terms of y, or both may be expressed in terms of a parameter. In any case the limits are the values at A and B of the variable that remains.

Example 1. Find the length of the arc of the parabola $y^2 = 4x$ between $x = 0$ and $x = 1$.

In this case $\frac{dx}{dy} = \frac{y}{2}$. The limiting values of y are 0 and 2. Hence

$$s = \int^2 \sqrt{1+\left(\frac{dx}{dy}\right)^2}\,dy = \int_0^2 \frac{1}{2}\sqrt{y^2+4}\,dy = \sqrt{2}+\ln(1+\sqrt{2}).$$

Ex. 2. Find the perimeter of the curve

$$x = a\cos^3\phi, \quad y = a\sin^3\phi.$$

In this case

$$ds = \sqrt{dx^2+dy^2} = \sqrt{9a^2\cos^4\phi\sin^2\phi + 9a^2\sin^4\phi\cos^2\phi}\,d\phi$$
$$= 3a\cos\phi\sin\phi\,d\phi.$$

One-fourth of the curve is described when ϕ varies from 0 to $\frac{\pi}{2}$. Hence the perimeter is

$$s = 4 \int_0^{\frac{\pi}{2}} 3\, a \, \cos\phi \sin\phi \, d\phi = 6\, a.$$

EXERCISES

1. Find the circumference of a circle by integration.
2. Find the length of $y^2 = x^3$ between $(0, 0)$ and $(4, 8)$.
3. Find the length of $x = \ln \sec y$ between $y = 0$ and $y = \frac{\pi}{3}$.
4. Find the length of $x = \frac{1}{4} y^2 - \frac{1}{2} \ln y$ between $y = 1$ and $y = 2$.
5. Find the length of $y = e^x$ between $(0, 1)$ and $(1, e)$.
6. Find the perimeter of the curve
$$x^{\frac{2}{3}} + y^{\frac{2}{3}} = a^{\frac{2}{3}}.$$
7. Find the length of the catenary
$$y = \frac{a}{2}\left(e^{\frac{x}{a}} + e^{-\frac{x}{a}}\right)$$
between $x = -a$ and $x = a$.
8. Find the length of one arch of the cycloid
$$x = a\,(\phi - \sin\phi), \qquad y = a\,(1 - \cos\phi).$$
9. Find the length of the involute of the circle
$$x = a\,(\cos\theta + \theta \sin\theta), \quad y = a\,(\sin\theta - \theta \cos\theta),$$
between $\theta = 0$ and $\theta = 2\pi$.
10. Find the length of an arc of the cycloid
$$x = a\,(\theta + \sin\theta), \quad y = a\,(1 - \cos\theta).$$

If s is the length of arc between the origin and any point (x, y) of the same arch, show that
$$s^2 = 8\,ay.$$

32. Length of a Curve. Polar Coördinates. — The differential of arc of a curve is (Differential Calculus, Arts. 54, 59)

$$ds = \sqrt{dx^2 + dy^2} = \sqrt{dr^2 + r^2\, d\theta^2}.$$

Equation (31) is, therefore, equivalent to

$$s = \int_A^B \sqrt{dr^2 + r^2 \, d\theta^2}. \tag{32}$$

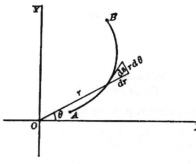

FIG. 32.

In using this formula, r must be expressed in terms of θ or θ in terms of r from the equation of the curve. The limits are the values at A and B of the variable that remains.

Example. Find the length of the first turn of the spiral $r = a\,\theta$.

In this case $dr = a \, d\theta$ and

$$s = \int_0^{2\pi} \sqrt{a^2 \, d\theta^2 + a^2\theta^2 \, d\theta^2} = a \int_0^{2\pi} \sqrt{1 + \theta^2} \, d\theta$$

$$= \pi a \sqrt{1 + 4\pi^2} + \frac{a}{2} \ln \left(2\pi + \sqrt{1 + 4\pi^2}\right).$$

EXERCISES

1. Find the circumference of the circle $r = a$.

2. Find the circumference of the circle $r = 2\,a \cos \theta$.

3. Find the length of the spiral $r = e^{a\theta}$ between $\theta = 0$ and $\theta = \dfrac{1}{a}$.

4. Find the distance along the straight line $r = a \sec \left(\theta - \dfrac{\pi}{3}\right)$ from $\theta = 0$ to $\theta = \dfrac{\pi}{2}$.

5. Find the arc of the parabola $r = a \sec^2 \tfrac{1}{2}\,\theta$ cut off by the y-axis.

6. Find the length of one loop of the curve

$$r = a \cos^4 \frac{\theta}{4}.$$

7. Find the perimeter of the cardioid
$$r = a\,(1 + \cos \theta).$$

8. Find the complete perimeter of the curve $r = a \sin^3 \dfrac{\theta}{3}$.

33. Area of a Surface of Revolution. — To find the area generated by revolving the arc AB about the x-axis.

Join A and B by a broken line with vertices on the arc.

Let x, y be the coördinates of P and $x + \Delta x$, $y + \Delta y$ those of Q. The chord PQ generates a frustum of a cone whose area is

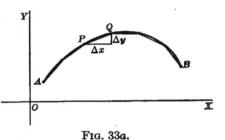

$\pi (2 y + \Delta y) PQ =$
$\pi (2 y + \Delta y) \sqrt{\Delta x^2 + \Delta y^2}.$

FIG. 33a.

The area generated by the broken line is then

$$\sum_{A}^{B} \pi (2 y + \Delta y) \sqrt{\Delta x^2 + \Delta y^2}.$$

The area S generated by the arc AB is the limit approached by this sum when Δx and Δy approach zero. Neglecting infinitesimals of higher order, $(2 y + \Delta y) \sqrt{\Delta x^2 + \Delta y^2}$ can be replaced by $2 y \sqrt{dx^2 + dy^2} = 2 y \, ds$. Hence the area generated is

$$S = \int_{A}^{B} 2 \pi y \, ds. \tag{33a}$$

In this formula y and ds must be calculated from the equation of the curve. The limits are the values at A and B of the variable in terms of which they are expressed.

Similarly, the area generated by revolving about the y-axis is

$$S = \int_{A}^{B} 2 \pi x \, ds. \tag{33b}$$

Example. Find the area of the surface generated by revolving about the y-axis the part of the curve $y = 1 - x^2$ above the x-axis.

In this case

$$ds = \sqrt{1 + \left(\frac{dy}{dx}\right)^2}\, dx = \sqrt{1 + 4\,x^2}\, dx.$$

The area required is generated by the part AB of the curve between $x = 0$ and $x = 1$. Hence

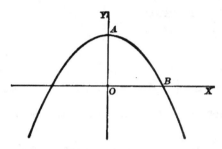

FIG. 33b.

$$S = \int_A^B 2\,\pi\,x\,ds = \int_0^1 2\,\pi x \sqrt{1 + 4\,x^2}\,dx$$

$$= \frac{\pi}{6}\,(1 + 4\,x^2)^{\frac{3}{2}}\Big|_0^1 = \frac{\pi}{6}\,(5\sqrt{5} - 1).$$

EXERCISES

1. Find the area of the surface of a sphere.

2. Find the area of the surface of a right circular cone.

3. Find the area of the spheroid generated by revolving an ellipse about its major axis.

4. Find the area generated by revolving the curve $x^{\frac{2}{3}} + y^{\frac{2}{3}} = a^{\frac{2}{3}}$ about the y-axis.

5. Find the area generated by revolving about OX, the part of the catenary

$$y = \frac{a}{2}\left(e^{\frac{x}{a}} + e^{-\frac{x}{a}}\right)$$

between $x = -a$ and $x = a$.

6. Find the area generated by revolving one arch of the cycloid

$$x = a\,(\phi - \sin\phi), \qquad y = a\,(1 - \cos\phi)$$

about OX.

7. Find the area generated by revolving the cardioid $r = a(1 + \cos \theta)$ about the initial line.

8. The arc of the circle

$$x^2 + y^2 = a^2$$

between $(a, 0)$ and $(0, a)$ is revolved about the line $x + y = a$. Find the area of the surface generated.

9. The arc of the parabola $y^2 = 4x$ between $x = 0$ and $x = 1$ is revolved about the line $y = -2$. Find the area generated.

10. Find the area of the surface generated by revolving the lemniscate $r^2 = 2a^2 \cos 2\theta$ about the line $\theta = \dfrac{\pi}{4}$.

34. Unconventional Methods. — The methods that have been given for finding lengths, areas, and volumes are the

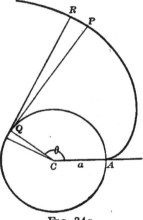

ones most generally applicable. In particular cases other methods may give the results more easily. To solve a problem by integration, it is merely necessary to express the required quantity in any way as a limit of the form used in defining the definite integral.

Example 1. When a string held taut is unwound from a fixed circle, its end describes a curve called the involute of the circle. Find the length of the part described when the first turn of the string is unwound.

FIG. 34a.

Let the string begin to unwind at A. When the end reaches P the part unwound QP is equal to the arc AQ. Hence

$$QP = AQ = a\theta.$$

When P moves to R the arc PR is approximately the arc of a circle with center at Q and central angle $\Delta\theta$. Hence

$$PR = a\theta \, \Delta\theta$$

approximately.   The length of the curve described when θ
varies from 0 to 2π is then

$$s = \lim_{\Delta\theta \to 0} \sum_0^{2\pi} a\theta \, \Delta\theta = \int_0^{2\pi} a\theta \, d\theta = 2\pi a^2.$$

Ex. 2.   Find the volume generated by rotating about the
y-axis the area bounded by the parabola $x^2 = y - 1$, the
x-axis, and the ordinates $x = \pm 1$.

Resolve the area into slices by ordinates at distances Δx
apart.   When revolved about the y-axis, the rectangle PM
between the ordinates x, $x + \Delta x$ generates a hollow cylinder
whose volume is

$$\pi \, (x + \Delta x)^2 \, y - \pi \, x^2 y = 2\pi x y \, \Delta x + \pi y \, (\Delta x)^2.$$

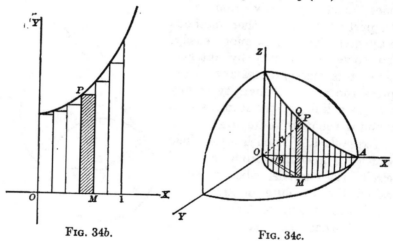

FIG. 34b.   FIG. 34c.

Since $\pi y \, (\Delta x)^2$ is an infinitesimal of higher order than Δx,
the required volume is

$$\lim_{\Delta x \to 0} \sum_0^1 2\pi x y \, \Delta x = \int_0^1 2\pi x \, (1 + x^2) \, dx = \tfrac{3}{2} \pi.$$

Ex. 3.   Find the area of the cylinder $x^2 + y^2 = ax$ within
the sphere $x^2 + y^2 + z^2 = a^2$.

Fig. 34c shows one-fourth of the required area.   Divide
the circle OA into equal arcs Δs.   The generators through

the points of division cut the surface of the cylinder into strips. Neglecting infinitesimals of higher order, the area of the strip MPQ is $MP \cdot \Delta s$. If r, θ are the polar coördinates of M, $r = a \cos \theta$ and

$$\Delta s = a \, \Delta \theta, \qquad MP = \sqrt{a^2 - r^2} = a \sin \theta.$$

The required area is therefore given by

$$\frac{S}{4} = \lim_{\Delta\theta \to 0} \sum_0^{\frac{\pi}{2}} a^2 \sin \theta \, \Delta\theta = \int_0^{\frac{\pi}{2}} a^2 \sin \theta \, d\theta.$$

Consequently

$$S = 4 a^2 \int_0^{\frac{\pi}{2}} \sin \theta \, d\theta = 4 a^2.$$

EXERCISES

1. Find the area swept over by the string in example 1, page 67.

2. Find the area of surface cut from a right circular cylinder by a plane passing through a diameter of the base and inclined 45° to the base.

3. The axes of two right circular cylinders of equal radius intersect at right angles. Find the area of the solid common to the two cylinders (Fig. 29c).

4. An equilateral triangle of side a is revolved about a line parallel to the base at distance b below the base. Find the volume generated.

5. The area bounded by the hyperbola $x^2 - y^2 = a^2$ and the lines $y = \pm a$ is revolved about the x-axis. Find the volume generated.

6. The vertex of a cone of vertical angle 2α is the center of a sphere of radius a. Find the volume common to the cone and sphere.

7. The axis of a cone of altitude h and radius of base $2 a$ is a generator of a cylinder of radius a. Find the area of the surface of the cylinder within the cone.

8. Find the area of the surface of the cone in Ex. 7 within the cylinder.

9. Find the volume of the cylinder in Ex. 7 within the cone.

CHAPTER VI

MECHANICAL AND PHYSICAL APPLICATIONS

35. Pressure. — The pressure of a liquid upon a horizontal area is equal to the weight of a vertical column of the liquid having the area as base and reaching to the surface. By the pressure at a point P in the liquid is meant the pressure upon a horizontal surface of unit area at that point. The

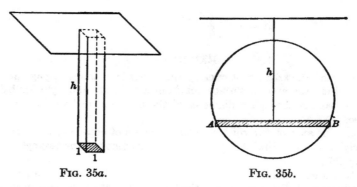

FIG. 35a.   FIG. 35b.

volume of a column of unit section and height h is h. Hence the pressure at depth h is

$$p = wh, \qquad (35a)$$

w being the weight of a cubic unit of the liquid.

To find the pressure upon a vertical plane area (Fig. 35b), we make use of the fact that the pressure at a point is the same in all directions. The pressure upon the strip AB parallel to the surface is then approximately

$$p \, \Delta A,$$

p being the pressure at any point of the strip and ΔA its area. The reason for this not being exact is that the pressure at the top of the strip is a little less than at the bottom. This difference is, however, infinitesimal, and, since it multiplies ΔA, the error is an infinitesimal of higher order than ΔA. The total pressure is, therefore,

$$P = \lim_{\Delta A \doteq 0} \sum p\,\Delta A = \int p\,dA = w \int h\,dA. \qquad (35b)$$

Before integration dA must be expressed in terms of h. The limits are the values of h at the top and bottom of the submerged area. In case of water the value of w is about 62.5 lbs. per cubic foot.

Example. Find the water pressure upon a semicircle of

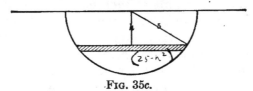

.Fig. 35c.

radius 5 ft., if its plane is vertical and its diameter in the surface of the water.

In this case the element of area is

$$dA = 2\sqrt{25 - h^2}\,dh.$$

Hence

$$P = w \int h\,dA = 2\,w \int_0^5 h\sqrt{25 - h^2}\,dh$$
$$= \tfrac{250}{3}\,w = \tfrac{250}{3}\,(62.5) = 5208.3\,\text{lbs.}$$

EXERCISES

1. Find the pressure sustained by a rectangular floodgate 10 ft. broad and 12 ft. deep, the upper edge being in the surface of the water.

2. Find the pressure on the lower half of the floodgate in the preceding problem.

3. Find the pressure on a triangle of base b and altitude h, submerged so that its vertex is in the surface of the water, and its altitude vertical.

4. Find the pressure upon a triangle of base b and altitude h, submerged so that its base is in the surface of the liquid and its altitude vertical.

5. Find the pressure upon a semi-ellipse submerged with one axis in the surface of the liquid and the other vertical.

6. A vertical masonry dam in the form of a trapezoid is 200 ft. long at the surface of the water, 150 ft. long at the bottom, and 60 ft. high. What pressure must it withstand?

7. One end of a water main, 2 ft. in diameter, is closed by a vertical bulkhead. Find the pressure on the bulkhead if its center is 40 ft. below the surface of the water.

8. A rectangular tank is filled with equal parts of water and oil. If the oil is half as heavy as water, show that the pressure on the sides is one-fourth greater than it would be if the tank were filled with oil.

36. Moment. — Divide a plane area or length into small parts such that the points of each part differ only infinitesimally in distance from a given axis. Multiply each part by the distance of one of its points from the axis, the distance being considered positive for points on one side of the axis and negative for points on the other. The limit approached by the sum of these products when the parts are taken smaller and smaller is called the *moment* of the area or length with respect to the axis.

Similarly, to find the moment of a length, area, volume, or mass in space with respect to a plane, we divide it into elements whose points differ only infinitesimally in distance from the plane and multiply each element by the distance of one of its points from the plane (considered positive for points on one side of the plane and negative on the other). The moment with respect to the plane is the limit approached by the sum of these products when the elements are taken smaller and smaller.

Example. Find the moment of a rectangle about an axis parallel to one of its sides at distance c.

Divide the rectangle into strips parallel to the axis (Fig. 36). Let y be the distance from the axis to a strip. The area of the strip is $b \, \Delta y$. Hence the moment is

$$\lim_{\Delta y \to 0} \sum_{c}^{c+a} yb \, \Delta y = \int_{c}^{c+a} by \, dy = ab\left(c + \frac{a}{2}\right).$$

Since ab is the area of the rectangle and $c + \dfrac{a}{2}$ is the distance
from the axis to its center, the moment is equal to the product
of the area and the distance from the axis to the center of the
rectangle.

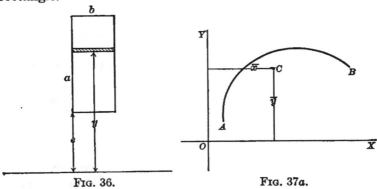

FIG. 36.   FIG. 37a.

**37. The Center of Gravity of a Length or Area in a
Plane.** — The center of gravity of a length or area in a
plane is the point at which it could be concentrated without
changing its moment with respect to any axis in the plane.

Let C $(\bar{x}, \bar{y})$ be the center of gravity of the arc AB (Fig.
37a), and let s be the length of the arc. The moment of AB
with respect to the x-axis is

$$\int_A^B y \, ds.$$

If the length s were concentrated at C, its moment would be
$s\bar{y}$. By the definition of center of gravity

$$s\bar{y} = \int_A^B y \, ds,$$

whence

$$\bar{y} = \frac{\displaystyle\int_A^B y \, ds}{s}.$$

Similarly,

$$\bar{x} = \frac{\displaystyle\int_A^B x \, ds}{s}.$$

The limits are the values at A and B of the variable in terms of which the integral is expressed.

Let $C(\bar{x}, \bar{y})$ be the center of gravity of an area (Figs. 37b, 37c). Divide the area into strips dA and let (x, y) be the center of gravity of the strip dA. The moment of the area with respect to the x-axis is

$$\int y\, dA.$$

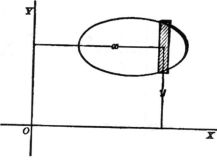

Fɪɢ. 37b.

If the area were concentrated at C, the moment would be $A\bar{y}$, where A is the total area. Hence

$$A\bar{y} = \int y\, dA,$$

or

$$\bar{y} = \frac{\int y\, dA}{A}.$$

Similarly,

$$\bar{x} = \frac{\int x\, dA}{A}.$$

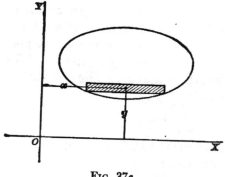

Fɪɢ. 37c.

The strip is usually taken parallel to a coördinate axis. The area can, however, be divided into strips of any other kind if convenient.

Example 1. Find the center of gravity of a quadrant of the circle $x^2 + y^2 = a^2$.

In this case

$$ds = \sqrt{dx^2 + dy^2} = \frac{a}{y}\, dx$$

and

$$\int y \, ds = \int_0^a y \cdot \frac{a}{y} \, dx = a^2.$$

The length of the arc is

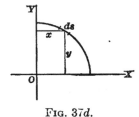

$$s = \frac{1}{4}(2\pi a) = \frac{\pi}{2}a.$$

Hence

$$\bar{y} = \frac{\int y \, ds}{s} = \frac{2a}{\pi}.$$

FIG. 37d.

It is evident from the symmetry of the figure that $\bar{x}$ has the same value.

Ex. 2.   Find the center of gravity of the area of a semi-circle.

From symmetry it is evident that the center of gravity is in the y-axis (Fig. 37e). Take the element of area parallel to OX. Then $dA = 2x \, dy$ and

$$\int y \, dA = \int 2xy \, dy = 2\int_0^a y \sqrt{a^2 - y^2} \, dy = \tfrac{2}{3}a^3.$$

The area is $A = \frac{\pi}{2}a^2$. Hence

$$\bar{y} = \int \frac{y \, dA}{A} = \frac{4a}{3\pi}.$$

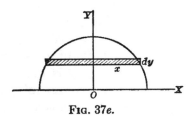

FIG. 37e.

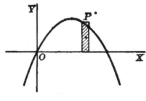

FIG. 37f.

Ex. 3.   Find the center of gravity of the area bounded by the x-axis and the parabola $y = 2x - x^2$.

Take the element of area perpendicular to OX. If (x, y)

are the coördinates of the top of the strip, its center of gravity is $\left(x, \dfrac{y}{2}\right)$. Hence its moment with respect to the x-axis is

$$\frac{y}{2} \cdot dA = \frac{1}{2} y^2 \, dx.$$

The moment of the whole area about OX is then

$$\int \frac{y^2}{2} \, dx = \int_0^2 \frac{1}{2} (2 x - x^2)^2 \, dx = \frac{16}{15}.$$

The area is

$$A = \int y \, dx = \int_0^2 (2 x - x^2) \, dx = \frac{4}{3}.$$

Hence $\bar{y} = \tfrac{2}{5}$. Similarly,

$$\bar{x} = \frac{\int x \, dA}{A} = \frac{\int_0^2 (2 x^2 - x^3) \, dx}{A} = 1.$$

38. Center of Gravity of a Length, Area, Volume, or Mass in Space. — The center of gravity is defined as the point at which the mass, area, length, or volume can be concentrated without changing its moment with respect to any plane.

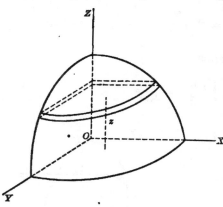

Fig. 38a.

Thus to find the center of gravity of a solid mass (Fig. 38a) cut it into slices of mass Δm. If (x, y, z) is the center of gravity of the slice, its moment with respect to the xy-plane is $z \Delta m$ and the moment of the whole mass is

$$\lim_{\Delta m \to 0} \sum z \, \Delta m = \int z \, dm.$$

$V ol \times \text{density} \cdot \int \text{Mass} = \int dm,$

If the whole mass M were concentrated at its center of gravity $(\bar{x}, \bar{y}, \bar{z})$, the moment with respect to the xy-plane would be $\bar{z}M$. Hence

$$\bar{z}M = \int z \, dm,$$

or

$$\bar{z} = \frac{\int z \, dm}{M}. \tag{38}$$

Similarly,

$$\bar{x} = \frac{\int x \, dm}{M}, \qquad \bar{y} = \frac{\int y \, dm}{M}. \tag{38}$$

The mass of a unit volume is called the density. If then dv is the volume of the element dm and ρ its density,

$$dm = \rho \, dv.$$

To find the center of gravity of a length, area, or volume it is merely necessary to replace M in these formulas by s, S, or v.

Example 1. Find the center of gravity of the volume of an octant of a sphere of radius a.

The volume of the slice (Fig. 38a) is

$$dv = \tfrac{1}{4}\pi x^2 \, dz = \tfrac{1}{4}\pi (a^2 - z^2) \, dz.$$

Hence

$$\int z \, dv = \int_0^a \frac{1}{4}\pi (a^2 - z^2) z \, dz = \frac{\pi}{16} a^4.$$

The volume of an octant of a sphere is $\tfrac{1}{6}\pi a^3$. Hence

$$\bar{z} = \frac{\int z \, dv}{v} = \frac{\dfrac{\pi}{16} a^4}{\dfrac{\pi}{6} a^3} = \frac{3}{8} a.$$

From symmetry it is evident that $\bar{x}$ and $\bar{y}$ have the same value.

Ex. 2.   Find the center of gravity of a right circular cone whose density is proportional to the distance from its base.

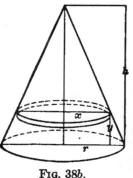

Cut the cone into slices parallel to the base.   Let y be the distance of a slice from the base.   Except for infinitesimals of higher order, its volume is $\pi x^2\, dy$, and its density is ky where K is constant.   Hence its mass is

$$\Delta m = k\pi x^2 y\, dy.$$

By similar triangles $x = \dfrac{r}{h}(h - y)$.

Fig. 38b.

Hence

$$\int y\, dm = \int_0^h \frac{k\pi r^2}{h^2}(h - y)^2\, y^2\, dy = \frac{k\pi r^2 h^3}{30}$$

$$M = \int dm = \int_0^h \frac{k\pi r^2}{h^2}(h - y)^2\, y\, dy = \frac{k\pi r^2 h^2}{12}.$$

Therefore, finally,

$$\bar{y} = \frac{\displaystyle\int y\, dm}{M} = \frac{2}{5}h.$$

EXERCISES

1. The wind produces a uniform pressure upon a rectangular door. Find the moment tending to turn the door on its hinges.

2. Find the moment of the pressure upon a rectangular floodgate about a horizontal line through its center, when the water is level with the top of the gate.

3. A triangle of base b and altitude h is submerged with its base horizontal, altitude vertical, and vertex c feet below the surface of the water.   Find the moment of the pressure upon the triangle about a horizontal line through the vertex.

4. Find the center of gravity of the area of a triangle.

5. Find the center of gravity of the segment of the parabola $y^2 = ax$, cut off by the line $x = a$.

6. Find the center of gravity of the area of a quadrant of the ellipse

$$\frac{x^2}{a^2} + \frac{y^2}{b^2} = 1.$$

7. Find the center of gravity of the area bounded by the coördinate axes and the parabola $x^{\frac{1}{2}} + y^{\frac{1}{2}} = a^{\frac{1}{2}}$.

8. Find the center of gravity of the area above the x-axis bounded by the curve $x^{\frac{1}{2}} + y^{\frac{1}{2}} = a^{\frac{1}{2}}$.

9. Find the center of gravity of the area bounded by the x-axis and one arch of the curve $y = \sin x$.

10. Find the center of gravity of the area bounded by the two parabolas $y^2 = ax$, $x^2 = ay$.

11. Find the center of gravity of the area of the upper half of the cardioid $r = a(1 + \cos\theta)$.

12. Find the center of gravity of the area bounded by the x-axis and one arch of the cycloid,

$$x = a(\phi - \sin\phi), \qquad y = a(1 - \cos\phi).$$

13. Find the center of gravity of the area within a loop of the lemniscate $r^2 = a^2 \cos 2\theta$.

14. Find the center of gravity of the arc of a semicircle of radius a.

15. Find the center of gravity of the arc of the catenary

$$y = \frac{a}{2}\left(e^{\frac{x}{a}} + e^{-\frac{x}{a}}\right)$$

between $x = -a$ and $x = a$.

16. Find the center of gravity of the arc of the curve $x^{\frac{1}{2}} + y^{\frac{1}{2}} = a^{\frac{1}{2}}$ in the first quadrant.

17. Find the center of gravity of the arc of the curve

$$x = \tfrac{1}{4}y^2 - \tfrac{1}{2}\ln y$$

between $y = 1$ and $y = 2$.

18. Find the center of gravity of an arch of the cycloid

$$x = a(\phi - \sin\phi), \qquad y = a(1 - \cos\phi).$$

19. Find the center of gravity of a right circular cone of constant density.

20. Find the center of gravity of a hemisphere of constant density.

21. Find the center of gravity of the solid generated by revolving about OX the area bounded by the parabola $y^2 = 4x$ and the line $x = 4$.

22. Find the center of gravity of a hemisphere whose density is proportional to the distance from the plane face.

23. Find the center of gravity of the solid generated by rotating a sector of a circle about one of its bounding radii.

24. Find the center of gravity of the solid generated by revolving the cardioid $r = a (1 + \cos \theta)$ about the initial line.

25. Find the center of gravity of the wedge cut from a right circular cylinder by a plane passing through a diameter of the base and making with the base the angle α.

26. Find the center of gravity of a hemispherical surface.

27. Show that the center of gravity of a zone of a sphere is midway between the bases of the zone.

28. The segment of the parabola $y^2 = 2 ax$ cut off by the line $x = a$ is revolved about the x-axis. Find the center of gravity of the surface generated.

39. Theorems of Pappus. *Theorem I.* — If the arc of a plane curve is revolved about an axis in its plane, and not crossing the arc, the area generated is equal to the product of the length of the arc and the length of the path described by its center of gravity.

Theorem II. If a plane area is revolved about an axis in its plane and not crossing the area, the volume generated is equal to the product of the area and the length of the path described by its center of gravity.

To prove the first theorem, let the arc be rotated about the x-axis. The ordinate of its center of gravity is

$$\bar{y} = \frac{\int y \, ds}{s},$$

whence

$$2 \pi \int y \, ds = 2 \pi \bar{y} s.$$

The left side of this equation represents the area of the surface generated. Also $2 \pi \bar{y}$ is the length of the path described by the center of gravity. This equation, therefore, expresses the result to be proved.

To prove the second theorem let the area be revolved about the x-axis. From the equation

$$\bar{y} = \frac{\int y \, dA}{A}$$

we get

$$2\pi \int y\, dA = 2\pi\bar{y}A.$$

Since $2\pi \int y\, dA$ is the volume generated, this equation is equivalent to theorem II.

Example 1. Find the area of the torus generated by revolving a circle of radius a about an axis in its plane at distance b (greater than a) from its center.

Since the circumference of the circle is $2\pi a$ and the length of the path described by its center $2\pi b$, the area generated is

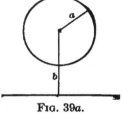

$$S = 2\pi a \cdot 2\pi b = 4\pi^2 ab.$$

FIG. 39a.

Ex. 2. Find the center of gravity of the area of a semicircle by using Pappus's theorems.

When a semicircle of radius a is revolved about its diameter, the volume of the sphere generated is $\frac{4}{3}\pi a^3$. If $\bar{y}$ is the distance of the center of gravity of the semicircle from this diameter, by the second theorem of Pappus,

$$\tfrac{4}{3}\pi a^3 = 2\pi\bar{y}\, A = 2\pi\bar{y} \cdot \tfrac{1}{2}\pi a^2,$$

whence

$$\bar{y} = \frac{\frac{4}{3}\pi a^3}{\pi^2 a^2} = \frac{4a}{3\pi}.$$

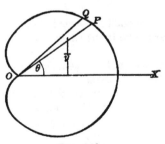

FIG. 39b.

Ex. 3. Find the volume generated by revolving the cardioid $r = a\,(1 + \cos\theta)$ about the initial line.

The area of the triangle OPQ is approximately

$$\tfrac{1}{2} r^2\, \Delta\theta,$$

and its center of gravity is $\frac{2}{3}$ of the distance from the vertex to the base.   Hence

$$\bar{y} = \tfrac{2}{3} r \sin\theta.$$

By the second theorem of Pappus, the volume generated by OPQ is then approximately

$$2\pi y\, \Delta A = \tfrac{2}{3}\pi r^3 \sin\theta\, \Delta\theta.$$

The entire volume is therefore

$$v = \int_0^\pi \tfrac{2}{3}\pi r^3 \sin\theta\, d\theta = \tfrac{2}{3}\pi a^3 \int_0^\pi (1+\cos\theta)^3 \sin\theta\, d\theta$$

$$= -\frac{2}{3}\pi a^3 \frac{(1+\cos\theta)^4}{4}\bigg|_0^\pi = \frac{8}{3}\pi a^3.$$

EXERCISES

1. By using Pappus's theorems find the lateral area and the volume of a right circular cone.

2. Find the volume of the torus generated by revolving a circle of radius a about an axis in its plane at distance b (greater than a) from its center.

3. A groove with cross-section an equilateral triangle of side $\frac{1}{2}$ inch is cut around a cylindrical shaft 6 inches in diameter. Find the volume of material cut away.

4. A steel band is placed around a cylindrical boiler 48 inches in diameter. A cross-section of the band is a semi-ellipse, its axes being 6 and $\sqrt{6}$ inches, respectively, the greater being parallel to the axis of the boiler. What is the volume of the band?

5. The length of an arch of the cycloid

$$x = a\,(\phi - \sin\phi), \qquad y = a\,(1 - \cos\phi)$$

is $8\,a$, and the area generated by revolving it about the x-axis is $\frac{64}{3}\pi a^2$. Find the area generated by revolving the arch about the tangent at its highest point.

6. By the method of Ex. 3, page 81, find the volume generated by revolving the lemniscate $r^2 = 2\,a^2 \cos 2\,\theta$ about the x-axis.

7. Obtain a formula for the volume generated by revolving the polar element of area about the line $x = -a$. Apply this formula to obtain the volume generated by revolving about $x = -a$ the sector of the circle $r = a$ bounded by the radii $\theta = -\alpha$, $\theta = +\alpha$.

8. A variable circle revolves about an axis in its plane. If the distance from the center of the circle to the axis is $2\,a$ and its radius is $a \sin\theta$, where θ is the angle of rotation, find the volume of the horn-shaped solid that is generated.

9. Can the area of the surface in Ex. 8 be found in a similar way?

I on any axis than C.g is $\sqrt{I_{cg} + Md^2}$ d = distance between // lines

10. The vertex of a right circular cone is on the surface of a right circular cylinder and its axis cuts the axis of the cylinder at right angles. Find the volume common to the cylinder and cone (use sections determined by planes through the vertex of the cone and the generators of the cylinder).

40. Moment of Inertia. — The moment of inertia of a particle about an axis is the product of its mass and the square of its distance from the axis.

To find the moment of inertia of a continuous mass, we divide it into parts such that the points of each differ only infinitesimally in distance from the axis. Let Δm be such a part and R the distance of one of its points from the axis. Except for infinitesimals of higher order, the moment of inertia of Δm about the axis is $R^2 \Delta m$. The moment of inertia of the entire mass is therefore

$$I = \lim_{\Delta m \to 0} \sum R^2 \Delta m = \int R^2 \, dm. \qquad (40)$$

By the moment of inertia of a length, area, or volume, we mean the value obtained by using the differential of length, area, or volume in place of dm in equation (40).

Example 1. Find the moment of inertia of a right circular cone of constant density about its axis.

Let ρ be the density, h the altitude, and a the radius of the base of the cone. Divide it into hollow cylindrical slices by means of cylindrical surfaces having the same axis as the cone. By similar triangles the altitude y of the cylindrical surface of radius r is

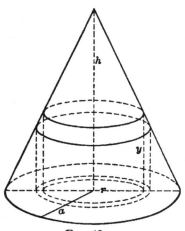

FIG. 40a.

$$y = \frac{h}{a}(a - r),$$

I of ...

Neglecting infinitesimals of higher order, the volume between the cylinders of radii r and $r + \Delta r$ is then

$$\Delta v = 2 \pi r y \, \Delta r = \frac{2 \pi h}{a} r (a - r) \, dr.$$

The moment of inertia is therefore

$$I = \int r^2 \, dm = \int r^2 \rho \, dv = \frac{2 \pi h \rho}{a} \int_0^a r^3 (a - r) \, dr = \frac{\pi \rho h a^4}{10}.$$

The mass of the cone is

$$M = \rho v = \tfrac{1}{3} \pi \rho a^2 h.$$

Hence

$$I = \tfrac{3}{10} M a^2.$$

FIG. 40b.

Ex. 2.   Find the moment of inertia of the area of a circle about a diameter of the circle.

Let the radius be a and let the x-axis be the diameter about which the moment of inertia is taken.

Divide the area into strips by lines parallel to the x-axis. Neglecting infinitesimals of higher order, the area of such a strip is $2 x \, \Delta y$ and its moment of inertia $2 x y^2 \, \Delta y$. The moment of inertia of the entire area is therefore

$$I = \int 2 x y^2 \, dy = 2 \int_{-a}^a \sqrt{a^2 - y^2} \, y^2 \, dy = \frac{\pi a^4}{4}.$$

EXERCISES

1. Find the moment of inertia of the area of a rectangle about one of its edges.

2. Find the moment of inertia of a triangle about its base.

3. Find the moment of inertia of a triangle about an axis through its vertex parallel to its base.

4. Find the moment of inertia about the y-axis of the area bounded by the parabola $y^2 = 4 ax$ and the line $x = a$.

5. Find the moment of inertia of the area in Ex. 4 about the line $x = a$.

6. Find the moment of inertia of the area of a circle about the axis perpendicular to its plane at the center. (Divide the area into rings with centers at the center of the circle.)

7. Find the moment of inertia of a cylinder of mass M and radius a about its axis.

8. Find the moment of inertia of a sphere of mass M and radius a about a diameter.

9. An ellipsoid is generated by revolving the ellipse

$$\frac{x^2}{a^2} + \frac{y^2}{b^2} = 1$$

about the x-axis. Find its moment of inertia about the x-axis.

10. Find the moment of inertia of a hemispherical shell of constant density about the diameter perpendicular to its plane face.

11. Prove that the moment of inertia about any axis is equal to the moment of inertia about a parallel axis through the center of gravity plus the product of the mass and the square of the distance between the two axes.

12. Use the answer to Ex. 6, and the theorem of Ex. 11 to determine the moment of inertia of a circular area about an axis, perpendicular to its plane at a point of the circumference.

41. Work Done by a Force. — Let a force be applied to a body at a fixed point. When the body moves work is done by the force. If the force is constant, the work is defined as the product of the force and the distance the point of application moves in the direction of the force. That is,

$$W = Fs, \tag{41a}$$

where W is the work, F the force, and s the distance moved in the direction of the force.

If the direction of motion does not coincide with that of the force, the work done is the product of the force and the projection of the displacement on the force.

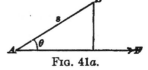

Fig. 41a.

Thus when the body moves from A to B (Fig. 41a) the work done by the force F is

$$W = Fs \cos \theta. \tag{41b}$$

If the force is variable, we divide the path into parts Δs. In moving the distance Δs, the force is nearly constant and so the work done is approximately $F \cos \theta \, \Delta s$. As the intervals Δs are taken shorter and shorter, this approximation becomes more and more accurate. The exact work is then the limit

$$W = \lim_{\Delta s \doteq 0} \sum F \cos\theta\, \Delta s = \int F \cos\theta\, ds. \qquad (41c)$$

To determine the value of W, we express $F \cos\theta$ and ds in terms of a single variable. The limits of integration are the values of this variable at the two ends of the path. If the displacement is in the direction of the force, $\theta = 0$, $\cos\theta = 1$ and

$$W = \int F\, ds. \qquad (41d)$$

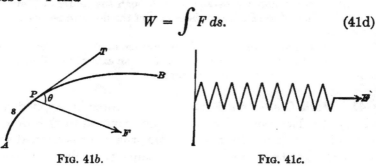

FIG. 41*b*.   FIG. 41*c*.

Example 1. The amount a helical spring is stretched is proportional to the force applied. If a force of 100 lbs. is required to stretch the spring 1 inch, find the work done in stretching it 4 inches.

Let s be the number of inches the spring is stretched. The force is then

$$F = ks,$$

k being constant. When $s = 1$, $F = 100$ lbs. Hence $k = 100$ and

$$F = 100\, s.$$

The work done in stretching the spring 4 inches is

$$\int_0^4 F\, ds = \int_0^4 100\, s\, ds = 800 \text{ inch pounds} = 66\tfrac{2}{3} \text{ foot pounds.}$$

Ex. 2.   A gas is confined in a cylinder with a movable piston. Assuming Boyle's law $pv = k$, find the work done by the pressure of the gas in pushing out the piston (Fig. 41d).

Let v be the volume of gas in the cylinder and p the pressure per unit area of the piston.   If A is the area of the piston, pA is the total pressure of the gas upon it.   If s is the distance the piston moves, the work done is

$$W = \int_{s_1}^{s_2} pA \, ds.$$

But $A \, ds = dv$.   Hence

$$W = \int_{v_1}^{v_2} p \, dv = \int_{v_1}^{v_2} \frac{k}{v} \, dv = k \ln \frac{v_2}{v_1}$$

is the work done when the volume expands from v_1 to v_2.

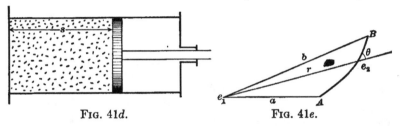

FIG. 41d.   FIG. 41e.

Ex. 3.   The force with which an electric charge e_1 repels a charge e_2 at distance r is

$$\frac{ke_1e_2}{r^2},$$

where k is constant.   Find the work done by this force when the charge e_2 moves from $r = a$ to $r = b$, e_1 remaining fixed.

Let the charge e_2 move from A to B along any path AB (Fig. 41e).   The work done by the force of repulsion is

$$W = \int F \cos \theta \, ds = \int F \, dr = \int_a^b \frac{ke_1e_2}{r^2} \, dr$$

$$= ke_1e_2 \left(\frac{1}{a} - \frac{1}{b} \right).$$

The work depends only on the end points A and B and not on the path connecting them.

EXERCISES

1. According to Hooke's law the force required to stretch a bar from the length a to the length $a + x$ is

$$\frac{kx}{a},$$

where K is constant. Find the work done in stretching the bar from the length a to the length b.

2. Supposing the force of gravity to vary inversely as the square of the distance from the earth's center, find the work done by gravity on a meteor of weight w lbs., when it comes from an indefinitely great distance to the earth's surface.

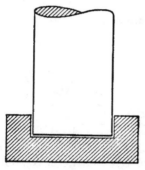

FIG. 41*f*.

3. If a gas expands without change of temperature, according to van der Waal's equation,

$$p = \frac{c}{v - b} - \frac{a}{v^2},$$

a, b, c being constant. Find the work done when the gas expands from the volume v_1 to the volume v_2.

4. The work in foot pounds required to move a body from one altitude to another is equal to the product of its weight in pounds and the height in feet that it is raised. Find the work required to pump the water out of a cylindrical cistern of diameter 4 ft. and depth 8 ft.

5. A vertical shaft is supported by a flat step bearing (Fig. 41*f*). The frictional force between a small part of the shaft and the bearing is μp, where p is the pressure between the two and μ is a constant. If the pressure per unit area is the same at all points of the supporting surface, and the weight of the shaft and its load is P, find the work of the frictional forces during each revolution of the shaft.

6. When an electric current flows a distance x through a homogeneous conductor of cross-section A, the resistance is

$$\frac{kx}{A},$$

where K is a constant depending on the material. Find the resistance when the current flows from the inner to the outer surface of a hollow cylinder, the two radii being a and b.

7. Find the resistance when the current flows from the inner to the outer surface of a hollow sphere.

8. Find the resistance when the current flows from one base of a truncated cone to the other.

9. When an electric current i flows an infinitesimal distance AB (Fig. 41g) it produces at any point O a magnetic force (perpendicular to the paper) equal to

$$\frac{id\theta}{r},$$

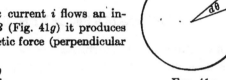

FIG. 41g.

where r is the distance between AB and O. Find the force at the center of a circle due to a current i flowing around it.

10. Find the magnetic force at the distance c from an infinite straight line along which a current i is flowing.

CHAPTER VII

APPROXIMATE METHODS

42. The Prismoidal Formula. — Let y_1, y_3, be two ordinates of a curve at distance h apart, and let y_2 be the

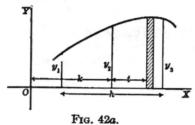

FIG. 42a.

ordinate midway between them. The area bounded by the x-axis, the curve, and the two ordinates is given approximately by the formula

$$A = \tfrac{1}{6} h \left(y_1 + 4 y_2 + y_3 \right). \quad (42a)$$

This is called the prismoidal formula because of its similarity to the formula for the volume of a prismoid.

If the equation of the curve is

$$y = a + bx + cx^2 + dx^3, \quad (42b)$$

where a, b, c, d, are constants (some of which may be zero), the prismoidal formula gives the exact area. To prove this let k be the abscissa of the middle ordinate and t the distance of any other ordinate from it (Fig. 42a). Then

$$x = k + t.$$

If we substitute this value for x, (42b) takes the form

$$y = A + Bt + Ct^2 + Dt^3,$$

where A, B, C, D are constants. The ordinates y_1, y_2, y_3 are obtained by substituting $t = -\dfrac{h}{2}, 0, \dfrac{h}{2}$. Hence

$$y_1 + 4 y_2 + y_3 = 6 A + \tfrac{3}{2} C h^2.$$

90

Also the area is

$$\int_{-\frac{h}{2}}^{\frac{h}{2}} y\, dt = Ah + C\, \frac{h^3}{12}.$$

This is equivalent to

$$\frac{h}{6}\left(6\,A + \frac{1}{2}Ch^2\right) = \frac{h}{6}\,(y_1 + 4\,y_2 + y_3),$$

which was to be proved.

If the equation of the curve does not have the form (42b), it may be approximately equivalent to one of that type and so the prismoidal formula may give an approximate value for the area.

While we have illustrated the prismoidal formula by the area under a curve, it may be used equally well to determine a length or volume or any other quantity represented by a definite integral,

$$\int_a^b f\,(x)\, dx.$$

Since such an integral represents the area under the curve $y = f\,(x)$, its value can be found by replacing h in (42a) by $b - a$ and y_1, y_2, y_3 by $f\,(a)$, $f\left(\dfrac{a+b}{2}\right)$, $f\,(b)$ respectively.

Example 1. Find the area bounded by the x-axis, the curve $y = e^{-x^2}$, and the ordinates $x = 0$, $x = 2$.

The integral

$$\int e^{-x^2}\, dx$$

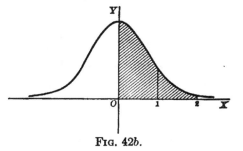

FIG. 42b.

cannot be expressed in terms of elementary functions. Therefore we cannot obtain the area by the methods that we have previously used. The ordinates y_1, y_2, y_3, in this case are

$$y_1 = 1, \qquad y_2 = e^{-1}, \qquad y_3 = e^{-2}.$$

The prismoidal formula, therefore, gives

$$A = \frac{2}{6}\left(1 + \frac{4}{e} + \frac{1}{e^2}\right) = 0.869.$$

The answer correct to 3 decimals (obtained from a table) is 0.882.

Ex. 2. Find the length of the parabola $y^2 = 4x$ from $x = 1$ to $x = 5$.

The length is given by the formula

$$s = \int_1^5 \sqrt{\frac{x+1}{x}}\, dx.$$

By integration we find $s = 4.726$. To apply the prismoidal formula, let

$$y = \sqrt{\frac{x+1}{x}}.$$

Then $h = 4$,

$$y_1 = \sqrt{2}, \qquad y_2 = \sqrt{\tfrac{4}{3}}, \qquad y_3 = \sqrt{\tfrac{6}{5}},$$

and

$$s = \tfrac{4}{6}\left(\sqrt{2} + 4\sqrt{\tfrac{4}{3}} + \sqrt{\tfrac{6}{5}}\right) = 4.752.$$

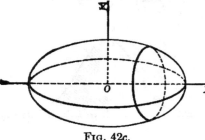

Fig. 42c.

Ex. 3. Find the volume of the spheroid generated by revolving the ellipse

$$\frac{x^2}{a^2} + \frac{y^2}{b^2} = 1$$

about the x-axis.

The section of the spheroid perpendicular to OX has the area

$$A = \pi y^2 = \pi b^2\left(1 - \frac{x^2}{a^2}\right).$$

Its volume is

$$V = \int_{-a}^{a} A \, dx.$$

Since $A.$ is a polynomial of the second degree in x (a special case of a third degree polynomial), the prismoidal formula gives the exact volume. The three cross-sections corresponding to $x = -a$, $x = 0$, $x = a$, are

$$A_1 = 0, \qquad A_2 = \pi b^2, \qquad A_3 = 0.$$

Hence

$$V = \frac{2\,a}{6} [A_1 + 4\,A_2 + A_3] = \frac{4}{3}\pi a b^2.$$

43. Simpson's Rule. — Divide the area between a curve and the x-axis into any even number of parts by means of equidistant ordinates $y_1, y_2, y_3, \ldots, y_n$. (An odd number of ordinates will be needed.) Simpson's rule for determining approximately the area between y_1 and y_n is

$$A = h \left(\frac{y_1 + 4\,y_2 + 2\,y_3 + 4\,y_4 + 2\,y_5 + \cdots + y_n}{1 + 4 + 2 + 4 + 2 + \cdots + 1} \right), \quad (43)$$

h being the distance between the ordinates y_1 and y_n. In the numerator the end coefficients are 1. The others are alternately 4 and 2. The denominator is the sum of the coefficients in the numerator.

This formula is obtained by applying the prismoidal formula to the strips taken two at a time and adding the results. Thus if the area

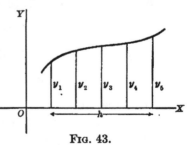

Fig. 43.

is divided into four strips by the ordinates $y_1, y_2, y_3, y_4, y_5,$ the part between y_1 and y_3 has a base equal to $\dfrac{h}{2}$. Its area as given by the prismoidal formula is

$$\frac{1}{6}\frac{h}{2} (y_1 + 4\,y_2 + y_3).$$

Similarly the area between y_3 and y_5 is

$$\frac{1}{6}\frac{h}{2}(y_3 + 4\,y_4 + y_5).$$

The sum of the two is

$$A = h\left(\frac{y_1 + 4\,y_2 + 2\,y_3 + 4\,y_4 + y_5}{12}\right).$$

By using a sufficiently large number of ordinates in Simpson's formula, the result can be made as accurate as desired.

Example. Find ln 5 by Simpson's rule. Since

$$\text{in } 5 = \int_1^5 \frac{dx}{x},$$

we take $y = \dfrac{1}{x}$ in Simpson's formula. Dividing the interval into 4 parts we get

$$\ln 5 = 4\left(\frac{1 + 4\cdot\frac{1}{2} + 2\cdot\frac{1}{3} + 4\cdot\frac{1}{4} + \frac{1}{5}}{12}\right) = 1.622.$$

If we divide the interval into 8 parts, we get

$$\ln 5 = \tfrac{4}{34}\left(1 + \tfrac{8}{3} + \tfrac{2}{2} + \tfrac{8}{5} + \tfrac{4}{3} + \tfrac{8}{7} + \tfrac{2}{4} + \tfrac{8}{9} + \tfrac{1}{5}\right) = 1.6108.$$

The value correct to 4 decimals is

$$\ln 5 = 1.6094.$$

44. Integration in Series. — In calculating integrals it is sometimes convenient to expand a function in infinite series and then integrate the series. This is particularly the case when the integral contains constants for which numerical values are not assigned. For the process to be valid all series used should converge.

Example. Find the length of a quadrant of the ellipse

$$\frac{x^2}{a^2} + \frac{y^2}{b^2} = 1.$$

Let a be greater than b. Introduce a parameter ϕ by the equation

$$x = a \sin \phi.$$

Substituting this value in the equation of the ellipse, we find

$$y = b \cos \phi.$$

Using these values of x and y we get

$$s = \int \sqrt{dx^2 + dy^2} = \int_0^{\frac{\pi}{2}} \sqrt{a^2 - (a^2 - b^2) \sin^2 \phi}\, d\phi.$$

This is an elliptic integral. It cannot be represented by an expression containing only a finite number of elementary functions. We therefore express it as an infinite series. By the binomial theorem

$$\sqrt{a^2 - (a^2 - b^2) \sin^2 \phi} = a\left[1 - \frac{1}{2} \frac{a^2 - b^2}{a^2} \sin^2 \phi - \frac{1}{2.4}\left(\frac{a^2 - b^2}{a^2}\right)^2 \sin^4 \phi \ldots\right].$$

Since

$$\int_0^{\frac{\pi}{2}} \sin^2 \phi\, d\phi = \frac{\pi}{4}, \qquad \int_0^{\frac{\pi}{2}} \sin^4 \phi\, d\phi = \frac{3\pi}{16},$$

we find by integrating term by term

$$s = a\left[\frac{\pi}{2} - \frac{\pi}{8} \frac{a^2 - b^2}{a^2} - \frac{3\pi}{128}\left(\frac{a^2 - b^2}{a^2}\right)^2 \ldots\right]$$
$$= \frac{\pi a}{2}\left[1 - \frac{a^2 - b^2}{4\, a^2} - \frac{3}{64}\left(\frac{a^2 - b^2}{a^2}\right)^2 \ldots\right].$$

If a and b are nearly equal, the value of s can be calculated very rapidly from the series.

EXERCISES

1. Show that the prismoidal formula gives the correct volume in each of the following cases: (a) sphere, (b) cone, (c) cylinder, (d) pyramid, (e) segment of a sphere, (f) truncated cone or pyramid.

2. Find the error when the value of the integral $\int_1^b x^4\, dx$ is found by the prismoidal formula.

In each of the following cases compare the value given by the prismoidal formula with the exact value determined by integration.

3. Area bounded by $y = \sqrt{x}$, $y = 0$, $x = 1$, $x = 3$.

4. Arc of the curve $y = x^3$ between $x = -2$, $x = +2$.

5. Volume generated by revolving about OX one arch of the sine curve $y = \sin x$.

6. Area of the surface of a hemisphere.

Compute each of the following by Simpson's rule using 4 intervals:

7. $\dfrac{\pi}{4} = \displaystyle\int_0^1 \dfrac{dx}{1 + x^2}$.

8. $\displaystyle\int_{1.1}^{9} \dfrac{dx}{\sqrt{1 + x^3}}$.

9. Length of the curve $y = \ln x$ from $x = 1$ to $x = 5$.

10. Surface of the spheroid generated by rotating the ellipse $x^2 + 4 y^2 = 4$ about the x-axis.

11. Volume of the solid generated by revolving about the x-axis the area bounded by $y = 0$, $y = \dfrac{1}{1 + x^2}$, $x = -2$, $x = 2$.

12. Find the value of

$$\int_0^1 \cos (x^2)\, dx,$$

by expanding in series.

13. Express

$$\int_0^a \frac{\sin (\lambda x)\, dx}{x}$$

as a series in powers of λ.

14. Find the length of a quadrant of the ellipse $x^2 + 2y^2 = 2$.

CHAPTER VIII

DOUBLE INTEGRATION

45. Double Integrals. — The notation

$$\int_a^b \int_c^d f(x, y) \, dx \, dy$$

is used to represent the result of integrating first with respect to y (leaving x constant) between the limits c, d and then with respect to x between the limits a, b.

As here defined the first integration is with respect to the variable whose differential stands last and its limits are attached to the last integral sign. Some writers integrate in a different order. In reading an article it is therefore necessary to know what convention the author uses.

Example. Find the value of the double integral

$$\int_0^1 \int_{-x}^x (x^2 + y^2) \, dx \, dy.$$

We integrate first with respect to y between the limits $-x$, x, then with respect to x between the limits $0, 1$. The result is

$$\int_0^1 \int_{-x}^x (x^2 + y^2) \, dx \, dy = \int_0^1 dx \, (x^2 y + \tfrac{1}{3} y^3)_{-x}^x = \int_0^1 \tfrac{8}{3} x^3 \, dx = \tfrac{2}{3}.$$

46. Area as a Double Integral. — Divide the area between two curves $y = f(x)$, $y = F(x)$ into strips of width Δx. Let P be the point (x, y) and Q the point $(x + \Delta x, y + \Delta y)$. The area of the rectangle PQ is $\Delta x \, \Delta y$. The area of the rectangle RS (Fig. 46a) is

$$\Delta x \sum_{f(x)}^{F(x)} \Delta y = \Delta x \int_{f(x)}^{F(x)} dy.$$

The area bounded by the ordinates $x = a$, $x = b$ is then

$$A = \lim_{\Delta x \doteq 0} \sum_a^b \Delta x \int_{f(x)}^{F(x)} dy = \int_a^b \int_{f(x)}^{F(x)} dx \, dy.$$

If it is simpler to cut the area into strips parallel to the x-axis, the area is

$$A = \int \int dy \, dx,$$

the limits in the first integration being the values of x at the ends of a variable strip; those in the second integration, the values of y giving the limiting strips.

Example. Find the area bounded by the parabola $y^2 = 4\,ax + 4\,a^2$ and the straight line $y = 2\,a - x$ (Fig. 46b).

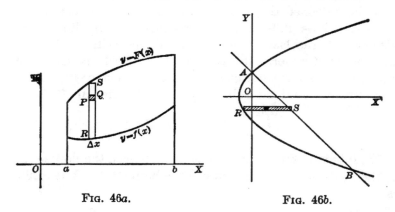

FIG. 46a.   FIG. 46b.

Solving simultaneously, we find that the parabola and the line intersect at A $(0, 2\,a)$ and B $(8\,a, -6\,a)$. Draw the strips parallel to the x-axis. The area is

$$A = \int_{-6a}^{2a} \int_{\frac{y^2-4a^2}{4a}}^{2a-y} dy \, dx = \int_{-6a}^{2a} \left(2\,a - y - \frac{y^2 - 4\,a^2}{4\,a} \right) dy = \frac{64}{3}\, a^2.$$

The limits in the first integration are the values of x at R and S, the ends of the variable strip. The limits in the second integration are the values of y at B and A, corresponding to the outside strips.

47. Volume by Double Integration. — To find the volume under a surface $z = f(x, y)$ and over a given region in the xy-plane.

The volume of the prism PQ standing on the base $\Delta x \, \Delta y$ (Fig. 47a) is

$$z \, \Delta x \, \Delta y.$$

The volume of the plate RT is then

$$\lim_{\Delta y \doteq 0} \sum_R^S z \, \Delta x \, \Delta y = \Delta x \int_{f(x)}^{F(x)} z \, dy,$$

$f(x)$, $F(x)$ being the values of y at R, S.   The entire volume is the limit of the sum of such plates

$$\lim_{\Delta x \doteq 0} \sum_a^b \Delta x \int_{f(x)}^{F(x)} z \, dy = \int_a^b \int_{f(x)}^{F(x)} z \, dx \, dy,$$

a, b being the values of x corresponding to the outside plates.

Example. Find the volume bounded by the surface $az = a^2 - x^2 - 4y^2$ and the xy-plane.

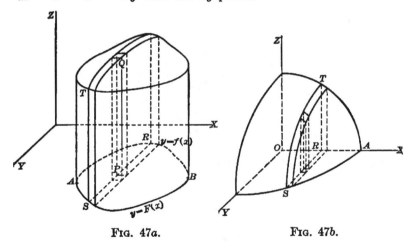

FIG. 47a.   FIG. 47b.

Fig. 47b shows one-fourth of the required volume.   At R, $y = 0$.   At S, $z = 0$ and so

$$y = \tfrac{1}{2} \sqrt{a^2 - x^2}.$$

The limiting values of x at O and A are 0 and a.   Therefore

$$v = 4 \int_0^a \int_0^{\frac{1}{2}\sqrt{a^2-x^2}} z\,dx\,dy = 4 \int_0^a \int_0^{\frac{1}{2}\sqrt{a^2-x^2}} \frac{1}{a}(a^2 - x^2 - 4y^2)\,dx\,dy$$

$$= \frac{4}{3a}\int_0^a (a^2 - x^2)^{\frac{3}{2}}\,dx = \frac{\pi a^3}{4}.$$

48. The Double Integral as the Limit of a Double Summation. — Divide a plane area by lines parallel to the coördinate axes into rectangles with sides Δx and Δy.   Let (x, y) be any point within one of these rectangles.   Form the product

$$f(x, y)\,\Delta x\,\Delta y.$$

This product is equal to the volume of the prism standing on the rectangle as base and reaching the surface $z = f(x, y)$ at some point over the base.   Take the sum of such products

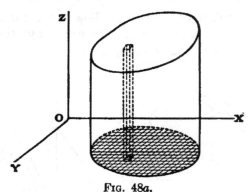

Fig. 48a.

for all the rectangles that lie entirely within the area.   We represent this sum by the notation

$$\sum \sum f(x, y)\,\Delta x\,\Delta y.$$

When Δx and Δy are taken smaller and smaller, this sum approaches as limit the double integral

$$\int \int f(x, y)\,dx\,dy,$$

with the limits determined by the given area; for it approaches the volume over the area and that volume is equal to the double integral.

Whenever then a quantity is a limit of a sum of the form

$$\sum \sum f(x, y) \, \Delta x \, \Delta y$$

its value can be found by double integration. Furthermore, in the formation of this sum, infinitesimals of higher order than $\Delta x \, \Delta y$ can be neglected without changing the limit. For, if $\epsilon \, \Delta x \, \Delta y$ is such an infinitesimal, the sum of the errors thus made is

$$\sum \sum \epsilon \, \Delta x \, \Delta y.$$

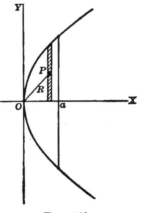

FIG. 48b.

When Δx and Δy approach zero, ϵ approaches zero. The sum of the errors approaches zero, since it is represented by a volume whose thickness approaches zero.

Example 1. An area is bounded by the parabola $y^2 = 4\,ax$ and the line $x = a$. Find its moment of inertia about the axis perpendicular to its plane at the origin.

Divide the area into rectangles $\Delta x \, \Delta y$. The distance of any point $P\,(x, y)$ from the axis perpendicular to the plane at O is $R = OP = \sqrt{x^2 + y^2}$. If then (x, y) is a point within one of the rectangles, the moment of inertia of that rectangle is

$$R^2 \, \Delta x \, \Delta y = (x^2 + y^2) \, \Delta x \, \Delta y,$$

approximately. That the result is approximate and not exact is due to the fact that different points in the rectangle differ slightly in distance from the axis. This difference is, however, infinitesimal and, since R^2 is multiplied by $\Delta x\,\Delta y$, the resulting error is of higher order than $\Delta x\,\Delta y$. Hence in the limit

$$I = \int_0^a \int_{-2\sqrt{ax}}^{2\sqrt{ax}} (x^2 + y^2)\,dx\,dy = \frac{344}{105}\,a^4.$$

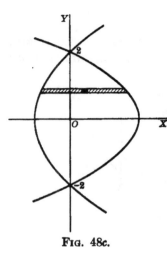

FIG. 48c.

Ex. 2.   Find the center of gravity of the area bounded by the parabolas $y^2 = 4x + 4$, $y^2 = -2x + 4$.

By symmetry the center of gravity is seen to be on the x-axis.   Its abscissa is

$$\bar{x} = \frac{\int x\,dA}{A}.$$

If we wish to use double integration we have merely to replace dA by $dx\,dy$ or $dy\,dx$.   From the figure it is seen that the first integration should be with respect to x.   Hence

$$\bar{x} = \frac{\displaystyle\int_{-2}^{2} \int_{\frac14(y^2-4)}^{\frac14(4-y^2)} x\,dy\,dx}{\displaystyle\int_{-2}^{2} \int_{\frac14(y^2-4)}^{\frac14(4-y^2)} dy\,dx} = \frac{\dfrac{16}{5}}{8} = \frac{2}{5}.$$

EXERCISES

Find the values of the following double integrals:

1. $\displaystyle\int_3^4 \int_1^2 \frac{dx\,dy}{(x+y)^2}.$

2. $\displaystyle\int_0^{2\pi} \int_{a\sin\theta}^{a} r\,d\theta\,dr.$

3. $\displaystyle\int_1^2 \int_x^{x\sqrt{3}} xy\,dx\,dy.$

4. $\displaystyle\int_0^{2\pi} \int_0^{\infty} e^{-kr^2} r\,d\theta\,dr.$

5. $\displaystyle\int_0^3 \int_y^2 (x^2 + y^2)\,dy\,dx.$

6. $\displaystyle\int_0^a \int_0^{\sqrt{a^2-y^2}} dy\,dx.$

7. Find the area bounded by the parabola $y^2 = 2x$ and the line $x = y$.

8. Find the area bounded by the parabola $y^2 = 4ax$, the line $x + y = 3a$, and the x-axis.

9. Find the area enclosed by the ellipse

$$(y - x)^2 + x^2 = 1.$$

10. Find the volume under the paraboloid $z = 4 - x^2 - y^2$ and over the square bounded by the lines $x = \pm 1$, $y = \pm 1$ in the xy-plane.

11. Find the volume bounded by the xy-plane, the cylinder $x^2 + y^2 = 1$, and the plane $x + y + z = 3$.

12. Find the volume in the first octant bounded by the cylinder $(x - 1)^2 + (y - 1)^2 = 1$ and the paraboloid $xy = z$.

13. Find the moment of inertia of the triangle bounded by the coördinate axes and the line $x + y = 1$ about the line perpendicular to its plane at the origin.

14. Find the moment of inertia of a square of side a about the axis perpendicular to its plane at one corner.

15. Find the moment of inertia of the triangle bounded by the lines $x + y = 2$, $x = 2$, $y = 2$ about the x-axis.

16. Find the moment of inertia of the area bounded by the parabola $y^2 = ax$ and the line $x = a$ about the line $y = -a$.

17. Find the moment of inertia of the area bounded by the hyperbola $xy = 4$ and the line $x + y = 5$ about the line $y = x$.

18. Find the moment of inertia of a cube about an edge.

19. A wedge is cut from a cylinder by a plane passing through a diameter of the base and inclined 45° to the base. Find its moment of inertia about the axis of the cylinder.

20. Find the center of gravity of the triangle formed by the lines $x = y$, $x + y = 4$, $x - 2y = 4$.

21. Find the center of gravity of the area bounded by the parabola $y^2 = 4ax + 4a^2$ and the line $y = 2a - x$.

49. Double Integration. Polar Coördinates. — Pass through the origin a series of lines making with each other equal angles $\Delta\theta$. Construct a series of circles with centers at the origin and radii differing by Δr. The lines and circles divide the plane into curved quadrilaterals (Fig. 49a).

Let r, θ be the coördinates of P, $r + \Delta r$, $\theta + \Delta\theta$ those of Q. Since PR is the arc of a circle of radius r and subtends the angle $\Delta\theta$ at the center, $PR = r\,\Delta\theta$. Also $RQ = \Delta r$.

When Δr and $\Delta \theta$ are very small PRQ will be approximately a rectangle with area

$$PR \cdot RQ = r \, \Delta \theta \, \Delta r.$$

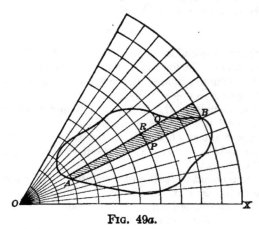

FIG. 49a.

It is very easy to show that the error is an infinitesimal of higher order than $\Delta \theta \, \Delta r$. (See Ex. 5, page 107.) Hence the sum

$$\sum \sum r \, \Delta \theta \, \Delta r,$$

taken for all the rectangles within a curve, gives in the limit the area of the curve in the form

$$A = \int \int r \, d\theta \, dr. \qquad (49a)$$

The limits in the first integration are the values of r at the ends A, B of the strip across the area. The limits in the second integration are the values of θ giving the outside strips.

If it is more convenient the first integration may be with respect to θ. The area is then

$$A = \int \int r \, dr \, d\theta.$$

The first limits are the values of θ at the ends of a strip between two concentric circles (Fig. 49b).   The second limits are the extreme values of r.

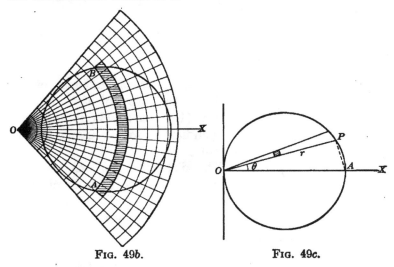

Fig. 49b.   Fig. 49c.

The element of area in polar coördinates is

$$dA = r\, d\theta\, dr. \qquad (49b)$$

We can use this in place of dA in finding moments of inertia, volumes, centers of gravity, or any other quantities expressed by integrals of the form

$$\int f(r, \theta)\, dA.$$

Example 1.   Change the double integral

$$\int_0^{2a} \int_0^{\sqrt{2ax-x^2}} (x^2 + y^2)\, dx\, dy$$

to polar coördinates.

The integral is taken over the area of the semicircle $y = \sqrt{2ax - x^2}$ (Fig. 49c).   In polar coördinates the equation of this circle is $r = 2a\cos\theta$.   The element of area

$dx\,dy$ can be replaced by $r\,d\theta\,dr$.*   Also $x^2 + y^2 = r^2$.   Hence

$$\int_0^{2a} \int_0^{\sqrt{2ax-x^2}} (x^2 + y^2)\,dx\,dy = \int_0^{\frac{\pi}{2}} \int_0^{2a\cos\theta} r^2 \cdot r\,d\theta\,dr.$$

The limits for r are the ends of the sector OP.   The limits for θ give the extreme sectors $\theta = 0$, $\theta = \dfrac{\pi}{2}$.

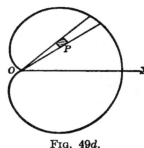

FIG. 49d.

Ex. 2.   Find the moment of inertia of the area of the cardioid $r = a\,(1 + \cos\theta)$ about the axis perpendicular to its plane at the origin.

The distance from any point P $(r,\,\theta)$ (Fig. 49d) to the axis of rotation is
$$OP = r.$$

Hence the moment of inertia is

$$I = 2 \int_0^{\pi} \int_0^{a\,(1+\cos\theta)} r^2 \cdot r\,d\theta\,dr = \frac{a^4}{2}\int_0^{\pi}(1 + \cos\theta)^4\,d\theta = \frac{35}{16}\pi a^4.$$

Ex. 3.   Find the center of gravity of the cardioid in the preceding problem.

The ordinate of the center of gravity is evidently zero. Its abscissa is

$$x = \frac{\int x\,dA}{\int dA} = \frac{2 \int_0^{\pi} \int_0^{a\,(1+\cos\theta)} r\cos\theta \cdot r\,d\theta\,dr}{2 \int \int r\,d\theta\,dr} = \frac{5}{6}a.$$

Ex. 4.   Find the volume common to a sphere of radius $2\,a$ and a cylinder of radius a, the center of the sphere being on the surface of the cylinder.

---

* This does not mean that
$$dx\,dy = r\,d\theta\,dr,$$
but merely that the sum of all the rectangular elements in the circle is equal to the sum of all the polar elements.

Fig. 49e shows one-fourth of the required volume. Take a system of polar coördinates in the xy-plane. On the element of area $r\,d\theta\,dr$ stands a prism of height

$$z = \sqrt{4\,a^2 - r^2},$$

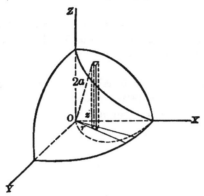

FIG. 49e.

The volume of the prism is $z \cdot r\,d\theta\,dr$ and the entire volume is

$$v = 4\int_0^{\frac{\pi}{2}} \int_0^{2\,a\cos\theta} \sqrt{4\,a^2 - r^2}\cdot r\,d\theta\,dr = 4\int_0^{\frac{\pi}{2}} \frac{(4\,a^2-r^2)^{\frac{3}{2}}}{-3}\bigg|_0^{2\,a\cos\theta} d\theta$$

$$= \frac{32\,a^3}{3}\int_0^{\frac{\pi}{2}} (1 - \sin^3\theta)\,d\theta = \frac{16}{9}\,a^3\,(3\,\pi - 4).$$

EXERCISES

Find the values of the following integrals by changing to polar coördinates:

1. $\displaystyle\int_0^a \int_0^{\sqrt{a^2-y^2}} (x^2 + y^2)\,dy\,dx.$ 3. $\displaystyle\int_0^\infty \int_0^\infty e^{-(x^2+y^2)}\,dx\,dy.$

2. $\displaystyle\int_0^{2a} \int_0^{\sqrt{2ax-x^2}} dx\,dy.$ 4. $\displaystyle\int_0^a \int_0^{\sqrt{a^2-x^2}} \sqrt{a^2 - x^2 - y^2}\,dx\,dy.$

5. Find the area bounded by two circles of radii a, $a + \Delta a$ and two lines through the origin, making with the initial line the angles α, $\alpha + \Delta\alpha$, respectively. Show that when Δa and $\Delta\alpha$ approach zero, the result differs from

$$a\,\Delta\alpha\,\Delta a$$

by an infinitesimal of higher order than $\Delta\alpha\,\Delta a$.

6. The central angle of a circular sector is 2α. Find the moment of inertia of its area about the bisector of the angle.

7. An area is bounded by the circle $r = a\sqrt{2}$ and the straight line $r = a \sec\left(\theta - \frac{\pi}{4}\right)$. Find its moment of inertia about the axis perpendicular to its plane at the origin.

8. Find the center of gravity of the area in Ex. 6.

9. The center of a circle of radius $2a$ lies on a circle of radius a. Find the moment of inertia of the area between them about the common tangent.

10. Find the moment of inertia of the area of the lemniscate $r^2 = 2a^2 \cos 2\theta$ about the axis perpendicular to its plane at the origin.

11. Find the moment of inertia of the area of the circle $r = 2a$ outside the parabola, $r = a \sec^2\frac{\theta}{2}$ about the axis perpendicular to its plane at the origin.

12. Find the moment of inertia about the y-axis of the area within the circle $(x - a)^2 + (y - a)^2 = 2a^2$.

13. The density of a square lamina is proportional to the distance from one corner. Find its moment of inertia about an edge passing through that corner.

14. Find the moment of inertia of a cylinder about a generator.

15. Find the moment of inertia of a cone about its axis.

16. Find the volume under the spherical surface $x^2 + y^2 + z^2 = a^2$ and over the lemniscate $r^2 = a^2 \cos 2\theta$ in the xy-plane.

17. Find the volume bounded by the xy-plane, the paraboloid $az = x^2 + y^2$ and the cylinder $x^2 + y^2 = 2ax$.

18. Find the moment of inertia of a sphere of density ρ about a diameter.

19. Find the volume generated by revolving one loop of the curve $r = a \cos 2\theta$ about the initial line.

50. Area of a Surface. — Let an area A in one plane be projected upon another plane. The area of the projection is

$$A' = A \cos\phi,$$

when ϕ is the angle between the planes.

To show this divide A into rectangles by two sets of lines respectively parallel and perpendicular to the intersection MN of the two planes. Let a and b be the sides of one of these rectangles, a being parallel to MN. The projection of this rectangle will be a rectangle with sides

$$a' = a, \qquad b' = b \cos \phi,$$

and area

$$a'b' = ab \cos \phi.$$

The sum of the projections of all the rectangles is

$$\sum a'b' = \sum ab \cos \phi.$$

As the rectangles are taken smaller and smaller this approaches as limit

$$A' = A \cos \phi,$$

which was to be proved.

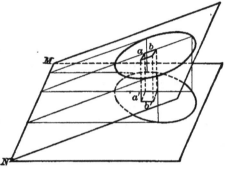

FIG. 50a.

To find the area of a curved surface, resolve it into elements whose projections on a coördinate plane are equal to the differential of area dA in that plane. The element of surface can be considered as lying approximately in a tangent plane. Its area is, therefore, approximately

$$\frac{dA}{\cos \phi},$$

where ϕ is the angle between the tangent plane and the coördinate plane on which the area is projected. The area of the surface is the limit

$$S = \int \frac{dA}{\cos \phi}.$$

The angle between two planes is equal to that between the perpendiculars to the planes. Therefore ϕ is equal to

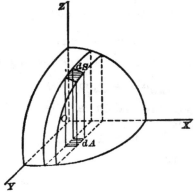

FIG. 50b.

the angle between the normal to the surface and the co-ordinate axis perpendicular to the plane on which we project.

If the equation of the surface is

$$F(x, y, z) = 0,$$

the cosine of the angle between its normal and the z-axis is (Differential Calculus, Art. 101)

$$\cos \gamma = \frac{\dfrac{\partial F}{\partial z}}{\sqrt{\left(\dfrac{\partial F}{\partial x}\right)^2 + \left(\dfrac{\partial F}{\partial y}\right)^2 + \left(\dfrac{\partial F}{\partial z}\right)^2}}.$$

The cosines of the angles between the normal and the x-axis or y-axis are obtained by replacing $\dfrac{\partial F}{\partial z}$ by $\dfrac{\partial F}{\partial x}$ or $\dfrac{\partial F}{\partial y}$. In finding areas the algebraic sign is assumed to be positive.

Example 1. Find the area of the sphere $x^2 + y^2 + z^2 = a^2$ within the cylinder $x^2 + y^2 = ax$.

Project on the xy-plane. The angle ϕ is then the angle γ between the normal to the sphere and the z-axis. Its cosine is

$$\cos \gamma = \frac{z}{\sqrt{x^2 + y^2 + z^2}} = \frac{z}{a}.$$

Using polar coördinates in the xy-plane,
$$z = \sqrt{a^2 - x^2 - y^2} = \sqrt{a^2 - r^2}.$$

Hence the area of the surface is

$$S = \int \frac{dA}{\cos \gamma} = 4 \int_0^{\frac{\pi}{2}} \int_0^{a \cos \theta} \frac{a r \, d\theta \, dr}{\sqrt{a^2 - r^2}} = 2 a^2 \, (\pi - 2).$$

Ex. 2. Find the area of the surface of the cone $y^2 + z^2 = x^2$ in the first octant bounded by the plane $y + z = a$.
Project on the yz-plane. Then $\phi = \alpha$ and

$$\cos \alpha = \frac{x}{\sqrt{x^2 + y^2 + z^2}} = \frac{x}{\sqrt{2 x^2}} = \frac{1}{\sqrt{2}}.$$

The area on the cone is therefore

$$S = \int_0^a \int_0^{a-y} \sqrt{2} \, dy \, dz = \frac{a^2 \sqrt{2}}{2}.$$

EXERCISES

1. Find the area of the triangle cut from the plane
$$x + 2y + 3z = 6$$
by the coördinate planes.

2. Find the area of the surface of the cylinder $x^2 + y^2 = a^2$ between the planes $z = 0$, $z = mx$.

3. Find the area of the surface of the cone $x^2 + y^2 = z^2$ cut out by the cylinder $x^2 + y^2 = 2 ax$.

4. Find the area of the plane $x + y + z = 2a$ in the first octant bounded by the cylinder $x^2 + y^2 = a^2$.

5. Find the area of the surface $z^2 = 2 xy$ above the xy-plane bounded by the planes $y = 1$, $x = 2$.

6. Find the area of the surface of the cylinder $x^2 + y^2 = 2 ax$ between the xy-plane and the cone $x^2 + y^2 = z^2$.

7. Find the area of the surface of the paraboloid $y^2 + z^2 = 2 ax$, intercepted by the parabolic cylinder $y^2 = ax$ and the plane $x = a$.

8. Find the area intercepted on the cylinder in Ex. 4.

9. A square hole of side a is cut through a sphere of radius a. If the axis of the hole is a diameter of the sphere, find the area of the surface cut out.

CHAPTER IX

TRIPLE INTEGRATION

51. Triple Integrals. — The notation

$$\int_{x_1}^{x_2} \int_{y_1}^{y_2} \int_{z_1}^{z_2} f(x, y, z)\, dx\, dy\, dz$$

is used to represent the result of integrating first with respect to z (leaving x and y constant) between the limits z_1 and z_2, then with respect to y (leaving x constant) between the limits y_1 and y_2, and finally with respect to x between the limits x_1 and x_2.

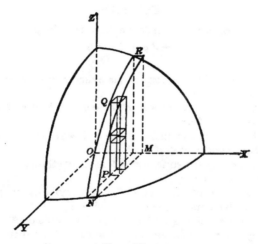

FIG. 52a.

52. Rectangular Coördinates. — Divide a solid into rectangular parallelepipeds of volume $\Delta x\, \Delta y\, \Delta z$ by planes parallel to the coördinate planes. To find the volume of

112

the solid, first take the sum of the parallelepipeds in a vertical column PQ. The result is

$$\sum \Delta x\, \Delta y\, \Delta z = \Delta x\, \Delta y \int_{z_1}^{z_2} dz,$$

z_1 and z_2 being the values of z at the ends of the column. Then sum these columns along a base MN and so obtain the volume of the plate MNR. The result is

$$\lim_{\Delta y \doteq 0} \sum \Delta x\, \Delta y \int_{z_1}^{z_2} dz = \Delta x \int_{y_1}^{y_2} \int_{z_1}^{z_2} dy\, dz,$$

y_1 and y_2 being the limiting values of y in the plate. Finally, take the sum of these plates. The result is the triple integral

$$v = \lim_{\Delta x \doteq 0} \sum \Delta x \int_{y_1}^{y_2} \int_{z_1}^{z_2} dy\, dz = \int_{x_1}^{x_2} \int_{y_1}^{y_2} \int_{z_1}^{z_2} dx\, dy\, dz,$$

x_1, x_2 being the limiting values of x.

It may be more convenient to begin by integrating with respect to x or y. In any case the limits can be obtained from the consideration that the first integration is a summation of parallelepipeds to form a prism, the second a summation of prisms to form a plate, and the third integration a summation of plates.

Let (x, y, z) be any point of the parallelepiped $\Delta x\, \Delta y\, \Delta z$. Multiply $\Delta x\, \Delta y\, \Delta z$ by $f(x, y, z)$ and form the sum

$$\sum \sum \sum f(x, y, z)\, \Delta x\, \Delta y\, \Delta z$$

taken for all parallelepipeds in the solid. When Δx, Δy, and Δz approach zero, this sum approaches the triple integral

$$\int \int \int f(x, y, z)\, dx\, dy\, dz$$

as limit. It can be shown that terms of higher order than $\Delta x\, \Delta y\, \Delta z$ can be neglected in the sum without changing the limit.

The differential of volume in rectangular coördinates is

$$dv = dx\, dy\, dz.$$

This can be used in the formulas for moment of inertia, center of gravity, etc., those quantities being then determined by triple integration.

Example 1. Find the volume of the ellipsoid

$$\frac{x^2}{a^2} + \frac{y^2}{b^2} + \frac{z^2}{c^2} = 1.$$

Fig. 52a shows one-eighth of the required volume. Therefore

$$v = 8 \int \int \int dx\, dy\, dz.$$

The limits in the first integration are the values $z = 0$ at P and $z = c\sqrt{1 - \dfrac{x^2}{a^2} - \dfrac{y^2}{b^2}}$ at Q. The limits in the second integration are the values of y at M and N. At M, $y = 0$ and at N, $z = 0$, whence $y = b\sqrt{1 - \dfrac{x^2}{a^2}}$. Finally, the limits for x are 0 and a. Therefore

$$v = 8 \int_0^a \int_0^{b\sqrt{1-\frac{x^2}{a^2}}} \int_0^{c\sqrt{1-\frac{x^2}{a^2}-\frac{y^2}{b^2}}} dx\, dy\, dz = \tfrac{4}{3}\pi abc.$$

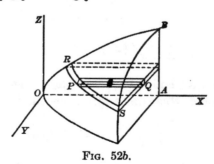

FIG. 52b.

Ex. 2. Find the center of gravity of the solid bounded by the paraboloid $y^2 + 2z^2 = 4x$ and the plane $x = 2$.

By symmetry $\bar{y}$ and $\bar{z}$ are zero. The x-coördinate is

$$\bar{x} = \frac{\int x \, dv}{\int dv} = \frac{4 \int_0^2 \int_0^{\sqrt{8-2z^2}} \int_{\frac{1}{4}(y^2+2z^2)}^2 x \, dz \, dy \, dx}{4 \int \int \int dz \, dy \, dx} = \frac{4}{3}.$$

The limits for x are the values $x = \frac{1}{4} (y^2 + 2 z^2)$ at P and $x = 2$ at Q. At S, $x = 2$ and $y = \sqrt{4 x - 2 z^2} = \sqrt{8 - 2 z^2}$. The limits for y are, therefore, $y = 0$ at R and $y = \sqrt{8 - 2 z^2}$ at S. The limits for z are $z = 0$ at A and $z = 2$ at B.

Ex. 3. Find the moment of inertia of a cube about an edge.

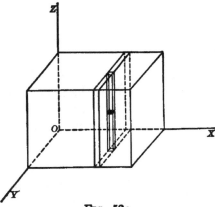

FIG. 52c.

Place the cube as shown in Fig. 52c and determine its moment of inertia about the z-axis. The distance of any point (x, y, z) from the z-axis is

$$R = \sqrt{x^2 + y^2}.$$

Hence the moment of inertia is

$$I = \int_0^a \int_0^a \int_0^a (x^2 + y^2) \, dx \, dy \, dz = \frac{2}{3} a^5,$$

where a is the edge of the cube.

EXERCISES

1. Find by triple integration the volume of the pyramid determined by the coördinate planes and the plane $x + y + z = 1$.

2. Find the moment of inertia of the pyramid in Ex. 1 about. the x-axis.

3. A wedge is cut from a cylinder of radius a by a plane passing through a diameter of the base and inclined 45° to the base. Find its center of gravity.

4. Find the volume bounded by the paraboloid $\frac{y^2}{b^2} + \frac{z^2}{c^2} = 2\frac{x}{a}$ and the plane $x = a$.

5. Express the volume of the cone

$$(z - 1)^2 = x^2 + y^2$$

in the first octant as a triple integral in 6 ways by integrating with dx, dy, dz, arranged in all possible orders.

6. Find the volume bounded by the surfaces $y^2 = 4a^2 - 3ax$, $y^2 = ax$, $z = \pm h$.

7. Find the volume bounded by the cylinder $z^2 = 1 - x - y$ and the coördinate planes.

53. Cylindrical Coördinates. — Let M be the projection of P on the xy-plane. Let r, θ be the polar coördinates of M

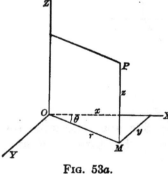

FIG. 53a.

in the xy-plane. The cylindrical coördinates of P are r, θ, z.

From Fig. 53a it is evident that

$$x = r \cos \theta, \qquad y = r \sin \theta.$$

By using these equations we can change any rectangular into a cylindrical equation.

The element of volume in cylindrical coördinates is the volume PQ, Fig. 53b, bounded by two cylindrical surfaces of radii r, $r + \Delta r$, two horizontal planes z, $z + \Delta z$, and two planes through the z-axis making angles θ, $\theta + \Delta \theta$ with OX. The base of PQ is equal to the polar element MN in the xy-plane. Its altitude PR is Δz. Hence

$$dv = r \, d\theta \, dr \, dz. \tag{53}$$

This value of dv can be used in the formulas for volume, center of gravity, moment of inertia, etc. In problems con-

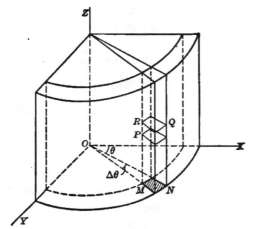

FIG. 53b.

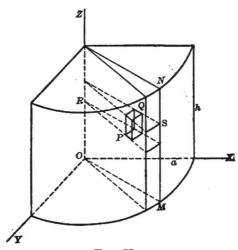

FIG. 53c.

nected with cylinders, cones, and spheres, the resulting integrations are usually much easier in cylindrical than in rectangular coördinates.

Example 1. Find the moment of inertia of a cylinder about a diameter of its base.

Let the moment of inertia be taken about the x-axis, Fig. 53c. The square of the distance from the element PQ to the x-axis is

$$R^2 = y^2 + z^2 = r^2 \sin^2 \theta + z^2.$$

The moment of inertia is therefore

$$\int R^2 \, dv = \int_0^{2\pi} \int_0^h \int_0^a (r^2 \sin^2 \theta + z^2) \, r \, d\theta \, dz \, dr$$

$$= \frac{\pi a^2 h}{12} (3 \, a^2 + 4 \, h^2).$$

The first integration is a summation for elements in the wedge RS, the second a summation for wedges in the slice OMN, the third a summation for all such slices.

Ex. 2. Find the volume bounded by the xy-plane, the cylinder $x^2 + y^2 = ax$, and the sphere $x^2 + y^2 + z^2 = a^2$.

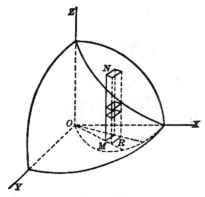

FIG. 53d.

In cylindrical coördinates, the equations of the cylinder and sphere are $r = a \cos \theta$ and $r^2 + z^2 = a^2$. The volume required is therefore

$$v = 2 \int_0^{\frac{\pi}{2}} \int_0^{a \cos \theta} \int_0^{\sqrt{a^2 - r^2}} r \, d\theta \, dr \, dz = \tfrac{1}{9} a^3 (3\pi - 4).$$

54. Spherical Coördinates. — The spherical coördinates of the point P (Fig. 54a) are $r = OP$ and the two angles θ and ϕ. From the diagram it is easily seen that

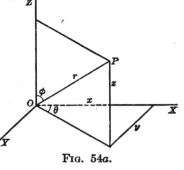

$$x = r \sin \phi \cos \theta,$$
$$y = r \sin \phi \sin \theta,$$
$$z = r \cos \phi.$$

The locus r = const. is a sphere with center at O; θ = const. is the plane through OZ making the angle θ with OX; ϕ = const. is the cone gener-

FIG. 54a.

ated by lines through O making the angle ϕ with OZ.

The element of volume is the volume $PQRS$ bounded

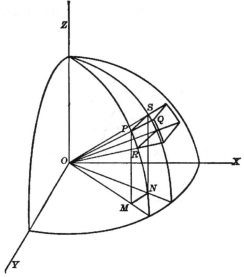

FIG. 54b.

by the spheres r, $r + \Delta r$, the planes θ, $\theta + \Delta \theta$, and the cones ϕ, $\phi + \Delta \phi$. When Δr, $\Delta \phi$, and $\Delta \theta$ are very small this is approximately a rectangular parallelepiped. Since $OP = r$ and $POR = \Delta\phi$,

$$PR = r\,\Delta\phi.$$

Also $OM = OP \sin\phi$ and the arc PS is approximately equal to its projection MN, whence

$$PS = MN = r \sin\phi\,\Delta\theta,$$

approximately. Consequently

$$\Delta v = PR \cdot PS \cdot PQ = r^2 \sin\phi\,\Delta\theta \cdot \Delta\phi \cdot \Delta r,$$

approximately. When the increments are taken smaller and smaller, the result becomes more and more accurate. Therefore

$$dv = r^2 \sin\phi\,d\theta\,d\phi\,dr. \tag{54}$$

Spherical coördinates work best in problems connected with spheres. They are also very useful in problems where the distance from a fixed point plays an important role.

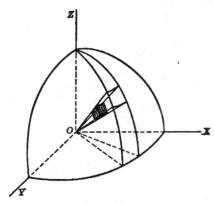

FIG. 54c.

Example. If the density of a solid hemisphere varies as the distance from the center, find its center of gravity.

Take the center of the sphere as origin and let the z-axis be perpendicular to the plane face of the hemisphere. By symmetry it is evident that $\bar{x}$ and $\bar{y}$ are zero. The density is $\rho = kr$, where k is constant. Also $z = r \cos \phi$. Hence

$$\bar{z} = \frac{\int z \, dm}{\int dm} = \frac{\int krz \, dv}{\int kr \, dv}$$

$$= \frac{\int_0^{2\pi} \int_0^{\frac{\pi}{2}} \int_0^a r^4 \cos \phi \sin \phi \, d\theta \, d\phi \, dr}{\int_0^{2\pi} \int_0^{\frac{\pi}{2}} \int_0^a r^3 \sin \phi \, d\theta \, d\phi \, dr} = \frac{2}{5} a.$$

EXERCISES

1. Find the volume bounded by the sphere $x^2 + y^2 + z^2 = 4$ and the paraboloid $x^2 + y^2 = 3 z$.

2. A right cone is scooped out of a right cylinder of the same height and base. Find the distance of the center of gravity of the remainder from the vertex.

3. Find the volume bounded by the surface $z = e^{-(x^2+y^2)}$ and the xy-plane.

4. Find the moment of inertia of a cone about a diameter of its base.

5. Find the volume of the cylinder $x^2 + y^2 = 2 ax$ intercepted between the paraboloid $x^2 + y^2 = 2 az$ and the xy-plane.

6. Find the center of gravity of the volume common to a sphere of radius a and a cone of vertical angle 2α, the vertex of the cone being at the center of the sphere.

7. Find the center of gravity of the volume bounded by a spherical surface of radius a and two planes passing through its center and including an angle of 60°.

8. The vertex of a cone of vertical angle $\frac{\pi}{2}$ is on the surface of a sphere of radius a. If the axis of the cone is a diameter of the sphere, find the moment of inertia of the volume common to the cone and sphere about this axis.

55. Attraction. — Two particles of masses m_1, m_2, separated by a distance r, attract each other with a force

$$\frac{km_1m_2}{r^2},$$

where k is a constant depending on the units of mass, distance, and force used.   A similar law expresses the attraction or repulsion between electric charges.

To find the attraction due to a continuous mass, resolve it into elements.   Each of these attracts with a force given by the above law.   Since the forces do not all act in the same direction we cannot obtain the total attraction by merely adding the magnitudes of the forces due to the several elements.

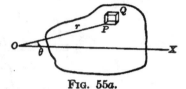

Fig. 55a.

The forces must be added geometrically. For this purpose we calculate the sum of the components along each coördinate axis.   The force having these sums as components is the resultant attraction.

If dm is the mass of an element at P, r its distance from O, and θ the angle between OX and OP, the attraction between this element and a unit particle at O is

$$k\,\frac{1 \cdot dm}{r^2} = \frac{k\,dm}{r^2}.$$

This force acts along OP.   Its component along OX is

$$\frac{\cos\theta \cdot k\,dm}{r^2}.$$

The component along OX of the total attraction is then

$$X = \int \frac{k\cos\theta\,dm}{r^2}.$$

The calculation of this integral may involve single, double, or triple integration, depending on the form of the attracting mass.

Example 1.   Find the attraction of a uniform wire of length $2\,l$, and mass M on a particle of unit mass at distance c along the perpendicular at the center of the wire.

Take the origin at the unit particle and the x-axis perpendicular to the wire.   Since particles below OX attract downward just as much as those above OX attract upward, the vertical component of the total attraction is zero. The component along OX is, therefore, the total attraction. The mass of the length dy of the wire is

$$\frac{M\,dy}{2\,l}.$$

Hence

$$X = \frac{kM}{2\,l} \int \frac{\cos\theta\,dy}{r^2}.$$

For simplicity of integration it is better to use θ as variable. Then $y = c \tan\theta$, $dy = c \sec^2\theta\,d\theta$, and

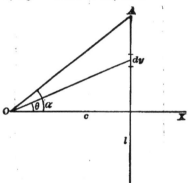

FIG. 55b.

$$X = \frac{kM}{2\,l} \int_{-\alpha}^{\alpha} \frac{\cos\theta \cdot c \sec^2\theta\,d\theta}{c^2 \sec^2\theta} = \frac{kM}{cl} \sin\alpha,$$

where α is the angle XOA.   In terms of l this is

$$X = \frac{kM}{c\sqrt{c^2 + l^2}}.$$

Ex. 2.   Find the attraction of a homogeneous cylinder of mass M upon a particle of unit mass on the axis at distance c from the end of the cylinder.

By symmetry it is clear that the total attraction will act along the axis of the cylinder.   Take the origin at the attracting particle and let the y-axis be the axis of the cylinder.

Divide the cylinder into rings generated by rotating the elements $dx\,dy$ about the y-axis. The volume of such a ring is

$$2\,\pi x\,dx\,dy$$

and its mass is

$$dm = \frac{M}{\pi a^2 h}\cdot 2\,\pi x\,dx\,dy = \frac{2\,M}{a^2 h}x\,dx\,dy.$$

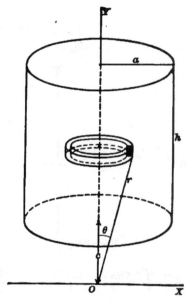

FIG. 55c.

Since all points of this ring are at the same distance from O and the joining lines make the same angle θ with OY, the vertical component of attraction is

$$k\int\frac{\cos\theta\,dm}{r^2} = k\int\frac{y\,dm}{r^3} = \frac{2\,Mk}{a^2 h}\int_c^{c+h}\int_0^a\frac{xy\,dy\,dx}{(x^2+y^2)^{\frac{3}{2}}}$$

$$= \frac{2\,Mk}{a^2 h}\Big[h + \sqrt{a^2+c^2} - \sqrt{a^2+(c+h)^2}\Big].$$

EXERCISES

1. Find the attraction of a uniform wire of mass M and length l on a particle of unit mass situated in the line of the wire at distance c from its end.

2. Find the attraction of a wire of mass M bent in the form of a semicircle of radius a on a unit particle at its center.

3. Find the attraction of a flat disk of mass M and radius a on a unit particle at the distance c in the perpendicular at the center of the disk.

4. Find the attraction of a homogeneous cone upon a unit particle situated at its vertex.

5. Show that, if a sphere is concentrated at its center, its attraction upon an outside particle will not be changed.

6. Find the attraction of a homogeneous cube upon a particle at one corner.

CHAPTER X

DIFFERENTIAL EQUATIONS

56. Definitions. — A differential equation is an equation containing differentials or derivatives. Thus

$$(x^2 + y^2)\, dx + 2\, xy\, dy = 0,$$

$$x \frac{d^2 y}{dx^2} - \frac{dy}{dx} = 2$$

are differential equations.

A *solution* of a differential equation is an equation connecting the variables such that the derivatives or differentials calculated from that equation satisfy the differential equation. Thus $y = x^2 - 2\, x$ is a solution of the second equation above; for when $x^2 - 2\, x$ is substituted for y the equation is satisfied.

A differential equation containing only a single independent variable, and so containing only total derivatives, is called an *ordinary* differential equation. An equation containing partial derivatives is called a *partial* differential equation. We shall consider only ordinary differential equations in this book.

The *order* of a differential equation is the order of the highest derivative occurring in it.

57. Illustrations of Differential Equations. — Whenever an equation connecting derivatives or differentials is known, the equation connecting the variables can be determined by solving the differential equation. A number of simple cases were treated in Chapter I.

The fundamental problem of integral calculus is to find the function

$$y = \int f(x)\, dx,$$

126

when $f(x)$ is given.   This is equivalent to solving the differential equation

$$dy = f(x)\, dx.$$

Often the slope of a curve is known as a function of x and y,

$$\frac{dy}{dx} = f(x, y).$$

The equation of the curve can be found by solving the differential equation.

In mechanical problems the velocity or acceleration of a particle may be known in terms of the distance s the particle has moved and the time t,

$$\frac{ds}{dt} = v, \qquad \frac{d^2s}{dt^2} = a.$$

The position s can be determined as a function of the time by solving the differential equation.

In physical or chemical problems the rates of change of the variables may be known as functions of the variables and the time.   The values of those variables at any time can be found by solving the differential equations.

Example.   Find the curve in which the cable of a suspension bridge hangs.

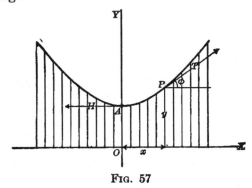

FIG. 57

Let the bridge be the x-axis and let the y-axis pass through the center of the cable.   The portion of the cable AP is in equilibrium under three forces, a horizontal tension H at A, a tension PT in the direction of the cable at P, and the weight of the portion of the bridge between A and P. The weight of the cable, being very small in comparison with that of the bridge, is neglected.

The weight of the part of the bridge between A and P is proportional to x. Let it be Kx. Since the vertical components of force must be in equilibrium

$$T \sin \phi = Kx.$$

Similarly, from the equilibrium of horizontal components, we have

$$T \cos \phi = H.$$

Dividing the former equation by this, we get

$$\tan \phi = \frac{K}{H} x.$$

But $\tan \phi = \frac{dy}{dx}$. Hence

$$\frac{dy}{dx} = \frac{K}{H} x.$$

The solution of this equation is

$$y = \frac{K}{2H} x^2 + c.$$

The curve is therefore a parabola.

58. Constants of Integration. Particular and General Solutions. — To solve the equation

$$\frac{dy}{dx} = f(x),$$

we integrate once and so obtain an equation with one arbitrary constant,

$$y = \int f(x)\, dx + c.$$

To solve the equation

$$\frac{d^2y}{dx^2} = f(x)$$

we integrate twice. The result

$$y = \int \int f(x)\, dx^2 + c_1 x + c_2$$

contains two arbitrary constants. Similarly, the integral of the equation

$$\frac{d^n y}{dx^n} = f(x)$$

contains n arbitrary constants.

These illustrations belong to a special type. The rule indicated is, however, general. *The complete, or general, solution of a differential equation of the nth order in two variables contains n arbitrary constants.* If particular values are assigned to any or all of these constants, the result is still a solution. Such a solution is called a *particular* solution.

In most problems leading to differential equations the result desired is a particular solution. To find this we usually find the general solution and then determine the constants from some extra information contained in the statement of the problem.

Example 1. Show that

$$x^2 + y^2 - 2cx = 0$$

is the general solution of the differential equation

$$y^2 - x^2 - 2xy\frac{dy}{dx} = 0.$$

Differentiating $x^2 + y^2 - 2cx = 0$, we get

$$2x + 2y\frac{dy}{dx} - 2c = 0,$$

whence

$$\frac{dy}{dx} = \frac{c - x}{y}.$$

Substituting this value in the differential equation, it becomes

$$y^2 - x^2 - 2xy\frac{dy}{dx} = y^2 - x^2 - 2x(c - x) = y^2 + x^2 - 2cx = 0.$$

Hence $x^2 + y^2 - 2cx = 0$ is a solution. Since it contains one constant and the differential equation is one of the first order, it is the general solution.

Ex. 2. Find the differential equation of which $y = c_1 e^x + c_2 e^{2x}$ is the general solution.

Since the given equation contains two constants, the differential equation is one of the second order. We therefore differentiate twice and so obtain

$$\frac{dy}{dx} = c_1 e^x + 2c_2 e^{2x},$$

$$\frac{d^2y}{dx^2} = c_1 e^x + 4c_2 e^{2x}.$$

Eliminating c_1, we get

$$\frac{d^2y}{dx^2} - \frac{dy}{dx} = 2c_2 e^{2x},$$

$$\frac{dy}{dx} - y = c_2 e^{2x}.$$

Hence

$$\frac{d^2y}{dx^2} - \frac{dy}{dx} = 2\left(\frac{dy}{dx} - y\right)$$

or

$$\frac{d^2y}{dx^2} - 3\frac{dy}{dx} + 2y = 0.$$

This is an equation of the second order having $y = c_1 e^x + c_2 e^{2x}$ as solution. It is the differential equation required.

EXERCISES

In each of the following exercises, show that the equation given is a solution of the differential equation and state whether it is the general or a particular solution.

1. $y = ce^x + e^{-x}$, $\frac{d^2y}{dx^2} = y.$

2. $x^2 - y^2 = cx,$ $(x^2 + y^2)\, dx - 2\, xy\, dy = 0.$

3. $y = ce^x \sin x,$ $\dfrac{d^2y}{dx^2} - 2\dfrac{dy}{dx} + 2\,y = 0.$

4. $y = c_1 + c_2 \sin(x + c_3),$ $\dfrac{d^3y}{dx^3} + \dfrac{dy}{dx} = 0.$

Find the differential equation of which each of the following equations is the general solution:

5. $y = c_1 x + \dfrac{c_2}{x}.$ **7.** $y = c_1 \sin x + c_2 \cos x.$

6. $y = cxe^x.$ **8.** $x^2 y = c_1 + c_2 \ln x + c_3 x^3.$

          9. $x^2 + c_1 xy + c_2 y^2 = 0.$

59. Differential Equations of the First Order in Two Variables. — By solving for $\dfrac{dy}{dx}$ an equation of the first order in two variables x and y can be reduced to the form

$$\frac{dy}{dx} = f(x, y).$$

To solve this equation is equivalent to finding the curves with slope equal to $f(x, y)$. The solution contains one

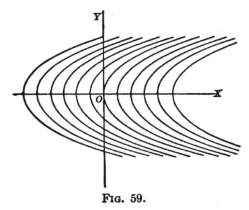

FIG. 59.

arbitrary constant. There is consequently an infinite number of such curves, usually one through each point of the plane.

We cannot always solve even this simple type of equation. In the following articles some cases will be discussed

which frequently occur and for which general methods of
solution are known.

60. Variables Separable. — A differential equation of
the form

$$M\,dx + N\,dy = 0$$

is called separable if each of the coefficients M and N contains only one of the variables or is the product of a function
of x and a function of y. By division the x's and dx can be
brought together in the first term, the y's and dy in the
second. The two terms can then be integrated separately
and the sum of the integrals equated to a constant.

Example 1. $(1 + x^2)\,dy - xy\,dx = 0.$
Dividing by $(1 + x^2)\,y$, this becomes

$$\frac{dy}{y} = \frac{x\,dx}{1 + x^2},$$

whence

$$\ln y = \tfrac{1}{2}\ln(1 + x^2) + c.$$

If $c = \ln k$, this is equivalent to

$$\ln y = \ln\sqrt{1 + x^2} + \ln k = \ln k\sqrt{1 + x^2},$$

and so

$$y = k\sqrt{1 + x^2},$$

where k is an arbitrary constant.

Ex. 2.   Find the curve in which the area bounded by the
curve, coördinate axes, and a variable ordinate is proportional
to the arc forming part of the boundary

Let A be the area and s the length of arc.   Then

$$A = ks.$$

Differentiating with respect to x,

$$\frac{dA}{dx} = k\frac{ds}{dx},$$

or

$$y = k\sqrt{1 + \left(\frac{dy}{dx}\right)^2}.$$

Solving for $\dfrac{dy}{dx}$,

$$\frac{dy}{dx} = \frac{\sqrt{y^2 - k^2}}{k},$$

whence

$$\frac{dy}{\sqrt{y^2 - k^2}} = \frac{dx}{k}.$$

The solution of this is

$$\ln\left(y + \sqrt{y^2 - k^2}\right) = \frac{x}{k} + c.$$

Therefore

$$y + \sqrt{y^2 - k^2} = e^{\frac{x}{k} + c} = e^c e^{\frac{x}{k}} = c_1 e^{\frac{x}{k}},$$

where c_1 is a new constant. Transposing y and squaring, we get

$$y^2 - k^2 = \left(c_1 e^{\frac{x}{k}}\right)^2 - 2 c_1 e^{\frac{x}{k}} y + y^2.$$

Hence, finally,

$$y = \frac{c_1}{2} e^{\frac{x}{k}} + \frac{k^2}{2\,c_1} e^{-\frac{x}{k}}.$$

61. Exact Differential Equations. — An equation

$$du = 0,$$

obtained by equating to zero the total differential of a function u of x and y, is called an *exact* differential equation. The solution of such an equation is

$$u = c.$$

The condition that $M\,dx + N\,dy$ be an exact differential is (Diff. Cal., Art. 100)

$$\frac{\partial M}{\partial y} = \frac{\partial N}{\partial x}. \tag{61}$$

This equation, therefore, expresses the condition that

$$M\,dx + N\,dy = 0$$

be an exact differential equation.

An exact equation can often be solved by inspection. To find u it is merely necessary to obtain a function whose total differential is $M\,dx + N\,dy$.

If this cannot be found by inspection, it can be determined from the fact that

$$du = M\,dx + N\,dy$$

and so

$$\frac{\partial u}{\partial x} = M.$$

By integrating with y constant, we therefore get

$$u = \int M\,dx + f(y).$$

Since y is constant in the integration, the constant of integration may be a function of y. This function can be found by equating the total differential of u to $M\,dx + N\,dy$. Since $df(y)$ gives terms containing y only, $f(y)$ *can usually be found by integrating the terms in $N\,dy$ that do not contain x.* In exceptional cases this may not give the correct result. The answer should, therefore, be tested by differentiation.

Example 1. $(2\,x - y)\,dx + (4\,y - x)\,dy = 0.$

The equation is equivalent to

$$2\,x\,dx + 4\,y\,dy - (y\,dx + x\,dy) = d(x^2 + 2\,y^2 - xy) = 0.$$

It is therefore exact and its solution is

$$x^2 + 2\,y^2 - xy = c.$$

Ex. 2. $(\ln y - 2\,x)\,dx + \left(\dfrac{x}{y} - 2\,y\right)dy = 0.$

In this case

$$\frac{\partial M}{\partial y} = \frac{\partial}{\partial y}(\ln y - 2\,x) = \frac{1}{y},$$

$$\frac{\partial N}{\partial x} = \frac{\partial}{\partial x}\left(\frac{x}{y} - 2\,y\right) = \frac{1}{y}.$$

These derivatives being equal, the equation is exact. Its solution is

$$x \ln y - x^2 - y^2 = c.$$

The part $x \ln y - x^2$ is obtained by integrating $(\ln y - 2x)\,dx$ with y constant. The term $-y^2$ is the integral of $-2y\,dy$, which is the only term in $\left(\dfrac{x}{y} - 2y\right) dy$ that does not contain x.

62. Integrating Factors. — If an equation of the form $M\,dx + N\,dy = 0$ is not exact it can be made exact by multiplying by a proper factor. Such a multiplier is called an *integrating factor*.

For example, the equation

$$x\,dy - y\,dx = 0$$

is not exact. But if it is multiplied by $\dfrac{1}{x^2}$, it takes the form

$$\frac{x\,dy - y\,dx}{x^2} = d\left(\frac{y}{x}\right) = 0$$

which is exact. It also becomes exact when multiplied by $\dfrac{1}{y^2}$ or $\dfrac{1}{xy}$. The functions $\dfrac{1}{x^2}, \dfrac{1}{y^2}, \dfrac{1}{xy}$ are all integrating factors of $x\,dy - y\,dx = 0$.

While an equation of the form $M\,dx + N\,dy = 0$ always has integrating factors, there is no general method of finding them.

Example 1. $y(1 + xy)\,dx - x\,dy = 0.$

This equation can be written

$$y\,dx - x\,dy + xy^2\,dx = 0.$$

Dividing by y^2,

$$\frac{y\,dx - x\,dy}{y^2} + x\,dx = 0.$$

Both terms of this equation are exact differentials. The solution is

$$\frac{x}{y} + \frac{1}{2}x^2 = c.$$

Ex. 2. $(y^2 + 2xy)\, dx + (2x^2 + 3xy)\, dy = 0$.

This is equivalent to

$$y^2\, dx + 3xy\, dy + 2xy\, dx + 2x^2\, dy = 0.$$

Multiplying by y, it becomes

$$y^2\, dx + 3xy^2\, dy + 2xy^2\, dx + 2x^2y\, dy = d\,(xy^3 + x^2y^2) = 0.$$

Hence

$$xy^3 + x^2y^2 = c.$$

63. Linear Equations. — A differential equation of the form

$$\frac{dy}{dx} + Py = Q, \tag{63a}$$

where P and Q are functions of x or constants, is called *linear*. The linear equation is one of the first degree in one of the variables (y in this case) and its derivative. Any functions of the other variable can occur.

If the linear equation is written in the form (63a),

$$e^{\int P\, dx}$$

is an integrating factor; for when multiplied by this factor the equation becomes

$$e^{\int P\, dx}\frac{dy}{dx} + ye^{\int P\, dx} P = e^{\int P\, dx} Q.$$

The left side is the derivative of

$$ye^{\int P\, dx}.$$

Hence

$$ye^{\int P\, dx} = \int e^{\int P\, dx}\, Q\, dx + c \tag{63b}$$

is the solution.

Example 1. $\dfrac{dy}{dx} + \dfrac{2}{x} y = x^3$.

In this case

$$\int P\,dx = \int \frac{2}{x}\,dx = 2\ln x = \ln x^2.$$

Hence

$$e^{\int P\,dx} = e^{\ln x^2} = x^2.$$

The integrating factor is, therefore, x^2. Multiplying by x^2 and changing to differentials, the equation becomes

$$x^2\,dy + 2\,xy\,dx = x^5\,dx.$$

The integral is

$$x^2 y = \tfrac{1}{6}\,x^6 + c.$$

Ex. 2. $(1 + y^2)\,dx - (xy + y + y^3)\,dy = 0.$

This is an equation of the first degree in x and dx. Dividing by $(1 + y^2)\,dy$, it becomes

$$\frac{dx}{dy} - \frac{y}{1 + y^2}\,x = y.$$

P is here a function of y and

$$\int P\,dy = \int \frac{-y\,dy}{1 + y^2} = -\frac{1}{2}\ln(1 + y^2) = \ln \frac{1}{\sqrt{1 + y^2}},$$

$$e^{\int P\,dy} = \frac{1}{\sqrt{1 + y^2}}.$$

Multiplying by the integrating factor, the equation becomes

$$\frac{dx}{\sqrt{1 + y^2}} - \frac{xy\,dy}{(1 + y^2)^{\frac{3}{2}}} = \frac{y\,dy}{\sqrt{1 + y^2}},$$

whence

$$\frac{x}{\sqrt{1 + y^2}} = \sqrt{1 + y^2} + c$$

and

$$x = 1 + y^2 + c\sqrt{1 + y^2}.$$

64. Equations Reducible to Linear Form. — An equation of the form

$$\frac{dy}{dx} + Py = Qy^n, \tag{64}$$

where P and Q are functions of x, can be made linear by a change of variable.   Dividing by y^n, it becomes

$$y^{-n}\frac{dy}{dx} + Py^{-n+1} = Q.$$

If we take

$$y^{1-n} = u$$

as a new variable, the equation takes the form

$$\frac{1}{1-n}\frac{du}{dx} + Pu = Q,$$

which is linear.

Example. $\dfrac{dy}{dx} + \dfrac{2}{x}y = \dfrac{y^3}{x^3}.$

Division by y^3 gives

$$y^{-3}\frac{dy}{dx} + \frac{2}{x}y^{-2} = \frac{1}{x^3}.$$

Let

$$u = y^{-2}.$$

Then

$$\frac{du}{dx} = -2y^{-3}\frac{dy}{dx},$$

whence

$$y^{-3}\frac{dy}{dx} = -\frac{1}{2}\frac{du}{dx}.$$

Substituting these values, we get

$$-\frac{1}{2}\frac{du}{dx} + \frac{2}{x}u = \frac{1}{x^3},$$

and so

$$\frac{du}{dx} - \frac{4}{x}u = -\frac{2}{x^3}.$$

This is a linear equation with solution

$$u = \frac{1}{3x^2} + cx^4,$$

or, since $u = y^{-2}$,

$$\frac{1}{y^2} = \frac{1}{3x^2} + cx^4.$$

65. Homogeneous Equations. — A function $f(x, y)$ is said to be a homogeneous function of the nth degree if

$$f(tx, ty) = t^n f(x, y).$$

Thus $\sqrt{x^2 + y^2}$ is a homogeneous function of the first degree; for

$$\sqrt{x^2 t^2 + y^2 t^2} = t \sqrt{x^2 + y^2}.$$

It is easily seen that a polynomial whose terms are all of the nth degree is a homogeneous function of the nth degree.

The differential equation

$$M\, dx + N\, dy = 0$$

is called homogeneous if M and N are homogeneous functions of the same degree. To solve a homogeneous equation substitute

$$y = vx.$$

The new equation will be separable.

Example 1. $x \dfrac{dy}{dx} - y = \sqrt{x^2 + y^2}.$

This is a homogeneous equation of the first degree. Substituting $y = vx$, it becomes

$$x\left(v + x \frac{dv}{dx}\right) - vx = \sqrt{x^2 + v^2 x^2}$$

whence

$$x \frac{dv}{dx} = \sqrt{1 + v^2}.$$

This is a separable equation with solution

$$x = c\left(v + \sqrt{1 + v^2}\right).$$

Replacing v by $\dfrac{y}{x}$, transposing, squaring, etc., the equation becomes

$$x^2 - 2\, cy = c^2.$$

Ex. 2. $\quad y \left(\dfrac{dy}{dx} \right)^2 + 2\, x \dfrac{dy}{dx} - y = 0.$

Solving for $\dfrac{dy}{dx}$, we get

$$\frac{dy}{dx} = \frac{-x \pm \sqrt{x^2 + y^2}}{y},$$

or

$$y\, dy + x\, dx = \pm \sqrt{x^2 + y^2}\, dx.$$

This is a homogeneous equation of the first degree. It is much easier, however, to divide by $\sqrt{x^2 + y^2}$ and integrate at once. The result is

$$\frac{x\, dx + y\, dy}{\sqrt{x^2 + y^2}} = \pm\, dx,$$

whence

$$\sqrt{x^2 + y^2} = c \pm x$$

and

$$y^2 = c^2 \pm 2\, cx.$$

Since c may be either positive or negative, the answer can be written

$$y^2 = c^2 + 2\, cx.$$

66. Change of Variable. — We have solved the homogeneous equation by taking as new variable

$$v = \frac{y}{x}.$$

It may be possible to reduce any equation to a simpler form by taking some function u of x and y as a new variable or by taking two functions u and v as new variables. Such functions are often suggested by the equation. In other cases they may be indicated by the problem in the solution of which the equation occurs.

Example. $\quad (x - y)^2 \dfrac{dy}{dx} = a^2.$

Let $x - y = u$. Then

$$1 - \frac{dy}{dx} = \frac{du}{dx}$$

and the differential equation becomes

$$u^2 \left(1 - \frac{du}{dx}\right) = a^2,$$

whence

$$u^2 - a^2 = u^2 \frac{du}{dx}.$$

The variables are separable. The solution is

$$x = u + \frac{a}{2} \ln \frac{u - a}{u + a} + c$$

$$= x - y + \frac{a}{2} \ln \frac{x - y - a}{x - y + a} + c,$$

or

$$y = \frac{a}{2} \ln \frac{x - y - a}{x - y + a} + c.$$

EXERCISES

Solve the following differential equations:

1. $x^3 \, dy - y^3 \, dx = 0$.

2. $\tan x \sin^2 y \, dx + \cos^2 x \cot y \, dy = 0$.

3. $(xy^2 + x) \, dx + (y - x^2 y) \, dy = 0$.

4. $(xy^2 + x) \, dx + (x^2 y - y) \, dy = 0$.

5. $(3 x^2 + 2 xy - y^2) \, dx + (x^2 - 2 xy - 3 y^2) \, dy = 0$.

6. $x \dfrac{dy}{dx} - y = y^3$.

7. $x \, dx + y \, dy = a \, (x^2 + y^2) \, dy$.

8. $x \dfrac{dy}{dx} + y = y^2$.

9. $\dfrac{dy}{dx} - ay = e^{bx}$.

10. $x^2 \dfrac{dy}{dx} - 2 xy = 3$.

11. $x^3 \dfrac{dy}{dx} - 2 xy = 3 y$.

12. $(2 xy^3 - y) \, dx + x \, dy = 0$.

13. $(1 - x^2) \dfrac{dy}{dx} + 2 xy = (1 - x^2)^2$.

14. $\tan x \dfrac{dy}{dx} - y = a$.

15. $x \dfrac{dy}{dx} - 3 y + x^4 y^2 = 0$.

16. $\dfrac{dy}{dx} + y = xy^2$.

17. $(x^2 - 1)^{\frac{3}{2}} dy + (x^3 + 3xy \sqrt{x^2 - 1}) dx = 0.$

18. $x\,dx + (x + y)\,dy = 0.$

19. $(x^2 + y^2)\,dx - 2xy\,dy = 0.$

20. $y\,dx + (x + y)\,dy = 0.$

21. $(x^3 - 3x^2y)\,dx + (y^3 - x^3)\,dy = 0.$

22. $ye^y\,dx = (y^3 + 2xe^y)\,dy.$

23. $\left(xye^{\frac{x}{y}} + y^2\right) dx - x^2 e^{\frac{x}{y}}\,dy = 0.$

24. $(x + y - 1)\,dx + (2x + 2y - 3)\,dy = 0.$

25. $3y^3 \dfrac{dy}{dx} - y^3 = x.$

26. $e^y \left(\dfrac{dy}{dx} + 1\right) = e^x.$

27. $x \left(\dfrac{dy}{dx}\right)^2 - 2y \dfrac{dy}{dx} - x = 0.$

28. $\left(\dfrac{dy}{dx}\right)^2 - (x + y) \dfrac{dy}{dx} + xy = 0.$

29. $y^2 \left(\dfrac{dy}{dx}\right)^2 + 2xy \dfrac{dy}{dx} - y^3 = 0.$

30. The differential equation for the charge q of a condenser having a capacity C connected in series with a circuit of resistance R is

$$R \frac{dq}{dt} + \frac{q}{C} = E,$$

where E is the electromotive force. Find v as a function of t if E is constant and $q = 0$ when $t = 0$.

31. The differential equation for the current induced by an electromotive force $E \sin \alpha t$ in a circuit having the inductance L and resistance R is

$$L \frac{di}{dt} + Ri = E \sin \alpha t.$$

Solve for i and determine the constants so that $i = I$ when $t = 0$.

Let PT be the tangent and PN the normal to a plane curve at $P(x, y)$ (Fig. 66a). Determine the curve or curves in each of the following cases:

32. The subtangent $TM = 3$ and the curve passes through $(2, 2)$.

33. The subnormal $MN = a$ and the curve passes through $(0, 0)$.

34. The intercept OT of the tangent on the x-axis is one-half the abscissa OM.

35. The length PT of the tangent is a constant a.

36. The length PN of the normal is a constant a.

37. The perpendicular from M to PT is a constant a.

Using polar coördinates (Fig. 66*b*), find the curve or curves in each of the following cases:

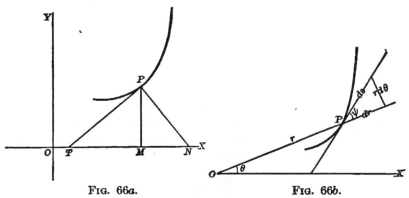

FIG. 66*a*.   FIG. 66*b*.

38. The curve passes through $(1, 0)$ and makes with OP a constant angle $\psi = \frac{\pi}{4}$.

39. The angles ψ and θ are equal.

40. The distance from O to the tangent is a constant a.

41. The projection of OP on the tangent at P is a constant a.

42. Find the curve passing through the origin in which the area bounded by the curve, x-axis, a fixed, and a variable ordinate is proportional to that ordinate.

43. Find the curve in which the length of arc is proportional to the angle between the tangents at its end.

44. Find the curve in which the length of arc is proportional to the difference of the abscissas at its ends.

45. Find the curve in which the length of any arc is proportional to the angle it subtends at a fixed point.

46. Find the curve in which the length of arc is proportional to the difference of the distances of its ends from a fixed point.

47. Oxygen flows through one tube into a liter flask filled with air while the mixture of oxygen and air escapes through another. If the action is so slow that the mixture in the flask may be considered uniform, what percentage of oxygen will the flask contain after 10 liters of gas have passed through? (Assume that air contains 21 per cent by volume of oxygen.)

67. Certain Equations of the Second Order. — There are two forms of the second order differential equation that

occur in mechanical problems so frequently that they deserve special attention.   These are

(1)
$$\frac{d^2y}{dx^2} = f\left(x, \frac{dy}{dx}\right),$$

(2)
$$\frac{d^2y}{dx^2} = f\left(y, \frac{dy}{dx}\right).$$

The peculiarity of these equations is that one of the variables (y in the first, x in the second) does not appear directly in the equation.   They are both reduced to equations of the first order by the substitution

$$\frac{dy}{dx} = p.$$

This substitution reduces the first equation to the form

$$\frac{dp}{dx} = f(x, p).$$

This is a first order equation whose solution has the form

$$p = F(x, c_1),$$

or, since $p = \dfrac{dy}{dx}$,

$$\frac{dy}{dx} = F(x, c_1).$$

This is again an equation of the first order.   Its solution is the result required.

In case of an equation of the second type, write the second derivative in the form

$$\frac{d^2y}{dx^2} = \frac{dp}{dx} = \frac{dp}{dy} \cdot \frac{dy}{dx} = p\frac{dp}{dy}.$$

The differential equation then becomes

$$p\frac{dp}{dy} = f(y, p).$$

Solve this for p and proceed as before.

Example 1. $(1 + x^2)\dfrac{d^2y}{dx^2} + 1 + \left(\dfrac{dy}{dx}\right)^2 = 0.$

Substituting p for $\dfrac{dy}{dx}$, we get

$$(1 + x^2)\frac{dp}{dx} + 1 + p^2 = 0.$$

This is a separable equation with solution

$$p = \frac{c_1 - x}{1 + c_1 x},$$

whence

$$dy = \frac{c_1 - x}{1 + c_1 x}\, dx.$$

The integral of this is

$$y = -\frac{x}{c_1} + \frac{c_1^2 + 1}{c_1^2}\ln\,(1 + c_1 x) + c_2.$$

By a change of constants this becomes

$$y = cx + (1 + c^2)\ln\,(c - x) + c'.$$

Ex. 2. $y\dfrac{d^2y}{dx^2} + \left(\dfrac{dy}{dx}\right)^2 = 1.$

Substituting

$$\frac{dy}{dx} = p, \qquad \frac{d^2y}{dx^2} = p\frac{dp}{dy},$$

we get

$$yp\frac{dp}{dy} + p^2 = 1.$$

The solution of this is

$$y^2 p^2 = y^2 + c_1.$$

Replacing p by $\dfrac{dy}{dx}$ and solving again, we get

$$y^2 + c_1 = (x + c_2)^2.$$

Ex. 3. Under the action of gravitation the acceleration of a falling body is $\dfrac{k}{r^2}$, where k is constant and r the distance from the center of the earth. Find the time required for the body to fall to the earth from a distance equal to that of the moon.

Let r_1 be the radius of the earth (about 4000 miles), r_2 the distance from the center of the earth to the moon (about 240,000 miles) and g the acceleration of gravity at the surface of the earth (about 32 feet per second). At the surface of the earth $r = r_1$ and

$$a = \frac{k}{r_1^2} = -g.$$

The negative sign is used because the acceleration is toward the origin ($r = 0$). Hence $k = -gr_1^2$ and the general value of the acceleration is

$$a = \frac{v\,dv}{dr} = -\frac{gr_1^2}{r^2},$$

where v is the velocity. The solution of this equation is

$$v^2 = \frac{2\,gr_1^2}{r} + C.$$

When $r = r_2$, $v = 0$. Consequently,

$$C = -2\,g\frac{r_1^2}{r_2^2}$$

and

$$v = \frac{dr}{dt} = -\sqrt{2\,gr_1^2\left(\frac{1}{r} - \frac{1}{r_2}\right)}.$$

The time of falling is therefore

$$t \doteq \int_{r_1}^{r_2}\sqrt{\frac{rr_2}{2\,gr_1^2\,(r_2 - r)}}\;dr = 116 \text{ hours.}$$

This result is obtained by using the numerical values of r_1 and r_2 and reducing g to miles per hour.

68. Linear Differential Equations with Constant Coefficients. — A differential equation of the form

$$\frac{d^n y}{dx^n} + a_1 \frac{d^{n-1} y}{dx^{n-1}} + a_2 \frac{d^{n-2} y}{dx^{n-2}} + \cdots + a_n y = f(x), \quad (68a)$$

where $a_1, a_2, \ldots a_n$ are constants, is called a linear differential equation with constant coefficients. For practical applications this is the most important type of differential equation.

In discussing these equations we shall find it convenient to represent the operation $\frac{d}{dx}$ by D. Then

$$\frac{dy}{dx} = Dy, \qquad \frac{d^2 y}{dx^2} = D^2 y, \text{ etc.}$$

Equation (68a) can be written

$$(D^n + a_1 D^{n-1} + a_2 D^{n-2} + \cdots + a_n) y = f(x). \quad (68b)$$

This signifies that if the operation

$$D^n + a_1 D^{n-1} + a_2 D^{n-2} + \cdots + a_n \quad (68c)$$

is performed on y, the result will be $f(x)$. The operation consists in differentiating y, n times, $n-1$ times, $n-2$ times, etc., multiplying the results by 1, a_1, a_2, etc., and adding.

With the differential equation is associated an algebraic equation

$$r^n + a_1 r^{n-1} + a_2 r^{n-2} + \cdots + a_n = 0.$$

If the roots of this *auxiliary* equation are $r_1, r_2, \ldots r_n$, the polynomial (68c) can be factored in the form

$$(D - r_1)(D - r_2) \cdots (D - r_n). \quad (68d)$$

If we operate on y with $D - a$, we get

$$(D - a) y = \frac{dy}{dx} - ay.$$

If we operate on this with $D - b$, we get

$$(D - b) \cdot (D - a)\, y = (D - b)\left(\frac{dy}{dx} - ay\right)$$

$$= \frac{d^2y}{dx^2} - (a + b)\frac{dy}{dx} + ab.$$

The same result is obtained by operating on y with

$$(D - a)(D - b) = D^2 - (a + b)\,D + ab.$$

Similarly, if we operate in succession with the factors of (68d), we get the same result that we should get by operating directly with the product (68c).

69. Equation with Right Hand Member Zero. — To solve the equation

$$(D^n + a_1 D^{n-1} + a_2 D^{n-2} + \cdots + a_n)\, y = 0 \qquad (69a)$$

factor the symbolic operator and so reduce the equation to the form

$$(D - r_1)(D - r_2) \cdots (D - r_n)\, y = 0.$$

The value $y = c_1 e^{r_1 x}$ is a solution; for

$$(D - r_1)\, c_1 e^{r_1 x} = c_1 r_1 e^{r_1 x} - r_1 c_1 e^{r_1 x} = 0$$

and the equation can be written

$$(D - r_2) \cdots (D - r_n) \cdot (D - r_1)\, y = (D - r_2) \cdots (D - r_n) \cdot 0 = 0.$$

Similarly, $y = c_2 e^{r_2 x}$, $y = c_3 e^{r_3 x}$, etc., are solutions. Finally

$$y = c_1 e^{r_1 x} + c_2 e^{r_2 x} + \cdots + c_n e^{r_n x} \qquad (69b)$$

is a solution; for the result of operating on y is the sum of the results of operating on $c_1 e^{r_1 x}$, $c_2 e^{r_2 x}$, etc., each of which is zero.

If the roots $r_1, r_2, \ldots, r_n$ are all different, (69b) contains n constants and so is the complete solution of (69a). If, however, two roots r_1 and r_2 are equal

$$c_1 e^{r_1 x} + c_2 e^{r_2 x} = (c_1 + c_2)\, e^{r_1 x}$$

contains only one abitrary constant $c_1 + c_2$ and (69b) contains only $n - 1$ arbitrary constants. In this case, however, xe^{r_1x} is also a solution; for

$$(D - r_1)\, xe^{r_1x} = r_1 xe^{r_1x} + e^{r_1x} - r_1 xe^{r_1x} = e^{r_1x}$$

and so

$$(D - r_1)^2\, xe^{r_1x} = (D - r_1)\, e^{r_1x} = 0.$$

If then two roots r_1 and r_2 are equal, the part of the solution corresponding to these roots is

$$(c_1 + c_2 x)e^{r_1x}.$$

More generally, if m roots $r_1, r_2, \ldots r_m$ are equal, the part of the solution corresponding to them is

$$(c_1 + c_2 x + c_3 x^2 + \cdots + c_m x^{m-1})e^{r_1x}. \tag{69c}$$

If the coefficients $a_1, a_2, \ldots a_n$, are real, imaginary roots occur in pairs

$$r_1 = \alpha + \beta\sqrt{-1}, \qquad r_2 = \alpha - \beta\sqrt{-1}.$$

The terms $c_1 e^{r_1x}$, $c_2 e^{r_2x}$ are imaginary but they can be replaced by two other terms that are real. Using these values of r_1 and r_2, we have

$$(D - r_1)\, (D - r_2) = (D - \alpha)^2 + \beta^2.$$

By performing the differentiations it can easily be verified that

$$[(D - \alpha)^2 + \beta^2] \cdot e^{\alpha x} \sin \beta x = 0,$$
$$[(D - \alpha)^2 + \beta^2] \cdot e^{\alpha x} \cos \beta x = 0.$$

Therefore

$$e^{\alpha x} [c_1 \sin \beta x + c_2 \cos \beta x] \tag{69d}$$

is a solution. This function, in which α and β are real, can, therefore, be used as the part of the solution corresponding to two imaginary roots $r = \alpha \pm \beta\sqrt{-1}$.

To solve the differential equation

$$(D^n + a_1 D^{n-1} + a_2 D^{n-2} + \cdots + a_n)\, y = 0,$$

let $r_1, r_2, \ldots, r_n$ be the roots of the auxiliary equation

$$r^n + a_1 r^{n-1} + a_2 r^{n-2} + \cdots + a_n = 0.$$

If these roots are all real and different, the solution of the equation is

$$y = c_1 e^{r_1 x} + c_2 e^{r_2 x} + \cdots + c_n e^{r_n x}.$$

If m of the roots $r_1, r_2, \ldots, r_m$ are equal, the corresponding part of the solution is

$$(c_1 + c_2 x + c_3 x^2 + \cdots + c_m x^{m-1})\, e^{r_1 x}.$$

The part of the solution corresponding to two imaginary roots $r = \alpha \pm \beta \sqrt{-1}$ is

$$e^{\alpha x}\, [c_1 \sin \beta x + c_2 \cos \beta x].$$

Example 1. $\dfrac{d^2 y}{dx^2} - \dfrac{dy}{dx} - 2y = 0.$

This is equivalent to

$$(D^2 - D - 2)\, y = 0.$$

The roots of the auxiliary equation

$$r^2 - r - 2 = 0$$

are -1 and 2. Hence the solution is

$$y = c_1 e^{-x} + c_2 e^{2x}.$$

Ex. 2. $\dfrac{d^3 y}{dx^3} + \dfrac{d^2 y}{dx^2} - 5\dfrac{dy}{dx} + 3y = 0.$

The roots of the auxiliary equation

$$r^3 + r^2 - 5r + 3 = 0$$

are $1, 1, -3$. The part of the solution corresponding to the two roots equal to 1 is

$$(c_1 + c_2 x)\, e^x.$$

Hence

$$y = (c_1 + c_2 x)\, e^x + c_3 e^{-3x}.$$

Ex. 3. $(D^2 + 2D + 2) y = 0.$

The roots of the auxiliary equation are

$$- 1 \pm \sqrt{-1}.$$

Therefore $\alpha = -1$, $\beta = 1$ in (69d) and

$$y = e^{-x} [c_1 \sin x + c_2 \cos x].$$

70. Equation with Right Hand Member a Function of x.—
Let $y = u$ be the *general solution* of the equation

$$(D^n + a_1 D^{n-1} + a_2 D^{n-2} + \cdots + a_n) y = 0$$

and let $y = v$ be *any solution* of the equation

$$(D^n + a_1 D^{n-1} + a_2 D^{n-2} + \cdots a_n) y = f(x). \qquad (70)$$

Then

$$y = u + v$$

is a solution of (70); for the operation

$$D^n + a_1 D^{n-1} + a_2 D^{n-2} + \cdots + a_n$$

when performed on u gives zero and when performed on v
gives $f(x)$.   Furthermore, $u + v$ contains n arbitrary constants.   Hence it is the general solution of (70).

The part u is called the *complementary function*, v the
particular integral.   To solve an equation of the form (70),
first solve the equation with right hand member zero and
then add to the result any solution of (70).

A particular integral can often be found by inspection.
If not, the general form of the integral can usually be determined by the following rules:

1. If $f(x) = ax^n + a_1 x^{n-1} + \cdots + a_n$, assume

$$y = A x^n + A_1 x^{n-1} + \cdots + A_n.$$

But, if 0 occurs m times as a root in the auxiliary equation,
assume

$$y = x^m [A x^n + A_1 x^{n-1} + \cdots + A_m].$$

2. If $f(x) = ce^{ax}$, assume

$$y = A e^{ax}.$$

But, if a occurs m times as a root of the auxiliary equation, assume

$$y = Ax^m e^{ax}.$$

3. If $f(x) = a \cos \beta x + b \sin \beta x$, assume

$$y = A \cos \beta x + B \sin \beta x.$$

But, if $\cos \beta x$ and $\sin \beta x$ occur in the complementary function, assume

$$y = x [A \cos \beta x + B \sin \beta x].$$

4. If $f(x) = ae^{ax} \cos \beta x + be^{ax} \sin \beta x$, assume

$$y = A e^{ax} \cos \beta x + \beta e^{ax} \sin \beta x.$$

But, if $e^{ax} \cos \beta x$ and $e^{ax} \sin \beta x$ occur in the complementary function, assume

$$y = xe^{ax} [A \cos \beta x + B \sin \beta x].$$

If $f(x)$ contains terms of different types, take for y the sum of the corresponding expressions. Substitute the value of y in the differential equation and determine the constants so that the equation is satisfied.

Example 1. $\quad \dfrac{d^2y}{dx^2} + 4y = 2x + 3.$

A particular solution is evidently

$$y = \tfrac{1}{4}(2x + 3).$$

Hence the complete solution is

$$y = c_1 \cos 2x + c_2 \sin 2x + \tfrac{1}{4}(2x + 3).$$

Ex. 2. $\quad (D^2 + 3D + 2)y = 2 + e^x.$

Substituting $y = A + Be^x$, we get

$$2A + 6Be^x = 2 + e^x.$$

Hence

$$2A = 2, \qquad 6B = 1$$

and

$$y = 1 + \tfrac{1}{6}e^x + c_1 e^{-x} + c_2 e^{-2x}.$$

Ex. 3. $\quad \dfrac{d^3y}{dx^3} + \dfrac{d^2y}{dx^2} = x^2.$

The roots of the auxiliary equation are 0, 0, -1. Since 0 is twice a root, we assume

$$y = x^2(Ax^2 + Bx + C) = Ax^4 + Bx^3 + Cx^2.$$

Substituting this value,

$$12Ax^2 + (24A + 6B)x + 6B + 2C = x^2.$$

Consequently,

$$12A = 1, \qquad 24A + 6B = 0, \qquad 6B + 2C = 0,$$

whence

$$A = \tfrac{1}{12}, \qquad B = -\tfrac{1}{3}, \qquad C = 1.$$

The solution is

$$y = \tfrac{1}{12}x^4 - \tfrac{1}{3}x^3 + x^2 + c_1 + c_2 x + c_3 e^{-x}.$$

71. Simultaneous Equations. — We consider only linear equations with constant coefficients containing one independent variable and as many dependent variables as equations. All but one of the dependent variables can be eliminated by a process analogous to that used in solving linear algebraic equations. The one remaining dependent variable is the solution of a linear equation. Its value can be found and the other functions can then be determined by substituting this value in the previous equations.

Example.
$$\frac{dx}{dt} + 2x - 3y = t,$$

$$\frac{dy}{dt} - 3x + 2y = e^{2t}.$$

Using D for $\dfrac{d}{dt}$, these equations can be written

$$(D + 2)x - 3y = t,$$
$$(D + 2)y - 3x = e^{2t}.$$

To eliminate y, multiply the first equation by $D + 2$ and the second by 3. The result is

$$(D + 2)^2 x - 3(D + 2)y = 1 + 2t,$$
$$3(D + 2)y - 9x = 3e^{2t}.$$

Adding, we get

$$[(D + 2)^2 - 9] x = 1 + 2t + 3 e^{2t}.$$

The solution of this equation is

$$x = -\tfrac{2}{9} t - \tfrac{13}{81} + \tfrac{3}{7} e^{2t} + c_1 e^{t} + c_2 e^{-5t}.$$

Substituting this value in the first equation, we find

$$y = \tfrac{1}{3} (D + 2) x - \tfrac{1}{3} t = -\tfrac{2}{9} t - \tfrac{13}{81} + \tfrac{3}{7} e^{2t} + c_1 e^{t} - c_2 e^{-5t}.$$

EXERCISES

Solve the following equations:

1. $x \dfrac{d^2 y}{dx^2} + \dfrac{dy}{dx} + x = 0.$

2. $(x + 1) \dfrac{d^2 y}{dx^2} - (x + 2) \dfrac{dy}{dx} + x + 2 = 0.$

3. $\dfrac{d^2 y}{dx^2} = a^2 y.$

4. $\dfrac{d^2 y}{dx^2} = -a^2 y.$

5. $\dfrac{d^2 s}{dt^2} = -\dfrac{k}{s^3}.$

6. $\dfrac{d^2 s}{dt^2} + a^2 \left(\dfrac{ds}{dt} \right)^2 = b^2.$

7. $x \dfrac{d^2 y}{dx^2} = \sqrt{1 + \left(\dfrac{dy}{dx} \right)^2}.$

8. $y \dfrac{d^2 y}{dx^2} = 1 + \left(\dfrac{dy}{dx} \right)^2.$

9. $\dfrac{d^2 y}{dx^2} - 4 \dfrac{dy}{dx} = 0.$

10. $\dfrac{d^2 y}{dx^2} - 5 \dfrac{dy}{dx} - 6 y = 0.$

11. $\dfrac{d^2 y}{dx^2} - 6 \dfrac{dy}{dx} + 9 y = 0.$

12. $\dfrac{d^2 y}{dx^2} + y = 0.$

13. $\dfrac{d^3 y}{dx^3} - 2 \dfrac{d^2 y}{dx^2} - 3 \dfrac{dy}{dx} = 0.$

14. $\dfrac{d^4 y}{dx^4} = y.$

15. $\dfrac{d^2 y}{dx^2} - 2 \dfrac{dy}{dx} + 3 y = 0.$

16. $\dfrac{d^2 y}{dx^2} + \dfrac{dy}{dx} + y = 0.$

17. $\dfrac{d^4 y}{dx^4} - 3 \dfrac{d^2 y}{dx^2} + 2 y = 0.$

18. $\dfrac{d^3 y}{dx^3} - 3 \dfrac{d^2 y}{dx^2} + 3 \dfrac{dy}{dx} - y = 0.$

19. $\dfrac{d^2 y}{dx^2} + y = x + 3.$

20. $\dfrac{d^2 y}{dx^2} - 4 y = e^{x}.$

21. $\dfrac{d^2 y}{dx^2} + \dfrac{dy}{dx} - 6 y = x^2.$

22. $\dfrac{dy}{dx} - y = \sin x.$

23. $\dfrac{d^2 y}{dx^2} - 2 \dfrac{dy}{dx} = 2 x - 3.$

24. $\dfrac{d^2 y}{dx^2} + 6 \dfrac{dy}{dx} + 5 y = x + e^{3x}.$

25. $\dfrac{d^2 y}{dx^2} - a^2 y = e^{ax}.$

26. $\dfrac{d^2 y}{dx^2} - \dfrac{dy}{dx} + y = \cos 2 x.$

27. $\dfrac{d^2 y}{dx^2} - y = x^3 - x^2.$

28. $\dfrac{d^2 y}{dx^2} - 4 \dfrac{dy}{dx} + 3 y = e^{2x} \sin x.$

29. $\dfrac{d^2y}{dx^2} - 9y = e^{3x} \cos x.$ **31.** $\dfrac{d^2y}{dx^2} + 4y = \cos 2x.$

30. $\dfrac{d^4y}{dx^4} + \dfrac{d^2y}{dx^2} = \cos 4x.$ **32.** $\dfrac{d^2y}{dx^2} + 2\dfrac{dy}{dx} + y = e^x + e^{-x}.$

33. $\dfrac{dy}{dt} + x = e^t,$ $\dfrac{dx}{dt} - y = e^{-t}.$

34. $\dfrac{dx}{dt} = x - 2y + 1,$ $\dfrac{dy}{dt} = x - y + 2.$

35. $4\dfrac{dx}{dt} - \dfrac{dy}{dt} + 3x = \sin t,$ $\dfrac{dx}{dt} + y = \cos t.$

36. $\dfrac{d^2y}{dt^2} = x,$ $\dfrac{d^2x}{dt^2} = y.$

37. Solve the equation

$$\frac{d^2y}{dx^2} + \left(\frac{dy}{dx}\right)^2 = 1$$

and determine the constants so that $y = 0$ and $\dfrac{dy}{dx} = 1$ when $x = 0$.

38. Solve $\dfrac{d^2y}{dx^2} = 3\sqrt{y}$ under the hypothesis that $y = 1$ and $\dfrac{dy}{dx} = 2$ when $x = 0$.

39. When a body sinks slowly in a liquid, its acceleration and velocity approximately satisfy the equation

$$a = g - kv,$$

g and k being constants. Find the distance passed over as a function of the time if the body starts from rest.

40. The acceleration and velocity of a body falling in the air approximately satisfy the equation $a = g - kv^2$, g and k being constants. Find the distance traversed as a function of the time if the body falls from rest.

41. A weight supported by a spiral spring is lifted a distance b and let fall. Its acceleration is given by the equation $a = -k^2s$, k being constant and s the displacement from the position of equilibrium. Find s in terms of the time t.

42. Find the velocity with which a meteor strikes the earth, assuming that it starts from rest at an indefinitely great distance and moves toward the earth with an acceleration inversely proportional to the square of its distance from the center.

43. A body falling in a hole through the center of the earth would have an acceleration toward the center proportional to its distance from the center. If the body starts from rest at the surface, find the time required to fall through.

44. A chain 5 feet long starts with one foot of its length hanging over the edge of a smooth table. The acceleration of the chain will be proportional to the amount over the edge. Find the time required to slide off.

45. A chain hangs over a smooth peg, 8 feet of its length being on one side and 10 on the other. Its acceleration will be proportional to the difference in length of the two sides. Find the time required to slide off.

SUPPLEMENTARY EXERCISES

CHAPTER II

1. $\int \dfrac{x\,dx}{a + bx^2}.$

2. $\int (a + bx)^2\,dx.$

3. $\int \dfrac{a + bx}{p + qx}\,dx.$

4. $\int x\sqrt{2 - 3x^2}\,dx.$

5. $\int \dfrac{(x + a)\,dx}{\sqrt{x^2 + 2ax + b}}.$

6. $\int \sqrt{\dfrac{x - 1}{x}}\,\dfrac{dx}{x^2}.$

7. $\int (x - 1)(x^2 - 2x)^{\frac{3}{2}}\,dx.$

8. $\int \dfrac{dx}{\sin ax}.$

9. $\int \dfrac{\sin ax}{\cos^2 ax}\,dx.$

10. $\int \dfrac{\cos 2x}{1 - \sin 2x}\,dx.$

11. $\int \dfrac{\sec^2 x \tan x\,dx}{a + b\sec^2 x}.$

12. $\int \dfrac{dx}{\sec x}.$

13. $\int \dfrac{\cot x\,dx}{1 - \sin x}.$

14. $\int \dfrac{\sin ax}{\cos ax}\,dx.$

15. $\int \dfrac{dx}{\cos x - \sin x}.$

16. $\int \dfrac{dx}{\sec x - \tan x}.$

17. $\int \dfrac{dx}{\sin^2 ax \cos^2 ax}.$

18. $\int \dfrac{\cos x\,dx}{\cos x + \sin x}.$

19. $\int \dfrac{dx}{\sqrt{\tan^2 x + 2}}.$

20. $\int \dfrac{dx}{x\sqrt{x^n - 1}}.$

21. $\int \dfrac{\sqrt{x^2 - 1}}{x}\,dx.$

22. $\int \dfrac{dx}{\sin^2 x - \cos^2 x}.$

23. $\int \dfrac{\cot x\,dx}{\sqrt{1 + \sin^2 x}}.$

24. $\int \dfrac{dx}{(2x - 1)\sqrt{4x^2 - 4x}}.$

25. $\int xe^{ax^2}\,dx.$

26. $\int \dfrac{e^{ax}\,dx}{b + ce^{ax}}.$

27. $\int \sec^2 x e^{\tan x}\,dx.$

28. $\int a^{b + cx}\,dx.$

29. $\int \dfrac{dx}{e^x + 1}.$

30. $\int \dfrac{dx}{e^x - e^{-x}}.$

31. $\int \tan x \ln \cos x\,dx.$

32. $\int \dfrac{dx}{a^2x^2 + 2abx + b^2}.$

33. $\int \dfrac{x\,dx}{\sqrt{x^2 - 2x + 3}}.$

34. $\int \dfrac{(2x + 3)\,dx}{(x - 1)\sqrt{x^2 - 2x}}.$

157

35. $\int \dfrac{dx}{x \sqrt{2x+3}}.$

36. $\int \dfrac{dx}{x^3 \sqrt{ax^2+b}}.$

37. $\int (a^2 - x^2)^{\frac{3}{2}}\, dx.$

38. $\int \dfrac{dx}{x \sqrt{ax^2+bx}}.$

39. $\int \sqrt{3-2x-x^2}\, dx.$

40. $\int (a^{\frac{2}{3}} - x^{\frac{2}{3}})^{\frac{3}{2}}\, dx.$

41. $\int \cos^6 x \sin^2 x\, dx.$

42. $\int (1+\cos x)^{\frac{3}{2}}\, dx.$

43. $\int \tan 2x \sec^4 2x\, dx.$

44. $\int \cot^4 x\, dx.$

45. $\int \dfrac{dx}{\tan x + \cot x}.$

46. $\int (\sec x + \tan x)^2\, dx.$

47. $\int \dfrac{\tan x - 1}{\tan x + 1}\, dx.$

48. $\int \dfrac{\cos^3 x\, dx}{\sin^3 x}.$

49. $\int \sin 2x \cos^2 x\, dx.$

50. $\int \sqrt{1+\cos^2 x} \sin 2x\, dx.$

51. $\int \dfrac{dx}{x \sqrt{a^2 x + b^2}}.$

52. $\int \dfrac{dx}{x^2 \sqrt{x-2}}.$

53. $\int \dfrac{dx}{(x-1) \sqrt{x+2}}.$

54. $\int x (ax+b)^{\frac{3}{2}}\, dx.$

55. $\int \dfrac{px+q}{\sqrt{ax+b}}\, dx.$

56. $\int x^3 \sqrt{a^2 - x^2}\, dx.$

57. $\int \dfrac{x^3\, dx}{\sqrt{a^2 - x^2}}.$

58. $\int \dfrac{x^2\, dx}{(x^2-1)^2}.$

59. $\int \dfrac{dx}{(a^2 - x^2)^{\frac{3}{2}}}.$

60. $\int \dfrac{x^5\, dx}{\sqrt{a^3 - x^3}}.$

61. $\int e^{x + \ln x}\, dx.$

62. $\int e^{ax} \sin bx\, dx.$

63. $\int \dfrac{x^2}{e^x}\, dx.$

64. $\int x \ln (cx+b)\, dx.$

65. $\int \dfrac{\ln (ax+b)}{x^2}\, dx$

66. $\int x \cot^{-1} x\, dx.$

67. $\int \dfrac{x\, dx}{(x^2-1)^2 (x^2+1)}.$

68. $\int \dfrac{x^2\, dx}{(x^3+1)(x^3-2)}.$

69. $\int \dfrac{x\, dx}{x^4+1}.$

70. $\int \dfrac{x^5}{(x-1)^5}\, dx.$

71. $\int x^3 \cos \tfrac{1}{2} x\, dx.$

72. $\int \dfrac{2x^2 + 3x}{(x-1)(x-2)(x+3)}\, dx.$

73. $\int \dfrac{(3x-5)\, dx}{x(x+3)^2}.$

74. $\int \dfrac{x\, dx}{x^3-8}.$

75. $\int \dfrac{dx}{(1-x^3)^{\frac{4}{3}}}.$

76. $\int \dfrac{x^3\, dx}{(1-2x^2)^{\frac{3}{2}}}.$

77. $\int \sec^4 x \tan^{\frac{3}{2}} x \, dx.$

78. $\int \sin 3x \cos 4x \, dx.$

79. $\int \sin^2 x \cos 2x \, dx.$

80. $\int \sin x \sin 5x \, dx.$

81. $\int \cos 2x \cos 3x \, dx.$

82. $\int (\cot x + \csc x)^2 \, dx.$

83. $\int \frac{(3x-1)\,dx}{\sqrt{2+3x-x^2}}.$

84. $\int \frac{x^2-3x+2}{\sqrt{x^2-4x+3}}\,dx.$

85. $\int \sqrt{\frac{a-x}{a+x}}\,dx.$

86. $\int (\sin x - \cos x)^3 \, dx.$

87. $\int \frac{x^5\,dx}{(x^2-a^2)^2}.$

88. $\int \frac{\log(x+\sqrt{x^2-1})}{\sqrt{x^2-1}}\,dx.$

89. $\int \sec^7 x \, dx.$

90. $\int (x^2+a^2)^{\frac{5}{2}}\,dx.$

CHAPTER IV

91. Find the area bounded by the x-axis and the parabola $y = x^2 - 4x + 5$.

92. Find the area bounded by the curves $y = x^3$, $y^2 = x$.

93. Find the area bounded by the parabola $y^2 = 2x$ and the witch $x = \frac{1}{y^2+1}$.

94. Find the area within a loop of the curve $y^2 = x^2 - x^4$.

95. Find the area of one of the sectors bounded by the hyperbola $x^2 - y^2 = 3$ and the lines $x = \pm 2y$.

96. Find the area bounded by the parabolas $y^2 = 2ax + a^2$, $y^2 + 2ax = 0$.

97. Find the area within the loop of the curve $x = \frac{3am}{1+m^3}$, $y = \frac{3am^2}{1+m^3}$.

98. Find the area bounded by the parabola $x = a\cos 2\phi$, $y = a\sin\phi$ and the line $x = -a$.

99. Find the area inclosed by the curve $x = a\cos^3\phi$, $y = b\sin^3\phi$.

100. Find the area bounded by the curve $x = a\sin\theta$, $y = a\cos^3\theta$.

101. Find the area of one loop of the curve $r = a\cos n\theta$.

102. Find the area of a loop of the curve $r = a(1 - 2\cos\theta)$.

103. Find the area between the curves $r = a(\cos\theta + 2)$, $r = a$.

104. Find the total area inclosed by the curve $r = a\sin\frac{1}{3}\theta$.

105. Find the area of the part of one loop of the curve $r^2 = a^2\sin 3\theta$ outside the curve $r^2 = a\sin\theta$.

106. By changing to polar coördinates find the area within one loop of the curve $(x^2 + y^2)^2 = a^2 xy$.

107. By changing to polar coördinates find the area of one of the regions between the circle $x^2 + y^2 = 2 a^2$ and hyperbola $x^2 - y^2 = a^2$.

108. Find the area of one of the regions bounded by $\theta = \sin r$ and the line $\theta = 1$.

109. Find the volume generated by revolving an ellipse about the tangent at one of its vertices.

110. Find the volume generated by revolving about the y-axis the area bounded by the curve $y^2 = x^3$ and the line $x = 4$.

111. Find the volume generated by rotating about the y-axis the area between the x-axis and one arch of the cycloid $x = a (\phi - \sin \phi)$, $y = a (1 - \cos \phi)$.

112. Find the volume generated by rotating the area of the preceding problem about the tangent at the highest point of the cycloid.

113. Find the volume generated by revolving about the x-axis the part of the ellipse $x^2 - xy + y^2 = 1$ in the first quadrant.

114. Find the volume generated by revolving about $\theta = \frac{\pi}{2}$ the area enclosed by the curve $r^2 = a^2 \sin \theta$.

115. The ends of an ellipse move along the parabolas $z^2 = ax$, $y^2 = ax$ and its plane is perpendicular to the x-axis. Find the volume swept out between $x = 0$ and $x = c$.

116. The ends of a helical spring lie in parallel planes at distance h apart and the area of a cross section of the spring perpendicular to its axis is A. Find the volume of the spring.

117. The axes of two right circular cylinders of equal radius intersect at an angle α. Find the common volume.

118. A rectangle moves from a fixed point, one side varying as the distance from the point, and the other as the square of this distance. At the distance of 10 feet the rectangle becomes a square of side 4 ft. What is the volume then generated?

119. A cylindrical bucket filled with oil is tipped until half the bottom is exposed; if the radius is 4 inches and the altitude 12 inches find the amount of oil poured out.

120. Two equal ellipses with semi-axes 5 and 6 inches have the same major axis and lie in perpendicular planes. A square moves with its center in the common axis and its diagonals chords of the ellipses. Find the volume generated.

121. Find the volume bounded by the paraboloid $12 z = 3 x^2 + y^2$ and the plane $z = 4$.

CHAPTER V

122. Find the length of the arc of the curve

$$y = \tfrac{1}{2} x \sqrt{x^2 - 1} - \tfrac{1}{2} \ln \left(x + \sqrt{x^2 - 1} \right) \text{ between } x = 1 \text{ and } x = 3.$$

123. Find the arc of the curve $9 y^2 = (2 x - 1)^3$ cut off by the line $x = 5$.

124. Find the perimeter of the loop of the curve

$$9 x^2 = (2 y - 1) (y - 2)^2.$$

125. Find the length of the curve $x = t^2 + t$, $y = t^2 - t$ below the x-axis.

126. Find the length of an arch of the curve

$$x = a\sqrt{3} (2 \phi - \sin 2 \phi), \quad y = \frac{a}{3} (1 - \cos 3 \phi).$$

127. Find the length of one quadrant of the curve

$$x = a \cos^3 \phi, \quad y = b \sin^3 \phi.$$

128. Find the circumference of the circle

$$r = 2 \sin \theta + 3 \cos \theta.$$

129. Find the perimeter of one loop of the curve

$$r = a \sin^5 \left(\frac{\theta}{5} \right).$$

130. Find the area of the surface generated by revolving the arc of the curve $9 y^2 = (2 x - 1)^3$ between $x = 0$ and $x = 2$ about the y-axis.

131. Find the area of the surface generated by revolving one arch of the cycloid $x = a (\phi - \sin \phi)$, $y = a (1 - \cos \phi)$ about the tangent at its highest point.

132. Find the area of the surface generated by rotating the curve $r^2 = a^2 \sin 2 \theta$ about the x-axis.

133. Find the area generated by revolving the loop of the curve $9 x^2 = (2 y - 1) (y - 2)^2$ about the x-axis.

134. Find the volume generated by revolving the area within the curve $y^2 = x^2 (1 - x^2)$ about the y-axis.

135. The vertical angle of a cone is $90°$, its vertex is on a sphere of radius a, and its axis is tangent to the sphere. Find the area of the cone within the sphere.

136. A cylinder with radius b intersects and is tangent to a sphere of radius a, greater than b. Find the area of the surface of the cylinder within the sphere.

137. A plane passes through the center of the base of a right circular cone and is parallel to an element of the cone. Find the areas of the two parts into which it cuts the lateral surface.

CHAPTER VI

138. Find the pressure on a square of side 4 feet if one diagonal is vertical and has its upper end in the surface.

139. Find the pressure on a segment of a parabola of base 2 b and altitude h, if the vertex is at the surface and the axis of the parabola is vertical.

140. Find the pressure on the parabolic segment of the preceding problem if the vertex is submerged and the base of the segment is in the surface.

141. Find the pressure on the ends of a cylindrical tank 4 feet in diameter, if the axis is horizontal and the tank is filled with water under a pressure of 10 lbs. per square inch at the top of the tank.

142. A barrel 3 ft. in diameter is filled with equal parts of water and oil. If the axis is horizontal and the weight of oil half that of water, find the pressure on one end.

143. Find the moment of the pressure in Ex. 138 about the other diagonal of the square.

144. Weights of 1, 2, and 3 pounds are placed at the points (0, 0), (2, 1), (4, − 3). Find their center of gravity.

145. A trapezoid is formed by connecting one vertex of a rectangle to the middle point of the opposite side. Find its center of gravity.

146. Find the center of gravity of a sector of a circle with radius a and central angle 2 α.

147. Find the center of gravity of the area within a loop of the curve $y^2 = x^2 - x^4$.

148. Find the center of gravity of the area bounded by the curve $y^2 = \dfrac{x^3}{2\,a - x}$ and its asymptote $x = 2\,a$.

149. Find the center of gravity of the area within one loop of the curve $r^2 = a^2 \sin \theta$.

150. Find the center of gravity of the area of the curve $x = a \sin^3 \phi$, $y = b \sin^3 \phi$ above the x-axis.

151. Find the center of gravity of the arc of the curve $9\,y^2 = (2\,x - 1)^3$ cut off by the line $x = 5$.

152. Find the center of gravity of the arc that forms the loop of the curve

$$9\,y^2 = (2\,x - 1)\,(x - 2)^2.$$

153. Find the center of gravity of the arc of the curve $x = t^2 + t$, $y = t^3 - t$ below the x-axis.

154. Show that the center of gravity of a pyramid of constant density is on the line joining the vertex to the center of gravity of the base, ¾ of the way from the vertex to the base.

155. Find the center of gravity of the surface of a right circular cone.

156. Show that the distance from the base to the center of gravity of the surface of an oblique cone is $\frac{1}{3}$ of the altitude. Is it on the line joining the vertex to the center of the base?

157. Find the center of gravity of the solid generated by rotating about the line $x = 4$, the area above the x-axis bounded by the parabola $y^2 = 4x$ and the line $x = 4$.

158. The arc of the curve $x^{\frac{2}{3}} + y^{\frac{2}{3}} = a^{\frac{2}{3}}$ above the x-axis is rotated about the y-axis. Find the center of gravity of the volume and that of the area generated.

159. Assuming that the specific gravity of sea water at depth h in miles is

$$\rho = e^{.0075\,h},$$

find the center of gravity of a section of the water with vertical sides five miles deep.

160. By using Pappus's theorems, find the center of gravity of the arc of a semicircle.

161. The ellipse

$$\frac{x^2}{a^2} + \frac{y^2}{b^2} = 1$$

is rotated about a tangent inclined 45° to its axis. Find the volume generated.

162. The volume of the ellipsoid

$$\frac{x^2}{a^2} + \frac{y^2}{b^2} + \frac{z^2}{c^2} = 1$$

is $\frac{4}{3}\pi abc$. Use this to find the center of gravity of a quadrant of the ellipse $\frac{x^2}{a^2} + \frac{y^2}{b^2} = 1$.

163. Find the volume generated by revolving one loop of the curve $r = a \sin \theta$ about the initial line.

164. A semicircle of radius a rotates about its bounding diameter while the diameter slides along the line in which it lies. Find the volume generated in one revolution.

165. The plane of a moving square is perpendicular to that of a fixed circle. One corner of the square is kept fixed at a point of the circle while the opposite corner moves around the circle. Find the volume generated.

166. Find the moment of inertia about the x-axis of the area bounded by the x-axis and the curve $y = 4 - x^2$.

167. Show that the moment of inertia of a plane area about an axis perpendicular to its plane at the origin is equal to the sum of its moments of inertia about the coordinate axes. Use this to find the moment of inertia of the ellipse $\frac{x^2}{a^2} + \frac{y^2}{b^2} = 1$ about the axis perpendicular to its plane at its center.

168. Find the moment of inertia of the surface of a right circular cone about its axis.

169. The area bounded by the x-axis and the parabola $y^2 = 4\,ax - x^2$ is revolved about the x-axis. Find the moment of inertia about the x-axis of the volume thus generated.

170. From a right circular cylinder a right cone with the same base and altitude is cut. Find the moment of inertia of the remaining volume about the axis of the cylinder.

171. A torus is generated by rotating a circle of radius a about an axis in its plane at distance b, greater than a, from the center. Find the moment of inertia of the volume of the torus about its axis.

172. Find the moment of inertia of the area of the torus about its axis.

173. The kinetic energy of a moving mass is

$$\int \tfrac{1}{2}\, v^2\, dm,$$

where v is the velocity of the element of mass dm. Show that the kinetic energy of a homogeneous cylinder of mass M and radius a rotating with angular velocity ω about its axis is $\tfrac{1}{4} M\omega^2 a^2$.

174. Show that the kinetic energy of a uniform sphere of mass M and radius a rotating with angular velocity ω about a diameter is $\tfrac{1}{5} M\omega^2 a^2$.

175. When a gas expands without receiving or giving out heat, its pressure and volume are connected by the equation

$$pv^\gamma = k$$

where γ and k are constant. Find the work done in expanding from the volume v_1 to the volume v_2.

176. The work done by an electric current of i amperes and E volts is iE joules per second. If

$$E = E_0 \cos \omega t, \qquad i = I_0 \cos (\omega t + \alpha),$$

where E_0, I_0, ω are constants, find the work done in one cycle.

177. When water is pumped from one vessel into another at a higher level, show that the work in foot pounds required is equal to the product of the total weight of water in pounds and the distance in feet its center of gravity is raised.

CHAPTER VII

178. Find the volume of an ellipsoid by using the prismoidal formula.

179. A wedge is cut from a right circular cylinder by a plane which passes through the center of the base and makes with the base an angle α. Find the volume of the wedge by the prismoidal formula.

180. Find approximately the volume of a barrel 30 inches long if its diameter at the ends is 20 inches and at the middle 24 inches.

181. The width of an irregular piece of land was measured at intervals of 10 yards, the measurements being 52, 56, 67, 49, 45, 53, and 62 yards. Find its area approximately by using Simpson's rule.

Find the values of the following integrals approximately by Simpson's rule:

182. $\int_0^4 \sqrt{x^3 + 1}\, dx.$

184. $\int_0^{\frac{1}{2}\pi} \sqrt{\sin x}\, dx.$

183. $\int_1^{10} \frac{1}{x^3} \ln x\, dx.$

185. $\int_{-4}^4 \frac{dx}{1 + x^4}.$

186. Find approximately the length of an arch of the curve $y = \sin x$.

187. Find approximately the area bounded by the x-axis, the curve $y = \dfrac{\sin x}{x}$, and the ordinates $x = 0$, $x = \pi$.

CHAPTER VIII

Express the following quantities as double integrals and determine the limits:

188. Area bounded by the parabola $y = x^2 - 2x + 3$ and the line $y = 2x$.

189. Area bounded by the circle $x^2 + y^2 = 2a^2$ and the curve

$$y^2 = \frac{x^3}{2a - x}.$$

190. Moment of inertia about the x-axis of the area within the circles

$$x^2 + y^2 = 5, \qquad x^2 + y^2 - 2x - 4y = 0.$$

191. Moment of inertia of the area within the loop of the curve $y^2 = x^2 - x^4$ about the axis perpendicular to its plane at the origin.

192. Volume bounded by the xy-plane the paraboloid $z = x^2 + y^2$ and the cylinder $x^2 + y^2 = 4$.

193. Volume bounded by the xy-plane the paraboloid $z = x^2 + y^2$ and the plane $z = 2x + 2y$.

194. Center of gravity of the solid bounded by the xz-plane, the cylinder $x^2 + z^2 = a^2$, and the plane $x + y + z = 4a$.

195. Volume generated by rotating about the x-axis one of the areas bounded by the circle $x^2 + y^2 = 5a^2$ and the parabola $y^2 = 4ax$.

In each of the following cases determine the region over which the integral is taken, interchange dx and dy, determine the new limits, and so find the value of the integral:

196. $\displaystyle\int_0^1 \int_0^x \frac{x\,dx\,dy}{\sqrt{x^2+y^2}}.$ **198.** $\displaystyle\int_0^1 \int_{\sqrt{y}}^1 \frac{1}{x} e^{-\frac{y}{x}}\,dy\,dx.$

197. $\displaystyle\int_0^a \int_{a-\sqrt{a^2-y^2}}^{a+\sqrt{a^2-y^2}} (x+y)\,dy\,dx.$ **199.** $\displaystyle\int_0^1 \int_0^2 \sqrt{x^2+xy}\,dy\,dx.$

Express the following quantities as double integrals using polar coördinates:

200. Area within the cardioid $r = a\,(1+\cos\theta)$ and outside the circle $r = \frac{1}{2} a$.

201. Center of gravity of the area within the circle $r = a$ and outside the circle $r = 2\,a \sin\theta$.

202. Moment of inertia of the area cut from the parabola

$$r = \frac{2\,a}{1-\cos\theta}$$

by the line $y = x$, about the x-axis.

203. Volume within the cylinder $r = 2\,a\sin\theta$ and the sphere

$$x^2 + y^2 + z^2 = 4\,a^2.$$

204. Moment of inertia of a sphere about a tangent line.

205. Volume bounded by the paraboloid $z = x^2 + y^2$ and the plane $z = 2\,x + 2\,y$.

206. Find the area cut from the cone $x^2 + y^2 = z^2$ by the plane $x = 2\,z - 3$.

207. Find the area cut from the plane by the cone in Ex. 206.

208. Find the area of the surface $z^2 + (x+y)^2 = a^2$ in the first octant.

209. Determine the area of the surface $z^2 = 2\,x$ cut out by the planes $y = 0,\ y = x,\ x = 1$.

CHAPTER IX

Express the following quantities as triple integrals:

210. Volume of an octant of a sphere of radius a.

211. Moment of inertia of the volume in the first octant bounded by the plane $\frac{x}{a} + \frac{y}{b} + \frac{z}{c} = 1$ about the x-axis.

212. Center of gravity of the region in the first octant bounded by the paraboloid $z = xy$ and the cylinder $x^2 + y^2 = a^2$.

213. Moment of inertia about the z-axis of the volume bounded by the paraboloid $z = x^2 + y^2$ and the plane $z = 2\,x + 3$.

214. Volume bounded by the cone $x^2 = y^2 + 2\,z^2$ and the plane $3\,x + y = 6$.

Express the following quantities as triple integrals in rectangular, cylindrical. and spherical coördinates, and evaluate one of the integrals:

215. Moment of inertia of a right circular cylinder about a line tangent to its base.

216. Moment of inertia of a segment cut from a sphere by a plane, about a diameter parallel to that plane.

217. Center of gravity of a right circular cone whose density varies as the distance from the center of the base.

218. Volume bounded by the xy-plane, the cylinder $x^2 + y^2 = 2\,ax$ and the cone $z^2 = x^2 + y^2$.

219. Find the attraction of a uniform wire of length l and mass M on a particle of unit mass at distance c from the wire in the perpendicular at one end.

220. Find the attraction of a right circular cylinder on a particle at the middle of its base.

221. Show that the attraction of a homogeneous shell bounded by two concentric spherical surfaces on a particle in the enclosed space is zero.

CHAPTER X

Solve the following differential equations:

222. $y\,dx + (x - xy)\,dy = 0.$

223. $\sin x \sin y\,dx + \cos x \cos y\,dy = 0.$

224. $(2\,xy - y^2 + 6\,x^2)\,dx + (3\,y^2 + x^2 - 2\,xy)\,dy = 0.$

225. $x\dfrac{dy}{dx} + y = x^3 y.$

226. $x\dfrac{dy}{dx} + y = \cot x.$

227. $x\,dy - \left(y + e^{\frac{1}{x}}\right) dx = 0.$

228. $(1 + x^2)\,dy + (xy + x)\,dx = 0.$

229. $x\,dx + y\,dy = x\,dy - y\,dx.$

230. $(\sin x + y)\,dy + (y \cos x - x^2)\,dx = 0.$

231. $y\,(e^x + 2)\,dx + (e^x + 2\,x)\,dy = 0.$

232. $(xy^2 - x)\,dx + (y + xy)\,dy = 0.$

233. $(1 + x^2)\dfrac{dy}{dx} + xy = 2\,y.$

234. $x\,dy - y\,dx = \sqrt{x^2 + y^2}\,dx.$

235. $(x - y)\,dx + x\,dy = 0.$

236. $x\,dy - y\,dx = x\sqrt{x^2 + y^2}\,dx.$

237. $e^{x+y}\,dy + (1 + e^y)\,dx = 0.$

238. $(2\,x + 3\,y - 1)\,dx + (4\,x + 6\,y - 5)\,dy = 0.$

239. $(3\,y^2 + 3\,xy + x^2)\,dx = (x^2 + 2\,xy)\,dy.$

240. $(1 + x^2)\,dy + (xy - x^2)\,dx = 0.$

241. $(x^2y + y^4)\,dx - (x^3 + 2\,xy^3)\,dy = 0.$

242. $(y + 1)\left(\dfrac{dy}{dx}\right)^2 = x^4 - x^3.$

243. $2\dfrac{dy}{dx} + y + xy^3 = 0.$

244. $y\,dx = (y^3 - x)\,dy.$

245. $y\,\dfrac{dy}{dx} + y^2 \cot x = \cos x.$

246. $(x^2 - y^2)\,(dx + dy) = (x^2 + y^2)\,(dy - dx).$

247. $x^2\,\dfrac{d^2y}{dx^2} + \dfrac{dy}{dx} = 1.$

248. $\dfrac{d^2s}{dt^2} = \dfrac{a^2}{s^3}.$

249. $y\,\dfrac{d^2y}{dx^2} + 2\,y\,\dfrac{dy}{dx} + \left(\dfrac{dy}{dx}\right)^2 = 0.$

250. $(1 + x)\,\dfrac{d^2y}{dx^2} = \dfrac{dy}{dx}.$

251. $\dfrac{d^2y}{dx^2} = k\sqrt{1 + \left(\dfrac{dy}{dx}\right)^2}.$

252. $\dfrac{d^2y}{dx^2} + 2\,\dfrac{dy}{dx} - 3\,y = x^3.$

253. $\dfrac{d^2y}{dx^2} - \dfrac{dy}{dx} = e^{2x}.$

254. $\dfrac{d^2y}{dx^2} + 4\,\dfrac{dy}{dx} + 4\,y = \cos x.$

255. $\dfrac{d^2y}{dx^2} - 4\,\dfrac{dy}{dx} + 8\,y = 3\,x - 4.$

256. $\dfrac{d^2y}{dx^2} + 2\,\dfrac{dy}{dx} = x + 1.$

257. $\dfrac{d^3y}{dx^3} + 2\,\dfrac{d^2y}{dx^2} - \dfrac{dy}{dx} - 2\,y = e^x + 3.$

258. $\dfrac{d^2y}{dx^2} + a^2y = \sin ax.$

259. $\dfrac{d^2y}{dx^2} - \dfrac{dy}{dx} - 2\,y = e^x \sin 2\,x.$

260. $\dfrac{d^2y}{dx^2} - \dfrac{dy}{dx} - 2\,y = e^{-x} \sin 2\,x.$

261. $\dfrac{d^2y}{dx^2} + 9\,y = 2 \cos 3\,x - 3 \cos 2\,x.$

262. $\dfrac{d^2y}{dx^2} + 6\,\dfrac{dy}{dx} + 5\,y = (e^x + 1)^2.$

263. $\dfrac{d^2y}{dx^2} - y = xe^{2x}$.

264. $\dfrac{d^2y}{dx^2} + 2\dfrac{dy}{dx} + 2y = x\cos x$.

265. $\dfrac{dy}{dt} + 2x = \sin t$, $\dfrac{dx}{dt} - 2y = \cos t$.

266. $\dfrac{dx}{dt} - \dfrac{dy}{dt} + x - y = t^2 - 3t - 3$, $x - y - \dfrac{dx}{dt} - \dfrac{dy}{dt} = t^2 - t - 3$.

267. According to Newton's Law, the rate at which a substance cools in air is proportional to the difference of the temperature of the substance and the temperature of air. If the temperature of air is 20° C. and the substance cools from 100° to 60° in 20 minutes, when will its temperature become 30°?

268. A particle moves in a straight line from a distance a towards a point with an acceleration which at distance r from the point is $k\,r^{-\frac{1}{2}}$. If the particle starts from rest, how long will be the time before it reaches the point?

269. A substance is undergoing transformation into another at a rate proportional to the amount of the substance remaining untransformed. If that amount is 34.2 when $t = 1$ hour and 11.6 when $t = 3$ hours, determine the amount at the start, $t = 0$, and find how many hours will elapse before only one per cent will remain.

270. Determine the shape of a reflector so that all the rays of light coming from a fixed point will be reflected in the same direction.

271. Find the curve in which a chain hangs when its ends are supported at two points and it is allowed to hang under its own weight. (See the example solved in Art. 57.)

272. By Hooke's Law the amount an elastic string of natural length l stretches under a force F is klF, k being constant. If the string is held vertical and allowed to elongate under its own weight w, show that the elongation is $\frac{1}{2} kwl$.

273. Assuming that the resistance of the air produces a negative acceleration equal to k times the square of the velocity, show that a projectile fired upward with a velocity v_1 will return to its starting point with the velocity

$$v_2 = \sqrt{\dfrac{gv_1^2}{g + kv_1^2}},$$

g being the acceleration of gravity.

274. Assuming that the density of sea water under a pressure of p pounds per square inch is

$$\rho = 1 + 0.000003\,p,$$

show that the surface of an ocean 5 miles deep is about 465 feet lower than it would be if water were incompressible. (A cubic foot of sea water weighs about 64 pounds.)

275. Show that when a liquid rotating with constant velocity is in equilibrium, its surface is a paraboloid of revolution.

276. Find the path described by a particle moving in a plane, if its acceleration is directed toward a fixed point and is proportional to the distance from the point.

ANSWERS TO EXERCISES

Page 5

1. $\frac{1}{5} x^5 - \frac{1}{2} x^4 + \frac{1}{3} x^3 + C.$

2. $\frac{1}{3} x^3 + \frac{1}{x} + C.$

3. $\frac{2}{3} x^{\frac{3}{2}} + 2 x^{\frac{1}{2}} + C.$

4. $\frac{1}{3} \sqrt{2x} \, (2x - 3) + C.$

5. $x^{\frac{1}{2}} \left(\frac{2}{7} x^3 + \frac{4}{5} x^2 + \frac{2}{3} x \right) + C.$

6. $a^{\frac{1}{2}} x - 2 a x^{\frac{1}{2}} + \frac{1}{2} a^{\frac{1}{2}} x^2 - \frac{2}{3} x^{\frac{3}{2}} + C.$

7. $\frac{1}{4} x^4 + \frac{1}{3} (a + b) x^3 + \frac{1}{2} ab x^2 + C.$

8. $2x + 3 \ln x + C.$

9. $\frac{1}{2} y^2 + 4y + 4 \ln y + C.$

10. $x^{\frac{1}{2}} \left(\frac{8}{13} x^4 - \frac{4}{9} x^2 - 6 \right) + C.$

11. $\ln (x + 1) + C.$

12. $-\dfrac{1}{x + 1} + C.$

13. $\sqrt{2x + 1} + C.$

14. $\frac{1}{2} \ln (x^2 + 2) + C.$

15. $\sqrt{x^2 - 1} + C.$

16. $-\dfrac{1}{4 b (a + bx^2)^2} + C.$

17. $-\frac{1}{3} (a^2 - x^2)^{\frac{3}{2}} + C.$

18. $\frac{1}{3} \ln (a^3 + x^3) + C.$

19. $\frac{2}{9} (x^3 - 1)^{\frac{3}{2}} + C.$

20. $\ln (x^2 + ax + b) + C.$

21. $2 \sqrt{x^2 + ax + b} + C.$

22. $-\dfrac{1}{5a} \ln (1 - at^5) + C.$

23. $-\frac{1}{3} (a^2 - t^2)^{\frac{3}{2}} + C.$

24. $x + 3 \ln (x - 2) + C.$

25. $\dfrac{1}{2} \ln (2x^2 + 1)$

$\qquad -\dfrac{1}{4 (2x^2 + 1)} + C.$

26. $\dfrac{1}{9} \left(1 - \dfrac{1}{x} \right)^9 + C.$

27. $-\dfrac{1}{n (n-1) (x^n + a)^{n-1}} + C.$

28. $\dfrac{\sqrt{2} \left(\sqrt{2x} - \sqrt{2a} \right)^{11}}{11} + C.$

29. $\frac{1}{3} x^3 - \frac{2}{3} \ln (x^3 + 2) + C.$

30. $\frac{1}{7} x^7 - \frac{2}{5} x^5 + \frac{1}{3} x^2 + C.$

Pages 12, 13

1. 138.

2. $\frac{1}{2} g t^2 + 30 t.$

3. $h = -\frac{1}{2} g t^2 + 100 t + 60.$ It reaches the highest point when $t = 3.1$ sec., $h = 215.3$ ft.

4. $\frac{1}{1000}$ sec.

171

5. $x = t^2 - t + 1$, $y = t - \frac{1}{2}t^2 + 2$. These are parametric equations of the path. The rectangular equation is $x^2 + 4xy + 4y^2 - 12x - 22y + 31 = 0$.

6. About 53 miles.

7. $x = \frac{k}{4}\sqrt{3}\, t^2$, $y = \frac{k}{4}t^2 + V_0 t$.

8. $y = 2x - \frac{1}{2}x^2 - \frac{1}{4}$.

9. $y = e^x$.

10. $\left(-\frac{5}{4}, -\frac{11}{4}\right)$.

11. $6y = x^3 - 3x^2 + 3x + 13$.

12. $-12\frac{1}{2}$.

14. About 4 per cent.

15. $x = x_0 e^{kt}$, where x is the number at time t, x_0 the number at time $t = 0$, and k is constant.

17. 17 minutes.

18. 11.4 minutes.

19. 11.6 years.

Pages 18, 19

1. $-\left(\frac{1}{4}\cos 2x + \frac{1}{4}\sin 2x\right) + C.$

2. $\frac{5}{2}\sin\left(\frac{2x - 3}{5}\right) + C.$

3. $-\frac{1}{n}\cos(nt + a) + C.$

4. $3\tan\frac{1}{3}\theta + C.$

5. $-4\csc\frac{\theta}{4} + C.$

6. $\frac{1}{2}\sin^2\theta + C.$

7. $\tan x + C.$

8. $-\frac{1}{2}\cot 2x + C.$

9. $-\csc x + C.$

10. $\frac{1}{4}\sec^4 x + C.$

11. $2\left(\csc\frac{\theta}{2} - \cot\frac{\theta}{2}\right) + C.$

12. $\frac{1}{2}\sin(x^2 - 1) + C.$

13. $\frac{1}{3}(\tan 3x + \sec 3x) + C.$

14. $\tan x + x - 2\ln(\sec x + \tan x) + C.$

15. $\ln(1 + \sin x) + C.$

16. $\theta + \cos^2\theta + C.$

17. $\sin x + \ln(\csc x - \cot x) + C.$

18. $\frac{1}{3}\sin^3 x + C.$

19. $\frac{1}{4}\tan^4 x + C.$

20. $\frac{1}{2}\tan^2 x + C.$

21. $-\frac{1}{6}\cos^6 x + C.$

22. $\frac{1}{2}\ln(1 + 2\tan x) + C.$

23. $-\frac{1}{2}\ln(1 - \sin 2x) + C.$

24. $\frac{1}{a}\ln(1 + \tan ax) + C.$

25. $\frac{1}{\sqrt{2}}\sin^{-1}\frac{x\sqrt{2}}{\sqrt{3}} + C.$

26. $\dfrac{1}{\sqrt{3}} \tan^{-1} \dfrac{x\sqrt{3}}{2} + C.$

27. $\dfrac{1}{2} \sec^{-1} \dfrac{x\sqrt{3}}{2} + C.$

28. $\frac{1}{6} \tan^{-1} 2y + C.$

29. $\dfrac{1}{\sqrt{7}} \ln\left(x\sqrt{7} + \sqrt{7x^2 + 1}\right) + C.$

30. $\dfrac{1}{3} \sec^{-1} \dfrac{ax}{3} + C.$

31. $\dfrac{1}{4\sqrt{3}} \ln \dfrac{2x + \sqrt{3}}{2x - \sqrt{3}} + C.$

32. $\ln\left(2x + \sqrt{4x^2 - 3}\right) + C.$

33. $-3\sqrt{4 - x^2} - 2\sin^{-1}\dfrac{x}{2} + C.$

34. $2\sqrt{x^2 + 4} + 3\ln\left(x + \sqrt{x^2 + 4}\right) + C.$

35. $\dfrac{1}{8}\ln(4x^2 - 5) + \dfrac{1}{\sqrt{5}}\ln\dfrac{2x - \sqrt{5}}{2x + \sqrt{5}} + C.$

36. $\dfrac{5}{3}\sqrt{3x^2 - 9} - \dfrac{2}{\sqrt{3}}\ln\left(x + \sqrt{x^2 - 3}\right) + C.$

37. $\sin^{-1}\left(\dfrac{\sin x}{\sqrt{2}}\right) + C.$

38. $-\sqrt{2 - \sin^2 x} + C.$

39. $\tan^{-1}(\sin x) + C.$

40. $\sec^{-1}(\tan x) + C.$

41. $\ln\left(\sec x + \sqrt{\sec^2 x + 1}\right).$

42. $2\sqrt{1 - \cos\theta} + C.$

43. $\dfrac{1}{4}\ln\dfrac{2 + \ln x}{2 - \ln x} + C.$

44. $-\frac{1}{2}\sqrt{\cos^2 x - \sin^2 x} + C.$

45. $\dfrac{1}{2}\sin^{-1}\dfrac{x^2}{a^2} + C.$

46. $-\dfrac{1}{k^2}e^{-k^2 x} + C.$

47. $\dfrac{1}{2a}(e^{2ax} - e^{-2ax}) + 2x + C.$

48. $\frac{1}{3}\ln(1 + e^{3x}) + C.$

49. $\ln(e^x + e^{-x}) + C.$

50. $e^{-\frac{1}{x}} + C.$

51. $\tan^{-1}(e^x) + C.$

52. $\ln\dfrac{1 - e^x}{1 + e^x} + C.$

53. $\dfrac{1}{a}\sin^{-1}(e^{ax}) + C.$

54. $\tan^{-1}(e^x) + C.$

Page 20

1. $\dfrac{1}{2}\tan^{-1}\dfrac{x + 3}{2} + C.$

2. $\dfrac{1}{2}\sin^{-1}\dfrac{2x - 1}{\sqrt{3}} + C.$

3. $\dfrac{1}{\sqrt{3}}\ln\left(3x + 2 + \sqrt{9x^2 + 12x + 6}\right) + C.$

4. $\dfrac{1}{\sqrt{5}}\sin^{-1}\dfrac{(2x - 1)\sqrt{5}}{3} + C.$

5. $\dfrac{1}{\sqrt{3}}\sec^{-1}\dfrac{(x - 3)\sqrt{6}}{3} + C.$

6. $\dfrac{1}{b-a}\ln\dfrac{x+a}{x+b}+C.$

7. $\dfrac{1}{4}\ln(4x^2-4x-2)+\dfrac{\sqrt{3}}{2}\ln\dfrac{2x-1-\sqrt{3}}{2x-1+\sqrt{3}}+C.$

8. $\dfrac{2}{3}\sqrt{3x^2-6x+1}+\dfrac{1}{\sqrt{3}}\ln[3(x-1)+\sqrt{9x^2-18x+3}]+C.$

9. $\dfrac{1}{6}\ln(3x^2+2x+2)+\dfrac{1}{3\sqrt{5}}\tan^{-1}\dfrac{3x+1}{\sqrt{5}}+C.$

10. $\dfrac{1}{\sqrt{2}}\sec^{-1}\dfrac{2x+1}{\sqrt{2}}+\dfrac{1}{2}\ln(2x+1+\sqrt{4x^2+4x-1})+C.$

11. $-\dfrac{3}{\sqrt{x^2-2x+3}}+C.$

12. $\sqrt{x^2-x-2}+\dfrac{1}{2}\ln(2x-1+\sqrt{4x^2-4x-8})+C.$

13. $\dfrac{1}{\sqrt{17}}\ln\left(\dfrac{4e^x+3-\sqrt{17}}{4e^x+3+\sqrt{17}}\right)+C.$

Page 25

1. $-\cos x+\dfrac{1}{3}\cos^3 x+C.$
2. $\sin x-\dfrac{2}{3}\sin^3 x+\dfrac{1}{5}\sin^5 x+C.$
3. $\sin x-\dfrac{2}{3}\cos^3 x+\dfrac{2}{3}\sin^3 x-\cos x+C.$
4. $-\dfrac{1}{3}\cos^3 x+\dfrac{1}{5}\cos^5 x+C.$
5. $\dfrac{2}{3}\sin^5\tfrac{1}{2}x-\dfrac{4}{7}\sin^7\tfrac{1}{2}x+\dfrac{2}{9}\sin^9\tfrac{1}{2}x+C.$
6. $\dfrac{1}{18}\sin^6 3\theta-\dfrac{1}{24}\sin^8 3\theta+C.$
7. $-\dfrac{2}{3}\cos^3\theta+\cos\theta+C.$
8. $\sin x+\dfrac{1}{3}\sin^3 x+C.$
9. $\cos x+\ln(\csc x-\cot x)+C.$
10. $\cos^2\theta-\dfrac{1}{4}\cos^4\theta-\ln\cos\theta+C.$
11. $\tan x+\dfrac{1}{3}\tan^3 x+C.$
12. $-(\cot y+\dfrac{4}{3}\cot^3 y+\dfrac{6}{5}\cot^5 y+\dfrac{4}{7}\cot^7 y+\dfrac{1}{9}\cot^9 y)+C.$
13. $\tan x-x+C.$
14. $2\tan\theta-\sec\theta-\theta+C.$
15. $\dfrac{1}{3}\sec^3\tfrac{1}{2}x+C.$
16. $\dfrac{1}{14}\sec^7 2x-\dfrac{1}{5}\sec^5 2x+\dfrac{1}{6}\sec^3 2x+C.$
17. $-\dfrac{1}{2}\csc^2 x-\ln\sin x+C.$
18. $\dfrac{1}{6}\sec^6 x-\dfrac{3}{4}\sec^4 x+\dfrac{3}{2}\sec^2 x+\ln\cos x+C.$
19. $-\dfrac{1}{5}\cot^5 x-\dfrac{1}{3}\cot^3 x+C.$
20. $\dfrac{1}{2}\tan^2 x+\ln\tan x+C.$
21. $\dfrac{x}{2}-\dfrac{1}{4a}\sin(2ax)+C.$
22. $\dfrac{x}{2}+\dfrac{1}{4a}\sin(2ax)+C.$

23. $\frac{3}{16} x - \frac{1}{64} \sin 4x - \frac{1}{48} \sin^3 2x + C.$

24. $\frac{3}{16} x - \frac{1}{32} \sin 2x + \frac{1}{24} \sin^3 x + C.$

25. $\frac{5}{16} x - \frac{1}{4} \sin 2x + \frac{3}{64} \sin 4x + \frac{1}{48} \sin^3 2x + C.$

26. $\tan x + \sec x + C.$

27. $\tan \frac{1}{2} x + C.$

28. $2 \left(\sin \frac{\theta}{2} - \cos \frac{\theta}{2} \right) + C.$

29. $\frac{x}{2} \sqrt{x^2 - a^2} - \frac{a^2}{2} \ln (x + \sqrt{x^2 - a^2}) + C.$

30. $\frac{x}{2} \sqrt{x^2 + a^2} + \frac{a^2}{2} \ln (x + \sqrt{x^2 + a^2}) + C.$

31. $\frac{x}{2} \sqrt{x^2 + a^2} - \frac{a^2}{2} \ln (x + \sqrt{x^2 + a^2}) + C.$

32. $-\dfrac{x}{a^2 \sqrt{x^2 - a^2}} + C.$

33. $\dfrac{1}{a} \ln \dfrac{x}{a + \sqrt{a^2 - x^2}} + C.$

34. $-\dfrac{\sqrt{2ax - x^2}}{ax} + C.$

35. $\dfrac{1}{\sqrt{a^2 - x^2}} + C.$

36. $\dfrac{1}{5} (x^2 + a^2)^{\frac{5}{2}} - \dfrac{a^2}{3} (x^2 + a^2)^{\frac{3}{2}} + C.$

37. $-\dfrac{\sqrt{x^2 + a^2}}{a^2 x} + C.$

38. $\dfrac{x-2}{2} \sqrt{x^2 - 4x + 5} + \dfrac{1}{2} \ln (x - 2 + \sqrt{x^2 - 4x + 5}) + C.$

39. $\dfrac{11 - 4x}{32} \sqrt{2 - 2x - 4x^2} + \dfrac{19}{64} \sin^{-1} \dfrac{4x+1}{3} + C.$

Page 30

1. $\dfrac{x^2}{2} + 4x - 2 \ln (x - 1) + 12 \ln (x - 2) + C.$

2. $3 \ln x - \ln (x + 1) + C.$

3. $\ln \dfrac{(x-1)(x+1)}{x} + C.$

4. $\dfrac{x}{4} + \ln x - \dfrac{7}{16} \ln (2x - 1) - \dfrac{9}{16} \ln (2x + 1) + C.$

5. $\frac{3}{4} \ln (x + 3) - \frac{1}{8} \ln (x + 1) - \frac{5}{8} \ln (x + 5) + C.$

6. $\frac{1}{2} \ln (2x - 1) - 3 \ln (2x - 3) + \frac{5}{2} \ln (2x - 5) + C.$

7. $x + \dfrac{1}{x} + \ln \dfrac{(x-1)^2}{x} + C.$

8. $\frac{1}{4}\ln(x+1) + \frac{3}{4}\ln(x-1) - \frac{1}{2(x-1)} + C.$

9. $\frac{1}{4}\left(\frac{2x}{1-x^2} + \ln\frac{x+1}{x-1}\right) + C.$

10. $x - 8\ln(x+1) - \frac{72x^2+96x+40}{3(x+1)^3} + C.$

11. $\frac{x^2+2x+3}{x^3} + \ln\frac{x-1}{x} + C.$

12. $\frac{1}{2}\ln\frac{x-2}{x+2} - \frac{1}{2}\frac{x}{x^2-4} + C.$

13. $\frac{1}{2(4-x^2)} + C.$

14. $x + \frac{1}{4}\ln\frac{x-1}{x+1} - \frac{1}{2}\tan^{-1}x + C.$

15. $\frac{1}{3}\ln\frac{x+1}{\sqrt{x^2-x+1}} + \frac{1}{\sqrt{3}}\tan^{-1}\frac{2x-1}{\sqrt{3}} + C.$

16. $\frac{1}{3}\ln(x^3+1) + C.$

17. $\frac{1}{6(x+1)} + \frac{1}{4}\ln\frac{x-1}{x+1} - \frac{2\sqrt{3}}{9}\tan^{-1}\frac{2x-1}{\sqrt{3}} + C.$

18. $\frac{1}{2(1-x^2)} + \ln\frac{x-1}{x+1} + C.$

19. $-\frac{8}{x^3-8} + \frac{1}{6}\ln\frac{x-2}{\sqrt{x^2+2x+4}} + \frac{1}{2\sqrt{3}}\tan^{-1}\frac{x+1}{\sqrt{3}} + C.$

20. $3(x+1)^{\frac{2}{3}} + \ln[(x+1)^{\frac{1}{3}}-1] - \sqrt{3}\tan^{-1}\frac{2(x+1)^{\frac{1}{3}}+1}{\sqrt{3}} + C.$

21. $-\frac{1}{5}x^{\frac{5}{12}} + \frac{1}{4}x^{\frac{1}{3}} - \frac{1}{3}x^{\frac{1}{4}} - x^{\frac{1}{12}} + \frac{1}{2}\ln\frac{1+x^{\frac{1}{12}}}{1-x^{\frac{1}{12}}} + C.$

22. $\frac{2}{5a^2}(ax+b)^{\frac{5}{2}} - \frac{2b}{3a^2}(ax+b)^{\frac{3}{2}} + C.$

23. $2\sqrt{x+2} - \ln(x+3) - 2\tan^{-1}\sqrt{x+2} + C.$

24. $4x^{\frac{1}{4}} + 2\ln(x^{\frac{1}{4}}-1) + \ln(x^{\frac{1}{2}}+1) - 2\tan^{-1}x^{\frac{1}{4}} + C.$

25. $\frac{1}{3}(x+1)^{\frac{3}{2}} + \frac{1}{3}(x-1)^{\frac{3}{2}} + C.$

Page 34

1. $\frac{1}{4}\cos 2x + \frac{x}{2}\sin 2x + C.$

2. $\frac{x^2}{2}\ln x - \frac{x^2}{4} + C.$

3. $x\sin^{-1}x + \sqrt{1-x^2} + C.$

4. $\frac{x^2+1}{2}\tan^{-1}x - \frac{1}{2}x + C.$

5. $x\ln(x+\sqrt{a^2+x^2}) - \sqrt{a^2+x^2} + C.$

6. $2\sqrt{x-1}\ln x - 4\sqrt{x-1} + 4\tan^{-1}\sqrt{x-1} + C.$

7. $\ln x \ln(\ln x) - \ln x + C.$

8. $\frac{1}{3}x^3\sec^{-1}x - \frac{x}{6}\sqrt{x^2-1} - \frac{1}{6}\ln(x+\sqrt{x^2-1}) + C.$

9. $x - (1+e^{-x})\ln(1+e^x) + C.$

10. $(x^2 - 2x + 2)e^x + C.$

11. $-(x^3 + 3x^2 + 6x + 6)e^{-x} + C.$

12. $\dfrac{x-1}{2}\sin 2x - \dfrac{2x^2 - 4x + 1}{4}\cos 2x + C.$

13. $\dfrac{x}{2}\sqrt{x^2-a^2} - \dfrac{a^2}{2}\ln(x+\sqrt{x^2-a^2}) + C.$

14. $\dfrac{x}{2}\sqrt{a^2+x^2} + \dfrac{a^2}{2}\ln(x+\sqrt{a^2+x^2}) + C.$

15. $\dfrac{e^{2x}}{13}(2\sin 3x - 3\cos 3x) + C.$

16. $\dfrac{e^x}{2}(\cos x + \sin x) + C.$

17. $-\dfrac{e^{-x}}{5}(\sin 2x + 2\cos 2x) + C.$

18. $\frac{1}{2}(\sec\theta\tan\theta + \ln(\sec\theta + \tan\theta)] + C.$

19. $\frac{1}{2}\cos x - \frac{1}{10}\cos 5x + C.$

Page 38

1. $\frac{4}{3}.$

2. $2.829.$

3. $-0.630.$

Pages 45, 46

1. $1 - \frac{1}{3}\sqrt{3}.$

2. $\dfrac{\pi}{3}.$

3. $-20.$

4. $2.$

5. $\frac{3}{4}.$

6. $1.807.$

7. $0.2877.$

8. $0.$

9. $\frac{3}{4}a.$

10. $2.$

11. $\infty.$

12. $\dfrac{\pi}{2}.$

13. $\dfrac{1}{2k^2}.$

14. $0.5493.$

15. $\dfrac{\pi}{4} + \dfrac{1}{2}.$

16. $1.786.$

17. $0.4055.$

18. $0.2877.$

19. $\dfrac{a^2}{2}(1 - \ln 2).$

Pages 49, 50

1. 11.
2. $\frac{1}{3}\sqrt{3}(4 - \sqrt{2})$.
3. $\frac{1}{2}\sqrt[3]{3} + 6$.
4. $\frac{1}{3}$.
5. 9.248.
6. πab.
7. $\frac{1}{6} a^2$.
8. $5\frac{1}{3}$.
9. $\frac{8}{15}$.
11. $\frac{14}{3} a^2$.
12. $\frac{9}{5}$.

13. $2\pi + \frac{1}{3},\ 6\pi - \frac{1}{3}$.
14. $4\sqrt{3} + \frac{14}{3}\pi$.
15. $5\left(\frac{\pi}{4} - \tan^{-1}\frac{1}{2}\right) + \frac{2}{3}$
17. $3\pi a^2$.
18. $\frac{3}{8}\pi a^2$.
19. $\pi(b^2 + 2ab)$.
20. $\pi\sqrt{3}$.
21. $3\pi a^2$.
22. $\frac{3}{4}\pi ab$.

Page 52

2. $\frac{\pi}{4} a^2$.
3. $\frac{2}{3} a^2 \sqrt{3}$.
4. $\frac{a^2}{4}(e^{4\pi} - 1)$.
5. $\frac{a^2}{2}$.
6. $\frac{3}{2}\pi$.
7. $\frac{1}{2}\pi a^2$.
8. $\frac{1}{3} a^2$.

9. $2 a^2(1 + \frac{1}{4}\sqrt{2})$.
10. $16\pi^3 a^2$.
11. $a^2\left(\frac{\pi}{3} + \frac{1}{2}\sqrt{3}\right)$.
13. $\frac{a^2}{4}(\pi - 1)$.
14. $(10\pi + 9\sqrt{3})\frac{a^2}{32}$.
15. πa^2.

Pages 55, 56

3. $\frac{16}{5}\pi$.
4. $\frac{\pi a^2}{6}$.

5. $\frac{\pi a^3}{4}\left(e^2 + 4 - \frac{1}{e^2}\right)$.
6. $\frac{1}{2}\pi^2$.

7. $\frac{4}{3}\pi a^3(1 - \cos^4\alpha)$, where a is the radius of the sphere and 2α the vertical angle of the cone.

8. $\frac{16}{5}\pi a^3$.
9. $\frac{32}{15}\pi a^3$.
10. $\frac{32}{4}\pi a^3$.
11. $5\pi^2 a^3$.
12. $\frac{32}{105}\pi a^3$.

13. $\frac{1}{3}\pi a^3$.
14. $\frac{13}{4}\pi^2 a^3$.
15. $8\pi\sqrt{3}$.
16. $\frac{\pi a^3}{16}\sqrt{2}$.

Page 59

2. $\frac{2}{3} a^3 \tan\alpha$.
3. $\frac{4}{3} a^3$.
4. $\frac{4}{3}\pi ab^2$.
5. $\frac{1}{3}\pi a^2 h$.
6. Ah.

8. $\frac{4}{3} a^3\left(1 + \frac{\pi}{2}\right)$
9. $\frac{4}{3} a^2 h$.
10. $\frac{4}{3\sqrt{2}}\pi a^3$.

Page 63

2. $\frac{8}{27}(10\sqrt{10}-1)$.

3. $\ln(2+\sqrt{3})$.

4. $\frac{1}{4}+\frac{1}{2}\ln 2$.

5. 2.003.

6. $6a$.

7. $a\left(1-\frac{1}{e}\right)$.

8. $8a$.

9. $2\pi^2 a$.

Page 64

3. $\frac{\sqrt{a^2+1}}{a}(e-1)$.

4. $\frac{4a}{\sqrt{3}}$.

5. $2a[\sqrt{2}+\ln(1+\sqrt{2})]$.

6. $\frac{14}{3}a$.

7. $8a$.

8. $\frac{1}{2}\pi a$.

Pages 66, 67

3. $2\pi b\left(b+\frac{a^2}{\sqrt{a^2-b^2}}\sin^{-1}\frac{\sqrt{a^2-b^2}}{a}\right)$.

4. $\frac{12}{5}\pi a^2$.

5. $\frac{a^2}{2}\left(e^2-\frac{1}{e^2}+4\right)$.

6. $\frac{44}{3}\pi a^2$.

7. $\frac{32}{5}\pi a^2$.

8. $\frac{1}{3}\pi a^2\sqrt{2}(4-\pi)$.

9. $8\pi[\sqrt{2}+\ln(1+\sqrt{2})]$.

10. $4\pi a^2$.

Page 69

1. $\frac{1}{4}\pi^2 a^2$.

2. $2a^2$.

3. $16a^3$.

4. $\frac{1}{4}\pi a^2(a+2b\sqrt{3})$.

5. $\frac{4}{3}\pi a^3(2\sqrt{2}-1)$.

6. $\frac{2}{3}\pi a^3(1-\cos\alpha)$.

7. $2ah(\pi-2)$.

8. $\frac{1}{2}\pi a\sqrt{h^2+4a^2}$.

9. $\frac{1}{3}a^2 h(9\pi-16)$.

Pages 71, 72

1. $45{,}000$ lbs.

2. $33{,}750$ lbs.

3. $\frac{1}{3}wbh^2$.

4. $\frac{1}{6}wbh^2$.

5. $\frac{2}{3}wab^2$, where a is the semi-axis in the surface and b the vertical semi-axis.

6. $300{,}000\,w$.

7. $40\,\pi w$.

Pages 78–80

1. $\frac{1}{2}pa^2 b$, where p is the pressure per unit area, a the width, and b the height of the door.

2. $\frac{1}{12}wa^3 b$.

3. $\frac{1}{12}wbh^2(4c+3h)$.

4. The intersection of the medians.

5. $(\tfrac{4}{5} a, 0)$.

6. $\bar{x} = \dfrac{4 a}{3 \pi}, \ \bar{y} = \dfrac{4 b}{3 \pi}$.

7. $\left(\dfrac{a}{5}, \dfrac{a}{5}\right)$.

8. $\left(0, \dfrac{256 a}{315 \pi}\right)$.

9. $\bar{y} = \dfrac{\pi}{8}$.

10. $(\tfrac{9}{10} a, \tfrac{9}{10} a)$.

11. $\left(\dfrac{5}{6} a, \dfrac{16 a}{9 \pi}\right)$.

12. $\bar{y} = \tfrac{4}{5} a$.

13. $\bar{x} = \tfrac{1}{4} \pi \sqrt{2} a$.

14. At distance $\dfrac{2 a}{\pi}$ from the bounding diameter.

15. $\bar{y} = \dfrac{a \left(e^4 + 4 e^2 - 1\right)}{4 e \left(e^2 - 1\right)}$.

16. $(\tfrac{2}{5} a, \tfrac{2}{5} a)$.

17. $(0.399, 1.520)$.

18. $\bar{y} = \tfrac{4}{5} a$.

19. On the axis $\tfrac{1}{4}$ of the distance from the base to the vertex.

20. At distance $\tfrac{3}{8} a$ from the plane face of the hemisphere, where a is the radius.

21. $(\tfrac{3}{5}, 0)$.

22. Its distance from the plane face is $\tfrac{3}{16}$ of the radius.

23. On the axis at distance $\tfrac{2}{3} a (1 + \cos \alpha)$ from he vertex, a being the radius and α the angle of the sector.

24. $(\tfrac{4}{5} a, 0)$.

25. The distance of the center of gravity from the base of the cylinder is $\tfrac{3}{32} \pi a \tan \alpha$.

26. At the middle of the radius perpendicular to the plane face.

28. $\bar{x} = \dfrac{6 \sqrt{3} + 1}{15 \sqrt{3} - 5}$.

Pages 82, 83

2. $2 \pi^2 a^2 b$.

3. $\dfrac{\pi}{32} \left(12 \sqrt{3} - 1\right)$.

4. $\pi \left(36 \pi + \sqrt{6}\right) \sqrt{6}$.

5. $\tfrac{32}{9} \pi a^2$.

6. $\tfrac{1}{3} \pi a^3 \left[3 \ln \left(1 + \sqrt{2}\right) - \sqrt{2}\right]$.

7. $\tfrac{2}{3} \pi a^3 \left(3 \alpha + 2 \sin \alpha\right)$.

8. $\pi^2 a^3$.

10. $\tfrac{2}{3} \pi a^3 \left(4 \sin \alpha - \sin^3 \alpha\right) \tan \alpha$, where a is the radius of the cylinder and 2α the vertical angle of the cone.

Pages 84, 85

1. $\tfrac{1}{3} a^3 b$, where b is the edge about which the rectangle is revolved.

2. $\tfrac{1}{12} b h^3$, where b is the base and h the altitude.

3. $\tfrac{1}{4} b h^3$, where b is the base and h the altitude.

4. $\tfrac{2}{7} a^4$.

5. $\tfrac{64}{105} a^4$.

6. $\tfrac{1}{2} \pi a^4$.

7. $\frac{1}{2} Ma^2 h$, where h is the altitude.

8. $\frac{2}{3} Ma^2$.

9. $\dfrac{8 \pi \rho a b^4}{15}$, where ρ is the density.

10. $\frac{2}{5} Ma^2$, where M is the mass and a the radius.

12. $\frac{1}{2} \pi a^4$

Pages 88, 89

1. $\dfrac{k (b - a)^2}{2 a}$.

2. aw ft. lbs., where a is the radius of the earth in feet.

3. $c \ln \dfrac{v_2 - b}{v_1 - b} + \dfrac{a}{v_2} - \dfrac{a}{v_1}$.

4. 25,133 ft. lbs.

5. $\frac{4}{3} \pi \mu P a$, where a is the radius of the shaft.

6. $\dfrac{k}{2 \pi h} \ln \dfrac{b}{a}$, where h is the altitude of the cylinder.

7. $\dfrac{k}{4 \pi} \left(\dfrac{1}{a} - \dfrac{1}{b} \right)$, where a and b are the inner and outer radii.

8. $\dfrac{kh}{\pi ab}$, where a and b are the radii of the ends and h the altitude

9. $\dfrac{2 \pi i}{r}$.   10. $\dfrac{2 i}{c}$.

Pages 95, 96

2. 8.5.

7. 0.785392.

8. 1.26.

9. 4.38.

10. 21.48.

11. 4.27.

12. 0.9045.

13. $a\lambda - \dfrac{a^3\lambda^3}{3\lfloor 3} + \dfrac{a^5\lambda^5}{5\lfloor 5} + \cdots$

14. 1.91.

Pages 102, 103

1. $\ln \frac{11}{4}$.

2. $\frac{1}{2} \pi a^2$.

3. $\frac{16}{4}$.

4. $\dfrac{\pi}{k}$.

5. -1.

6. $\dfrac{\pi a^2}{4}$.

7. $\frac{2}{3}$.

8. $\frac{10}{3} a^2$.

9. π.

10. $13\frac{1}{3}$.

11. 3π.

12. π.

13. $\frac{1}{6}$.

14. $\frac{4}{3} a^4$.

15. 4.

16. $\frac{4}{5} a^4$.

17. $16 \ln 2 - \frac{21}{4}$.

18. $\frac{2}{3} a^5$.

19. $\frac{4}{5} a^5$.

20. $(\frac{2}{3}, -\frac{2}{3})$.

21. $(\frac{12}{5} a, -2 a)$.

Pages 107, 108

1. $\dfrac{\pi a^4}{8}$.

2. $\dfrac{\pi a^2}{2}$.

3. $\dfrac{\pi}{4}$.

4. $\dfrac{\pi a^3}{6}$.

6. $\frac{1}{4} a^4 (2\alpha - \sin 2\alpha)$.

7. $\frac{1}{12} a^4 (6\pi - 8)$.

8. On the bisector at the distance $\dfrac{2 a \sin \alpha}{3 \alpha}$ from the center.

9. $\frac{71}{4} \pi a^4$.

10. $\frac{1}{2}\pi a^4$.

11. $a^4 (4\pi - \frac{22}{15})$.

12. $3 \pi a^4$.

15. $\frac{3}{10} M a^2$, M being the mass and a the radius of the base.

16. $\frac{1}{3} a^3 (3\pi - 4)$.

17. $\frac{1}{4} \pi a^3$.

18. $\frac{8}{15} \pi \rho a^5$.

19. $(8\sqrt{2} - 9) \dfrac{2 \pi a^3}{105}$.

Page 111

1. $3\sqrt{14}$.

2. There are two areas between the planes each equal to $2 ma^2$.

3. Two areas are determined each equal to $\pi a^2 \sqrt{2}$.

4. $\frac{1}{4} \pi a^2 \sqrt{3}$.

5. 4.

6. $8 a^2$.

7. $\frac{1}{12} \pi a^2 (3\sqrt{3} - 1)$.

8. $a^2 (\pi - 2)$.

9. $8 a^2 \tan^{-1} \frac{1}{2} \sqrt{2}$.

Page 116

1. $\frac{1}{6}$.

2. $\frac{1}{30}$.

3. Its distance from the base is $\frac{3}{32} \pi a$.

4. πabc.

6. $\frac{13}{9} a^2 h$.

7. $\frac{4}{15}$.

Page 121

1. $\frac{19}{6} \pi$.

2. $\frac{3}{4} h$, where h is the altitude.

3. π.

4. $\dfrac{\pi a^2 h}{60} (2 h^2 + 3 a^2)$.

5. $\frac{1}{2} \pi a^3$.

6. On the axis of the cone at the distance $\frac{3}{8} a (1 + \cos\alpha)$ from the vertex.

7. If the two planes are $\theta = \pm \dfrac{\pi}{6}$, the spherical coördinates of the center of gravity are $r = \dfrac{9}{16} a$, $\theta = 0$, $\phi = \dfrac{\pi}{2}$.

8. $\frac{11}{10} \pi a^5$.

Page 125

1. $\dfrac{kM}{c\,(c+l)}$.

2. $\dfrac{2\,kM}{\pi a^2}$.

3. $\dfrac{2\,kMc}{a^2}\left[\dfrac{1}{c} - \dfrac{1}{\sqrt{c^2+a^2}}\right]$.

4. $2\,\pi k\rho h\,(1-\cos\alpha)$, where ρ is the density, h the altitude, and $2\,\alpha$ the vertical angle of the cone.

6. The components along the edge through the corner are each equal to

$$\frac{2\,Mk}{a^2}\left[\frac{\pi}{12} + \ln\frac{2+\sqrt{2}}{1+\sqrt{3}}\right].$$

Pages 130, 131

5. $x^2\dfrac{d^2y}{dx^2} + x\dfrac{dy}{dx} - y = 0$.

6. $x\,dy - y\,(x+1)\,dx = 0$.

7. $\dfrac{d^2y}{dx^2} + y = 0$.

8. $x^3\dfrac{d^3y}{dx^3} + 6\,x^2\dfrac{d^2y}{dx^2} + 4\,x\dfrac{dy}{dx} - 4\,y = 0$.

9. $y\,dx = x\,dy$.

Pages 141–143

1. $x^2 - y^2 = cx^2y^2$.

2. $\tan^2 x - \cot^2 y = c$.

3. $y^2 + 1 = c\,(x^2 - 1)$.

4. $x^2y^2 + x^2 - y^2 = c$.

5. $x^3 + x^2y - xy^2 - y^3 = c$.

6. $y^2 = cx^2\,(y^2 + 1)$.

7. $x^2 + y^2 = ce^{2\,av}$.

8. $xy = c\,(y - 1)$.

9. $y = ce^{ax} + \dfrac{1}{b-a}\,e^{bx}$.

10. $y = cx^2 - \dfrac{1}{x}$.

11. $y = cx^2 e^{-\frac{3}{x}}$.

12. $x^2y = x + cy$.

13. $y = (1 - x^2)\,(x + c)$.

14. $y = c\sin x - a$.

15. $7\,x^3 = y\,(x^7 + c)$.

16. $\dfrac{1}{y^2} = x + \dfrac{1}{2} + ce^{2\,x}$.

17. $x^4 + 4\,y\,(x^2 - 1)^{\frac{3}{2}} = c$.

18. $\ln\,(x^2 + xy + y^2) + \dfrac{2}{\sqrt{3}}\,\tan^{-1}\dfrac{x+2\,y}{x\sqrt{3}} = c$.

19. $x^2 - y^2 = cx$.

20. $y^2 + 2\,xy = c$.

21. $x^4 - 4\,x^3y + y^4 = c$.

22. $\dfrac{x}{y^2} = c - e^{-y}$.

23. $e^{\frac{x}{y}} + \ln x = c$.

24. $x + 2y + \ln\,(x + y - 2) = c$.

25. $y^3 = ce^x - x - 1$.

26. $e^y = \tfrac{1}{2}\,e^x + ce^{-x}$.

27. $y = \dfrac{c}{2} - \dfrac{x^2}{2\,c}$.

28. $y = \tfrac{1}{2}\,x^2 + c$, or $y = ce^x$.

29. $y^2 = 2\,cx + c^2$.

30. $q = Ec\left(1 - e^{-\frac{t}{Rc}}\right)$.

31. $i = Ie^{-\frac{R}{L}t} + \dfrac{E}{R^2 + \alpha^2 L^2}\left[R\sin\alpha t - L\alpha\left(\cos\alpha t - e^{-\frac{R}{L}t}\right)\right]$.

32. $y^3 = 8 e^{x-2}$.   34. $y = cx^3$.

33. $y^3 = 2 ax$.

35. $x = a \ln \dfrac{y}{a + \sqrt{a^2 - y^2}} + \sqrt{a^2 - y^2} + c$.

36. $y^2 + (x - c)^2 = a^2$.

37. $y = \dfrac{c}{2} e^{\frac{x}{a}} + \dfrac{a^2}{2 c} e^{-\frac{x}{a}}$.

38. $r = e^{\theta}$.

39. $r = c \sin \theta$.

40. $r = a \sec (\theta + c)$.

41. $a\theta = \sqrt{r^2 - a^2} - a \sec^{-1} \dfrac{r}{a} + c$.

42. $y = e^{\frac{x}{k}}$.

43. A circle.

44. A straight line.

45. A circle with the fixed point on its circumference or at its center.

46. The logarithmic spirals $r = ce^{k\theta}$.

47. 0.999964.

Pages 154–156

1. $y = c_1 \ln x - \frac{1}{4} x^2 + c_2$.

2. $y = x + c_1 x e^x + c_2$.

3. $y = c_1 e^{ax} + c_2 e^{-ax}$.

4. $y = c_1 \sin ax + c_2 \cos ax$.

5. $t = \int \sqrt{\dfrac{s}{2 k + c_1 s}} \, ds + c_2$.

6. $s = \dfrac{1}{a^2} \ln (c_1 e^{abt} - e^{-abt}) + c_2$.

7. $y = \dfrac{c_1}{4} x^2 - \dfrac{1}{2 c_1} \ln x + c_2$.

8. $y = \dfrac{1}{2 c_1} [e^{c_1 x + c_2} + e^{-(c_1 x + c_2)}]$.

9. $y = c_1 + c_2 e^{4 x}$.

10. $y = c_1 e^{5 x} + c_2 e^{-x}$.

11. $y = (c_1 + c_2 x) e^{3 x}$.

12. $y = c_1 \cos x + c_2 \sin x$.

13. $y = c_1 + c_2 e^{-x} + c_3 e^{3 x}$.

14. $y = c_1 e^x + c_2 e^{-x} + c_3 \cos x + c_4 \sin x$.

15. $y = e^x [c_1 \cos (x \sqrt{2}) + c_2 \sin (x \sqrt{2})]$.

16. $y = e^{-\frac{1}{2} x} \left[c_1 \cos \dfrac{x \sqrt{3}}{2} + c_2 \sin \dfrac{x \sqrt{3}}{2} \right]$.

17. $y = c_1 e^x + c_2 e^{-x} + c_3 e^{x\sqrt{2}} + c_4 e^{-x\sqrt{2}}$.

18. $y = (c_1 + c_2 x + c_3 x^2)\, e^x$.

19. $y = x + 3 + c_1 \cos x + c_2 \sin x$.

20. $y = c_1 e^{2x} + c_2 e^{-2x} - \frac{1}{3} e^x$.

21. $y = c_1 e^{2x} + c_2 e^{-3x} - \frac{1}{6} x^2 - \frac{1}{18} x - \frac{7}{108}$.

22. $y = c e^x - \frac{1}{2}(\sin x + \cos x)$.

23. $y = c_1 + c_2 e^{2x} - \frac{1}{2} x^2 + x$.

24. $y = c_1 e^{-x} + c_2 e^{-5x} + \frac{1}{5} x - \frac{6}{25} + \frac{1}{32} e^{3x}$.

25. $y = c_1 e^{ax} + c_2 e^{-ax} + \dfrac{x}{2a} e^{ax}$.

26. $y = e^{\frac{1}{2}x}\left[c_1 \cos \dfrac{x\sqrt{3}}{2} + c_2 \sin \dfrac{x\sqrt{3}}{2} \right] - \dfrac{1}{13}(2\sin 2x + 3\cos 2x)$.

27. $y = c_1 e^x + e^{-\frac{1}{2}x}\left[c_1 \cos \dfrac{x\sqrt{3}}{2} + c_2 \sin \dfrac{x\sqrt{3}}{2} \right] - x^3 + x^2 - 6$.

28. $y = c_1 e^x + c_2 e^{3x} - \frac{1}{2} e^{2x} \sin x$.

29. $y = c_1 e^{3x} + c_2 e^{-3x} + \frac{1}{37} e^{3x}(6\sin x - \cos x)$.

30. $y = c_1 + c_2 x + c_3 x^2 + c_4 e^{-x} + \frac{1}{1088}(4\cos 4x - \sin 4x)$.

31. $y = c_1 \cos 2x + (c_2 + \frac{1}{4} x)\sin 2x$.

32. $y = e^{-x}(c_1 + c_2 x + \frac{1}{2} x^2) + \frac{1}{8} e^x$.

33. $x = c_1 \cos t + c_2 \sin t + \frac{1}{2}(e^t - e^{-t})$,
$y = c_1 \sin t - c_2 \cos t + \frac{1}{2}(e^t - e^{-t})$.

34. $y = c_1 \cos t + c_2 \sin t - 1$,
$x = (c_1 + c_2)\cos t + (c_2 - c_1)\sin t - 3$.

35. $x = c_1 e^t + c_3 e^{-3t}$,
$y = c_1 e^{-t} + 3 c_2 e^{-3t} + \cos t$.

36. $x = c_1 e^t + c_2 e^{-t} + c_3 \cos t + c_4 \sin t$,
$y = c_1 e^t + c_2 e^{-t} - c_3 \cos t - c_4 \sin t$.

37. $y = x$.

38. $2 y^{\frac{1}{2}} = x + 2$.

39. $s = \dfrac{g}{k} t + \dfrac{g}{k^2}(e^{-kt} - 1)$.

40. $s = \dfrac{1}{k} \ln \left(\dfrac{e^{t\sqrt{gk}} + e^{-t\sqrt{gk}}}{2} \right)$.

41. $s = b \cos (kt)$.

42. About 7 miles per second.

43. About $42\frac{1}{2}$ minutes.

44. $t = \sqrt{\dfrac{5}{g}} \ln (5 + \sqrt{24})$.

45. $t = \dfrac{3}{\sqrt{g}} \ln (9 + 4\sqrt{5})$.

TABLE OF INTEGRALS

1. $\int u^n \, du = \dfrac{u^{n+1}}{n+1}$, if n is not -1.

2. $\int \dfrac{du}{u} = \ln u$.

3. $\int \dfrac{du}{u^2 + a^2} = \dfrac{1}{a} \tan^{-1} \dfrac{u}{a}$.

4. $\int \dfrac{du}{u^2 - a^2} = \dfrac{1}{2a} \ln \dfrac{u-a}{u+a}$.

5. $\int e^u \, du = e^u$.

6. $\int a^u \, du = \dfrac{a^u}{\ln a}$.

INTEGRALS OF TRIGONOMETRIC FUNCTIONS

7. $\int \sin u \, du = -\cos u$.

8. $\int \sin^2 u \, du = \frac{1}{2} u - \frac{1}{4} \sin 2u = \frac{1}{2}(u - \sin u \cos u)$.

9. $\int \sin^4 u \, du = \frac{3}{8} u - \frac{1}{4} \sin 2u + \frac{1}{32} \sin 4u$.

10. $\int \sin^6 u \, du = \frac{5}{16} u - \frac{1}{4} \sin 2u + \frac{1}{48} \sin^3 2u + \frac{3}{64} \sin 4u$.

11. $\int \cos u \, du = \sin u$.

12. $\int \cos^2 u \, du = \frac{1}{2} u + \frac{1}{4} \sin 2u = \frac{1}{2}(u + \sin u \cos u)$.

13. $\int \cos^4 u \, du = \frac{3}{8} u + \frac{1}{4} \sin 2u + \frac{1}{32} \sin 4u$.

14. $\int \cos^6 u \, du = \frac{5}{16} u + \frac{1}{4} \sin 2u - \frac{1}{48} \sin^3 2u + \frac{3}{64} \sin 4u$.

15. $\int \tan u \, du = -\ln \cos u$.

16. $\int \cot u \, du = \ln \sin u$.

186

17. $\int \sec u \, du = \ln (\sec u + \tan u) = \ln \tan \left(\dfrac{u}{2} + \dfrac{\pi}{4} \right).$

18. $\int \sec^2 u \, du = \tan u.$

19. $\int \sec^3 u \, du = \frac{1}{2} \sec u \tan u + \frac{1}{2} \ln (\sec u + \tan u).$

20. $\int \csc u \, du = \ln (\csc u - \cot u) = \ln \tan \dfrac{u}{2}.$

21. $\int \csc^2 u \, du = -\cot u.$

22. $\int \csc^3 u \, du = - \frac{1}{2} \csc u \cot u + \frac{1}{2} \ln (\csc u - \cot u).$

INTEGRALS CONTAINING $\sqrt{a^2 - u^2}$

23. $\int \sqrt{a^2 - u^2} \, du = \dfrac{u}{2} \sqrt{a^2 - u^2} + \dfrac{a^2}{2} \sin^{-1} \dfrac{u}{a}.$

24. $\int u^2 \sqrt{a^2 - u^2} \, du = \dfrac{u}{8} (2u^2 - a^2) \sqrt{a^2 - u^2} + \dfrac{a^4}{8} \sin^{-1} \dfrac{u}{a}.$

25. $\int \dfrac{\sqrt{a^2 - u^2}}{u} \, du = \sqrt{a^2 - u^2} + a \ln \dfrac{a - \sqrt{a^2 - u^2}}{u}.$

26. $\int \dfrac{du}{\sqrt{a^2 - u^2}} = \sin^{-1} \dfrac{u}{a}.$

27. $\int \dfrac{u^2 \, du}{\sqrt{a^2 - u^2}} = - \dfrac{u}{2} \sqrt{a^2 - u^2} + \dfrac{a^2}{2} \sin^{-1} \dfrac{u}{a}.$

28. $\int \dfrac{du}{u \sqrt{a^2 - u^2}} = \dfrac{1}{a} \ln \dfrac{a - \sqrt{a^2 - u^2}}{u}.$

29. $\int \dfrac{du}{u^2 \sqrt{a^2 - u^2}} = - \dfrac{\sqrt{a^2 - u^2}}{a^2 u}.$

30. $\int (a^2 - u^2)^{\frac{3}{2}} \, du = \dfrac{u}{8} (5a^2 - 2u^2) \sqrt{a^2 - u^2} + \dfrac{3a^4}{8} \sin^{-1} \dfrac{u}{a}.$

31. $\int \dfrac{du}{(a^2 - u^2)^{\frac{3}{2}}} = \dfrac{u}{a^2 \sqrt{a^2 - u^2}}.$

INTEGRALS CONTAINING $\sqrt{u^2 - a^2}$

32. $\int \sqrt{u^2 - a^2} \, du = \dfrac{u}{2} \sqrt{u^2 - a^2} - \dfrac{a^2}{2} \ln (u + \sqrt{u^2 - a^2}).$

33. $\int u^2 \sqrt{u^2 - a^2} \, du = \dfrac{u}{8} (2u^2 - a^2) \sqrt{u^2 - a^2} - \dfrac{a^4}{8} \ln (u + \sqrt{u^2 - a^2}).$

34. $\int \dfrac{\sqrt{u^2 - a^2}}{u}\, du = \sqrt{u^2 - a^2} - a \sec^{-1} \dfrac{u}{a}.$

35. $\int \dfrac{du}{\sqrt{u^2 - a^2}}\, du = \ln\left(u + \sqrt{u^2 - a^2}\right).$

36. $\int \dfrac{u^2\, du}{\sqrt{u^2 - a^2}} = \dfrac{u}{2} \sqrt{u^2 - a^2} + \dfrac{a^2}{2} \ln\left(u + \sqrt{u^2 - a^2}\right).$

37. $\int \dfrac{du}{u\sqrt{u^2 - a^2}} = \dfrac{1}{a} \sec^{-1} \dfrac{u}{a}.$

38. $\int \dfrac{du}{u^2 \sqrt{u^2 - a^2}} = \dfrac{\sqrt{u^2 - a^2}}{a^2 u}.$

39. $\int (u^2 - a^2)^{\frac{3}{2}}\, du = \dfrac{u}{8} (2\, u^2 - 5\, a^2) \sqrt{u^2 - a^2} + \dfrac{3\, a^4}{8} \ln\left(u + \sqrt{u^2 - a^2}\right).$

40. $\int \dfrac{du}{(u^2 - a^2)^{\frac{3}{2}}} = -\dfrac{u}{\sqrt{u^2 - a^2}}.$

INTEGRALS CONTAINING $\sqrt{u^2 + a^2}$

41. $\int \sqrt{u^2 + a^2}\, du = \dfrac{u}{2} \sqrt{u^2 + a^2} + \dfrac{a^2}{2} \ln\left(u + \sqrt{u^2 + a^2}\right).$

42. $\int u^2 \sqrt{u^2 + a^2}\, du = \dfrac{u}{8} (2\, u^2 + a^2) \sqrt{u^2 + a^2} - \dfrac{a^4}{8} \ln\left(u + \sqrt{u^2 + a^2}\right).$

43. $\int \dfrac{\sqrt{u^2 + a^2}}{u}\, du = \sqrt{u^2 + a^2} + a \ln \dfrac{\sqrt{u^2 + a^2} - a}{u}.$

44. $\int \dfrac{du}{\sqrt{u^2 + a^2}} = \ln\left(u + \sqrt{u^2 + a^2}\right).$

45. $\int \dfrac{u^2\, du}{\sqrt{u^2 + a^2}} = \dfrac{u}{2} \sqrt{u^2 + a^2} - \dfrac{a^2}{2} \ln\left(u + \sqrt{u^2 + a^2}\right).$

46. $\int \dfrac{du}{u\sqrt{u^2 + a^2}} = \dfrac{1}{a} \ln \dfrac{\sqrt{u^2 + a^2} - a}{u}.$

47. $\int \dfrac{du}{u^2 \sqrt{u^2 + a^2}} = -\dfrac{\sqrt{u^2 + a^2}}{a^2 u}.$

48. $\int (u^2 + a^2)^{\frac{3}{2}}\, du = \dfrac{u}{8} (2\, u^2 + 5\, a^2) \sqrt{u^2 + a^2} + \dfrac{3\, a^4}{8} \ln\left(u + \sqrt{u^2 + a^2}\right).$

49. $\int \dfrac{du}{(u^2 + a^2)^{\frac{3}{2}}} = \dfrac{u}{a^2 \sqrt{u^2 + a^2}}.$

OTHER INTEGRALS

50. $\displaystyle\int\sqrt{\dfrac{px+q}{ax+b}}\,dx$

$\displaystyle =\frac{1}{a}\sqrt{(ax+b)\,(px+q)}$

$\displaystyle -\frac{bp-aq}{a\sqrt{ap}}\ln\left(\sqrt{p\,(ax+b)}+\sqrt{a\,(px+q)}\right)$

$\displaystyle =\frac{1}{a}\sqrt{(ax+b)\,(px+q)}-\frac{bp-aq}{a\sqrt{-ap}}\tan^{-1}\frac{\sqrt{-ap\,(ax+b)}}{a\sqrt{px+q}}.$

51. $\displaystyle\int e^{ax}\sin bx\,dx=\frac{e^{ax}\,(a\sin bx-b\cos bx)}{a^2+b^2}.$

52. $\displaystyle\int e^{ax}\cos bx\,dx=\frac{e^{ax}\,(b\sin bx+a\cos bx)}{a^2+b^2}.$

0-509

N	0	1	2	3	4	5	6	7	8	9
0	......	0.0000	0.6931	1.0986	1.3863	1.6094	1.7918	1.9459	2.0794	2.1972
1	2.3026	2.3979	2.4849	2.5649	2.6391	2.7081	2.7726	2.8332	2.8904	2.9444
2	9957	3.0445	3.0910	3.1355	3.1781	3.2189	3.2581	3.2958	3.3322	3.3673
3	3.4012	4340	4657	4965	5264	5553	5835	6109	6376	6636
4	6889	7136	7377	7612	7842	8067	8286	8501	8712	8918
5	9120	9318	9512	9703	9890	4.0073	4.0254	4.0431	4.0604	4.0775
6	4.0943	4.1109	4.1271	4.1431	4.1589	1744	1897	2047	2195	2341
7	2485	2627	2767	2905	3041	3175	3307	3438	3567	3694
8	3820	3944	4067	4188	4308	4427	4543	4659	4773	4886
9	4998	5109	5218	5326	5433	5539	5643	5747	5850	5951
10	6052	6151	6250	6347	6444	6540	6634	6728	6821	6913
11	7005	7095	7185	7274	7362	7449	7536	7622	7707	7791
12	7875	7958	8040	8122	8203	8283	8363	8442	8520	8598
13	8675	8752	8828	8903	8978	9053	9127	9200	9273	9345
14	9416	9488	9558	9628	9698	9767	9836	9904	9972	5.0039
15	5.0106	5.0173	5.0239	5.0304	5.0370	5.0434	5.0499	5.0562	5.0626	0689
16	0752	0814	0876	0938	0999	1059	1120	1180	1240	1299
17	1358	1417	1475	1533	1591	1648	1705	1761	1818	1874
18	1930	1985	2040	2095	2149	2204	2257	2311	2364	2417
19	2470	2523	2575	2627	2679	2730	2781	2832	2883	2933
20	2983	3033	3083	3132	3181	3230	3279	3327	3375	3423
21	3471	3519	3566	3613	3660	3706	3753	3799	3845	3891
22	3936	3982	4027	4072	4116	4161	4205	4250	4293	4337
23	4381	4424	4467	4510	4553	4596	4638	4681	4723	4765
24	4806	4848	4889	4931	4972	5013	5053	5094	5134	5175
25	5215	5255	5294	5334	5373	5413	5452	5491	5530	5568
26	5607	5645	5683	5722	5759	5797	5835	5872	5910	5947
27	5984	6021	6058	6095	6131	6168	6204	6240	6276	6312
28	6348	6384	6419	6454	6490	6525	6560	6595	6630	6664
29	6699	6733	6768	6802	6836	6870	6904	6937	6971	7004
30	7038	7071	7104	7137	7170	7203	7236	7268	7301	7333
31	7366	7398	7430	7462	7494	7526	7557	7589	7621	7652
32	7683	7714	7746	7777	7807	7838	7869	7900	7930	7961
33	7991	8021	8051	8081	8111	8141	8171	8201	8230	8260
34	8289	8319	8348	8377	8406	8435	8464	8493	8522	8551
35	8579	8608	8636	8665	8693	8721	8749	8777	8805	8833
36	8861	8889	8916	8944	8972	8999	9026	9054	9081	9108
37	9135	9162	9189	9216	9243	9269	9296	9322	9349	9375
38	9402	9428	9454	9480	9506	9532	9558	9584	9610	9636
39	9661	9687	9713	9738	9764	9789	9814	9839	9865	9890
40	9915	9940	9965	9989	6.0014	6.0039	6.0064	6.0088	6.0113	6.0137
41	6.0162	6.0186	6.0210	6.0234	0259	0283	0307	0331	0355	0379
42	0403	0426	0450	0474	0497	0521	0544	0568	0591	0615
43	0638	0661	0684	0707	0730	0753	0776	0799	0822	0845
44	0868	0890	0913	0936	0958	0981	1003	1026	1048	1070
45	1092	1115	1137	1159	1181	1203	1225	1247	1269	1291
46	1312	1334	1356	1377	1399	1420	1442	1463	1485	1506
47	1527	1549	1570	1591	1612	1633	1654	1675	1696	1717
48	1738	1759	1779	1800	1821	1841	1862	1883	1903	1924
49	1944	1964	1985	2005	2025	2046	2066	2086	2106	2126
50	2146	2166	2186	2206	2226	2246	2265	2285	2305	2324
N	0	1	2	3	4	5	6	7	8	9

500-1009

N	0	1	2	3	4	5	6	7	8	9
50	6.2146	6.2166	6.2186	6.2206	6.2226	6.2246	6.2265	6.2285	6.2305	6.2324
51	2344	2364	2383	2403	2422	2442	2461	2480	2500	2519
52	2538	2558	2577	2596	2615	2634	2653	2672	2691	2710
53	2729	2748	2766	2785	2804	2823	2841	2860	2879	2897
54	2916	2934	2953	2971	2989	3008	3026	3044	3063	3081
55	3099	3117	3135	3154	3172	3190	3208	3226	3244	3261
56	3279	3297	3315	3333	3351	3368	3386	3404	3421	3439
57	3456	3474	3491	3509	3526	3544	3561	3578	3596	3613
58	3630	3648	3665	3682	3699	3716	3733	3750	3767	3784
59	3801	3818	3835	3852	3869	3886	3902	3919	3936	3953
60	3969	3986	4003	4019	4036	4052	4069	4085	4102	4118
61	4135	4151	4167	4184	4200	4216	4232	4249	4265	4281
62	4297	4313	4329	4345	4362	4378	4394	4409	4425	4441
63	4457	4473	4489	4505	4520	4536	4552	4568	4583	4599
64	4615	4630	4646	4661	4677	4693	4708	4723	4739	4754
65	4770	4785	4800	4816	4831	4846	4862	4877	4892	4907
66	4922	4938	4953	4968	4983	4998	5013	5028	5043	5058
67	5073	5088	5103	5117	5132	5147	5162	5177	5191	5206
68	5221	5236	5250	5265	5280	5294	5309	5323	5338	5352
69	5367	5381	5396	5410	5425	5439	5453	5468	5482	5497
70	5511	5525	5539	5554	5568	5582	5596	5610	5624	5639
71	5653	5667	5681	5695	5709	5723	5737	5751	5765	5779
72	5793	5806	5820	5834	5848	5862	5876	5889	5903	5917
73	5930	5944	5958	5971	5985	5999	6012	6026	6039	6053
74	6067	6080	6093	6107	6120	6134	6147	6161	6174	6187
75	6201	6214	6227	6241	6254	6267	6280	6294	6307	6320
76	6333	6346	6359	6373	6386	6399	6412	6425	6438	6451
77	6464	6477	6490	6503	6516	6529	6542	6554	6567	6580
78	6593	6606	6619	6631	6644	6657	6670	6682	6695	6708
79	6720	6733	6746	6758	6771	6783	6796	6809	6821	6834
80	6846	6859	6871	6884	6896	6908	6921	6933	6946	6958
81	6970	6983	6995	7007	7020	7032	7044	7056	7069	7081
82	7093	7105	7117	7130	7142	7154	7166	7178	7190	7202
83	7214	7226	7238	7250	7262	7274	7286	7298	7310	7322
84	7334	7346	7358	7370	7382	7393	7405	7417	7429	7441
85	7452	7464	7476	7488	7499	7511	7523	7534	7546	7558
86	7569	7581	7593	7604	7616	7627	7639	7650	7662	7673
87	7685	7696	7708	7719	7731	7742	7754	7765	7776	7788
88	7799	7811	7822	7833	7845	7856	7867	7878	7890	7901
89	7912	7923	7935	7946	7957	7968	7979	7991	8002	8013
90	8024	8035	8046	8057	8068	8079	8090	8101	8112	8123
91	8134	8145	8156	8167	8178	8189	8200	8211	8222	8233
92	8244	8255	8265	8276	8287	8298	8309	8320	8330	8341
93	8352	8363	8373	8384	8395	8405	8416	8427	8437	8448
94	8459	8469	8480	8491	8501	8512	8522	8533	8544	8554
95	8565	8575	8586	8596	8607	8617	8628	8638	8648	8659
96	8669	8680	8690	8701	8711	8721	8732	8742	8752	8763
97	8773	8783	8794	8804	8814	8824	8835	8845	8855	8865
98	8876	8886	8896	8906	8916	8926	8937	8947	8957	8967
99	8977	8987	8997	9007	9017	9027	9037	9048	9058	9068
100	9078	9088	9098	9108	9117	9127	9137	9147	9157	9167
N	0	1	2	3	4	5	6	7	8	9

$a = \dfrac{dv}{dt}$ ① ⎫

$v = \dfrac{ds}{dt}$ ② ⎬ define

$dt = \dfrac{dv}{a} = \dfrac{ds}{v}$

Of time derivation   1943

acceleration   functional conditions

when $T = 0$
v_0
$s_0 = 0$

constant

Variable

∴ $v = a = \dfrac{dv}{dt}$

∴ $v = \dfrac{ds}{dt}$

3. $v\,dv = a\,ds$

1. $v = Kt + v_0$

2. $S = \dfrac{Kt^2}{2} + v_0 t$

3. $S_{mean} = \dfrac{K}{v}(2T-1) + v_0$

4. $v^2 = 2KS \perp v_0^2$

INDEX

193

& the line.

$(x y)$

$h x$

$?I$

$$\frac{\pi y^2 dx \, \delta \, y^2}{4} +$$

$(\pi y^2 dx \, \delta \, x^2)$

about base

Relation between $x y$

$$\frac{x}{h} + \frac{y}{a} = 1$$

Tan Plane to $F(x, y, z)$ at $x'y'z'$ is

$$(x - x')\left(\frac{\partial F}{\partial x}\right) + (y - y')\left(\frac{\partial F}{\partial y}\right) + (z - z')\left(\frac{\partial F}{\partial z}\right)_{/2}$$

normal line to surface at $F(xyz)$
= at $x'y'z'$ is

$$\frac{x - x'}{\left(\frac{\partial F}{\partial x}\right)'} = \frac{y - y'}{\left(\frac{\partial F}{\partial y}\right)} = \frac{z - z'}{\left(\frac{\partial F}{\partial z}\right)'}$$

x between normal line and z axis.

CPSIA information can be obtained
at www.ICGtesting.com
Printed in the USA
LVHW080711100822
725606LV00004B/111